CHRISTOLOGY AND SCIENCE

CHRISTOLOGY AND SCIENCE

F. LeRon Shults

WILLIAM B. EERDMANS PUBLISHING COMPANY
GRAND RAPIDS, MICHIGAN / CAMBRIDGE, U.K.

Published 2008
in the United Kingdom by
Ashgate Publishing Limited
Gower House, Croft Road
Aldershot, Hampshire GU11 3HR
www.ashgate.com

and in the United States of America by
Wm. B. Eerdmans Publishing Co.
2140 Oak Industrial Drive N.E., Grand Rapids, Michigan 49505
www.eerdmans.com

Printed and bound in Great Britain

13 12 11 10 09 08   7 6 5 4 3 2 1

Library of Congress Cataloging-in-Publication Data

Shults, F. LeRon.
Christology and science / F. LeRon Shults.
p.   cm.
Includes bibliographical references and index.
Eerdmans ISBN 978-0-8028-6248-8 (pbk.: alk. paper)
1. Religion and science. 2. Jesus Christ. 3. Science — Philosophy.
I. Title.

BL240.3.S58 2008
232 — dc22

2007021335

To Ken Reynhout

Contents

Acknowledgments

As I explain in more detail in the epilogue, this book is part of a broader theological project that has stretched over five years. During this time many people have provided feedback on various parts of the current volume, but I want to single out my friend Ken Reynhout for special thanks. As he did for so many of my other projects, including *Reforming the Doctrine of God*, Ken worked through early and late drafts of *Christology and Science*, providing careful comments that were both critical and constructive. We had many conversations on these (and other) themes while Ken was my research and teaching assistant at Bethel Seminary from 2002 to 2005. He has been (and continues to be) not only a great friend but the best kind of colleague an author could hope for. Even (and especially) when he does not agree, Ken has always taken the time to understand my rationale for an argument before offering insightful questions that drive me to pursue greater clarity and cohesion. In sincere gratitude for this ongoing gift of friendship and collegiality, I dedicate this book to him.

I also want to acknowledge the generosity of several other individuals and institutions whose support helped create the context within which writing this book became possible. Special thanks to J. Wentzel van Huyssteen and Roger Trigg for inviting me to contribute a volume to this Ashgate Science and Religion series. Sarah Lloyd and her editorial staff at Ashgate have been exceptionally responsive and professional (and patient) throughout the process of bringing this book to print. I am also grateful to Bill Eerdmans for agreeing to accept the book as part of Eerdmans' publishing line in North America. During the summers of 2003–2005, I participated in the *Oxford Seminars in Christianity and Science*, which were generously supported by the John Templeton Foundation. This provided me not only with time to research and write but also with the opportunity to share ideas with scientists, philosophers and other theologians. I have had the opportunity to present drafts of parts of this book not only at Oxford, but also at Bethel Theological Seminary, Fuller Theological Seminary, Garrett-Evangelical Theological Seminary, Princeton Theological Seminary and Tübingen University, as well as at the American Academy of Religion, the Society for the Study of Theology and the European Society for the Study of Science and Theology. I am thankful to my hosts and to all of the students and seminar participants who offered valuable feedback on my attempts at reforming Christology. I completed the final draft of the manuscript during my first year at the

University of Agder in Kristiansand, Norway, which was possible in large part because of my new colleagues' willingness to give me a "soft start" as I adjusted to my new European context. Finally, I am especially grateful to my wife and children who willingly embraced the idea of a Norwegian adventure and whose identity, agency and presence toward me and one another shape the intimate context of my own ongoing pursuit of reformation.

Chapter 1

Reforming Christology

In every generation Christian theology is faced with the task of articulating the intuitions of the biblical tradition about the significance of Jesus Christ in a way that engages its own cultural context. This task feels especially daunting and dangerous in the context of interdisciplinary dialogue with contemporary sciences such as evolutionary biology, cultural anthropology and physical cosmology, which question the coherence and plausibility of many traditional christological formulations. However, as we reflect on the philosophical shifts that have shaped the conceptual space of late modern discourse about human life in the cosmos we may find that these challenges also provide theology with new opportunities for explicating and clarifying the Christian experience and understanding of Jesus Christ. This book is my attempt to show that engaging in this interdisciplinary endeavor is both possible and promising.

The task of reforming Christology will indeed require the *reconstruction* of previous doctrinal formulations, as it has throughout church history. Many traditional depictions of the person, work and coming of Christ are shaped by assumptions about humanity and the world that no longer make sense in light of contemporary science. One way of responding to these challenges would be to try to insulate theology from science, defensively maintaining one's favored ancient or early modern doctrinal formulation. Or one might try to insulate science from theology, defensively reducing the human longing for redemptive transformation to one's favored disciplinary explanation. Extreme responses are often the easiest. However, the more difficult reconstructive response, which attempts to maintain the integrity of theology while integrating relevant scientific and philosophical insights, will also be the more rewarding. As we will see in the following chapters, reconstructing Christology has always been an important part of the ongoing reformation of the Christian church.

This brings us to a second sense in which this book aims at *reforming* Christology. The study of Jesus Christ ought to have a reformative effect on contemporary life. An articulation of Christian doctrine should not only help us make sense of our experience in the world; it should also facilitate the reformation of our ways of living in the world. Many traditional formulations of Christology rely so heavily on ancient concepts of substance or medieval concepts of jurisprudence that they seem irrelevant to the concrete concerns that shape late modern culture. Yet, the human longing to understand and be understood, to love and be loved, to hold and be held onto in healthy relations with others is as strong as ever in contemporary life. One of the functions of christological discourse is to illuminate the origin, condition and goal of these desires. Bringing Christology and science into explicit, concrete dialogue will have a disturbing effect on many of our comfortable assumptions about our life together, but this is an important part of any deeply transformative process.

It is important to face the fears that we bring to such an endeavor. Some theologians will be concerned that discussion of particular claims about Christ may offend the pluralist sensibilities of the interdisciplinary community, while others will be anxious that serious engagement with science will simply render implausible some cherished christological formulations. Some scientists will worry that talking about Jesus in public will undermine their reputation among their colleagues, while others will suspect that religionists are encroaching on their territory. Some laypersons will fear that any change in inherited formulations brings the destruction of faith itself, while others will wonder whether maintaining the centrality of Christology is really worth the effort.

How can we enhance the desirability of the reconstructive task of interdisciplinary dialogue without obscuring the real terror that it sometimes brings? Part of the problem is the way in which we have imagined the relation between the disciplines. Theology and science have often been depicted as enemies, sometimes as friends, and occasionally as disinterested acquaintances. These are quite obviously inter-*personal* metaphors for inter-*disciplinary* relations. Nevertheless, such similes can have a powerful heuristic function. The complexity of the relations between disciplines and disciplinarians calls for different ways of interacting in varying contexts, which means that no single metaphor will fit every situation. We may sometimes need to be friendly, sometimes antagonistic, sometimes to leave the other alone. Indeed there may be some dialogues in which the partners are both amicable and inimical during the same conversation.

Accepting a default image of interdisciplinary engagement, however, has an effect on the way one approaches the dialogue. I would like to suggest an interpersonal metaphor that is rarely considered appropriate (if considered at all) for the interaction between the disciplines. Is it possible that we might think of theology and science as *lovers?* Like the other metaphors, it has its limitations – most obviously its sexual innuendo. However, there are ways in which this simile can help us make sense of and even facilitate our interdisciplinary affairs. First and foremost, comparing theology and science to lovers provides us with a way to make sense of our mutual fear and fascination. We fear existential encounters that we cannot control. This inability to control the other, which evokes trembling in the presence of the beloved, is ingredient to true love. The risk of losing control is part of the delightful experience that binds lovers together.

Lovers are fascinated by their differences, as well as their shared interests. Self-discovery and discovery of the other are reciprocally related for lovers, as they search together for new ways of understanding one another and their place in a shared cosmos. A good lover delights in learning from the beloved and rejoices when the beloved experiences a transformative insight. However, real love takes hard work at mutual interpretation. Mature lovers do not spend all their time gazing into each other's eyes, blind to all faults. They are willing to confront one another for the sake of illumination and transformation. This interpersonal metaphor elicits an image of shared delightful terror in the other that promotes mutual understanding. In this sense, the disciplines of theology and science must learn to become better lovers.

Objections will arise from members of both disciplines. Some will object that if Christology (or theology) marries the science of today it will become a widow tomorrow, or soon be forced to seek divorce. This is a rather strange attitude toward marriage. Does one partner's transformation require the dissolution of the relationship? Tension arises in any relation in which one person is open to the transformative experience of discovery and critical interpretation while the other is not. Moreover, why should we assume that marriage is the only possible construct within which the delightful terror of love can emerge and grow? Theology once had her fair share of suitors. The problem today is not so much the danger of getting married to a particular science, as it is the unlikely prospect of getting a date. Isn't the former queen of the sciences even allowed to flirt a little? Many theologians and scientists find the prospect of serious engagement purely terrifying. The metaphor of disciplinary lovers may open up new ways of looking at each other, new ways of facing our fear that enhance mutual fascination and release us from our obsession with controlling one another.

Of course even lovers who are interested in learning together may still get annoyed with each other. Probably what annoys scientists the most is when theologians try to prove claims about Jesus by appealing to scientific theories or discoveries, or when they attempt to use specific christological beliefs to fill in alleged gaps in scientific knowledge. Probably what annoys theologians the most is when scientists try to protect their allegedly neutral fields of inquiry by dismissing all religious belief as delusional, or when they attempt to reduce religious experience to factors that may be wholly explained by their own disciplines. Although readers may find themselves perturbed by what follows for other reasons, I have attempted to avoid these particularly annoying habits.

How can these interdisciplinary lovers strengthen their relation to one another without one discipline alienating or becoming co-dependent on the other? One way is to attend to the mediating role of *philosophy* in this dialogue. Theology and science are both guided by a love of knowledge, and reflecting together on the way in which philosophical categories shape our inquiry can facilitate a deeper level of interaction. We are dealing here with a reciprocal triangular mediation. We should not imagine that philosophers do their work and then scientists and theologians are left to figure out how it helps (or hurts) them. Nor should we think of science as simply providing facts, which then must be dealt with by philosophy and theology, nor of theology as a finalized set of assertions which may or may not be engaged by the other disciplines. Theology, science and philosophy all search for ways of making sense of the human experience of life in the cosmos, often shaping each other in ways that are not immediately obvious; our attention will be on the interwoven dynamics of this reciprocity.

Throughout the course of this book we will concentrate on ways in which particular categories have shaped this reciprocal mediation. In this sense we are engaged in *philosophical* theology, which in my view is dialectically linked to *systematic* theology as part of a broader dynamic process (cf. Shults, 1999, 206–11). Although issues related to the interpretation of the biblical tradition will be woven throughout our discussion, our focus in this context will be on the ways in which these interpretations have been (and are) shaped by the triangular mediation of Christology, philosophy and science. In the remainder of this introductory chapter, we will explore three different ways of configuring the reciprocal relations among these disciplines.

Jesus Christ and the Philosophy of Science

The "philosophy of science" involves critical reflection on the relations among and self-understanding of organized fields of study. This form of inquiry analyzes the nature, process and outcome of inquiry itself, which requires abstraction from particular disciplines in order to attend to broader epistemological and hermeneutical issues. In cultures where universities play a significant role in public discourse, philosophers of science often focus on what counts as academic or positive knowledge (*Wissenschaft*, *vitenskap*) and how it is properly acquired, formulated and defended. The self-understanding of theology is shaped by this debate, even (or especially) when the response of theologians is one of attempted self-isolation from the threat of interdisciplinary discourse.

Does the study of Jesus Christ involve the acquisition of new knowledge and, if so, how ought such knowledge to be formulated and defended? This question may feel threatening for those who continue to operate within the assumptions of early modern philosophy of science. Before the Enlightenment, the themes that are now treated by science and theology were often self-consciously integrated as part of a holistic understanding of the world. The split between these disciplines had already begun to emerge in the late middle ages, but during the 17th and 18th centuries it was widened into a chasm. Increasingly, theology was associated with "faith" in distinction from science, which was associated with "reason." Whereas theology might be passionate and subjective, science was supposed to be neutral and objective. Truly "scientific" conclusions are those deduced from empirical analysis and experimentation that could be repeated by any dispassionate rational individual; nomological proofs were increasingly privileged over ideographic observations. In the 19th century this ideal contributed to the hardening of a separation between the "natural" sciences and the "human" sciences.

The dichotomies at the heart of this approach to the philosophy of science created an atmosphere in which some educators began to argue that theology should be excluded from the academy. Some theologians responded by trying to emulate the "hard" sciences (e.g., logically deducing propositions from "data" posited in the Bible) while others attempted to refigure theology as a "soft" science (e.g., merely interpreting the narrative or drama of church history). Others gave up on the idea that theology was a "science" at all. Each of these decisions affected the way in which the theologians understood the task of (or need for) acquiring, formulating and defending "knowledge" of Jesus Christ.

In the following chapters we will explore several concrete examples of the deleterious effects of this early modern view of "science" on the self-understanding of theology in general and on the task of christological reconstruction in particular. The main purpose of this sub-section, however, is to point to three developments within *late modern* philosophy of science that have shaped the contemporary conceptual landscape in a way that provides new opportunities for reforming Christology in dialogue with other disciplines.

The first development has to do with the growing appeal of *relationality* as a heuristic category in the philosophy of science. I have rehearsed this history in more detail elsewhere (Shults, 2003; 2005), but it is important to review it again briefly because understanding this shift is crucial for clarifying the task of reconstructing Christology in late modern culture. The suppression of the concept of *relation* goes back to Aristotle, whose influential philosophy of science privileged the concept of *substance* in human knowledge. In his

Categories he argued that knowing a thing involves defining its substance (or essence). We may also be interested in describing the way in which the thing is related to other things, but such relations are only "accidental" – not "essential" to knowing its thingyness.

The category of relation appears in Aristotle's list of categories but (like the others) it is subordinated to the category of substance. He was not alone here. "Relation" does not even appear on Plato's list, although he does include "the different" as we will see in chapter 2. The concept of *ousia* (substance) also played a central role in Plato's metaphysical distinction between perceptible and intelligible reality. Although the Stoics placed more emphasis on relationality, their typical listing of four categories exhibits the same prioritization: substance, quality, disposed in a certain way and disposed in a certain way in relation to something else. The demotion of relationality in ontology was mirrored in the epistemology of these ancient Greek philosophical schools.

As we will see in our exploration of the historical development of Christology, this privileging of the category of substance dominated patristic and medieval theology (and philosophy). Over the centuries, however, the difficulties with a theory of knowledge (and predication) that failed to attend sufficiently to the relations between things became increasingly evident. Alongside the rise of modern empirical science, philosophers like Locke and Hume began to recognize that *scientia* – knowledge of reality – requires more than simply defining the substances of things. Understanding the relations in which a "thing" is embedded is necessary for understanding what it *is*.

By the late 18th century Kant found it necessary to reverse Aristotle, making "substance and accidents" a sub-category of the broader category "of Relation." Hegel emphasized the concept of relationality even more, challenging the basic separation between substance and accidents. For him "absolute relation" is the highest category in objective logic. This intuition played itself out in various ways in other 19th century philosophical proposals, such as C.S. Peirce's "new list" of categories, in which scientific knowledge is parsed in terms of three "classes of relations." For our purposes here, the details of these proposals are less important than the major conceptual shift they illustrate in the philosophy of science.

This turn to relationality can also be traced in the history of the development of the philosophy of logic and mathematics, which shape the underlying structure of argumentation within the natural sciences. As Ernst Cassirer has shown in his *Substance and Function* (1923), the concept of a "thing" with its "attributes," which was essential to Aristotelian logic and dominated mathematics throughout most of the early modern period, proved to be unsuitable for the analysis of complex systems of logical *relations*. Defining the concept of "number" in generic (substantial) terms hindered the discovery of the way in which constitutive differentiated relations among numbers open up new possibilities for analysis (e.g., infinitesimal calculus, set theory). Eventually the category of substance lost its hold in meta-mathematics and was increasingly replaced by the concept of *function.* Once "freed of all thing-like being," the peculiar functional character of logical concepts was revealed. Cassirer demonstrates how shifting from reliance on the *generic* concept to the *relational* concept made it possible for Gauss to develop the theory of imaginary numbers, for Dedekind to offer an explanation of the irrational numbers, and for Cantor to use generating relations for the production of transfinite numbers.

As we will see in our case studies below, this shift had ramifications beyond pure mathematics. Physicists soon discovered that the natural world could be more adequately explained using relational concepts. So Einstein's field equations for general special relativity, for example, are based on the use of functional relations. Quantum physics pressed philosophers of science even further, leading them to challenge the adequacy of substance/attribute predication theory to make sense of the entanglement phenomena discovered at the subatomic level. Here reality itself resists the abstraction associated with the category of "thing" (substance), and physicists increasingly appealed to inherently relational and dynamic modes of talking about what "happens between" and within the unpredictable flow of "interphenomena" (cf. Reichenbach, 1988 [1944], 21, 176–7; Bohm, 1981, 28–47). The biological and social sciences have also progressively paid more attention to the constitutive function of relations within complex organizational systems in order to make better sense of the world.

In the chapters that follow we will attempt to clarify the challenges and opportunities that this philosophical turn to relationality creates for the task of articulating a Christian understanding of the significance of Jesus Christ today. As we will see, substance categories played a dominant role in many traditional formulations of Christology, sometimes obscuring the importance of interpreting the *relation* of Jesus Christ to God, humanity and the cosmos in these doctrines. As we theologians overcome our addiction to "substance abuse" we may find that we are able to recover some of the relational resources in the biblical tradition in creative ways that facilitate a healthier engagement with the efforts of our colleagues in the other disciplines.

A second development in the philosophy of science that is of particular relevance for the reconstructive task of Christology is the late modern emphasis on the *contextuality* of all scientific inquiry. The positivist notion that scientific theorizing involves objective analysis of data that are simply given (posited) has been criticized as an impossible and inappropriate epistemic ideal. All data are theory-laden. In other words, our experience of "the world" is always and already interpreted through our linguistic categories and shaped by our participation *within* a world of shared meaning schemes. Knowledge is not simply acquired by deducing universally true propositions from self-evident facts accessible to all rational observers. Our interpretive and explanatory efforts are immersed within and mediated by our participation in overlapping socio-linguistic contexts composed of dynamically interacting hermeneutical structures.

Philosophers of science have described the contextuality of disciplinary activity in various ways, referring to the "paradigms" (Kuhn, 1996), "research programs" (Lakatos, 1980), or "traditions" (MacIntyre, 1988) that guide our inquiry. Acknowledging the contextuality of theory-construction does not cripple science. On the contrary, the "fiduciary component" or "personal coefficient" (Polanyi, 1962) of knowledge is what motivates the scientific enterprise. Personal commitment and intellectual passion are an impetus for the pursuit of knowledge. This does not entail subjectivism or relativism. Participating self-consciously within a particular paradigm ought to be balanced with an openness to distanciate ourselves from our research program and humbly enter into transversal hermeneutical encounters with other traditions.

Traditional formulations of Christology have been shaped by their contexts throughout church history, as the following chapters will show. Critical awareness of this social embeddedness grew more intense during the 19th century. Sarah Coakley has demonstrated the influence of Ernst Troeltsch's call for a *Christ Without Absolutes* (Coakley, 1988) on theological engagement with the social sciences in the 20th century. Those who reacted violently to the claim that doctrine is always socially located and responded by attempting to insulate theology from culture illustrated (ironically) the very dynamic they were trying to deny. In light of these broader philosophical developments, Wesley Wildman argues that we should aim for *Fidelity with Plausibility* (1998), insisting that the contextuality of doctrine requires a "modest" rather than an "absolute" Christology. Yet, as both Coakley and Wildman point out, giving up the hubris of absolutism does not mean giving up on the intelligibility of Christian belief in (for example) the incarnation. It does mean, however, reformulating our explication of faith in Christ in ways that self-consciously engage the plausibility structures of our own contexts.

This may initially appear threatening to Christology, but this new conceptual space actually opens up opportunities for concrete interaction with the other sciences. The harsh dichotomy between faith and reason that created a barrier to dialogue can be refigured as a dialectical dynamic in which and out of which all our inquiry operates. Faith and reason are interwoven within every contextualized form of human inquiry. Making a rational judgment involves committing oneself to a belief, and faith involves making judgments about what is trustworthy. To believe something or to trust someone requires some knowledge of that thing or person. To know something or someone requires some level of commitment, a fiduciary connection to that which is known.

Christology is no longer forced to choose between beginning "from below" or "from above." Neither of these is really possible. Every judgment made about the significance of Jesus Christ is embedded within a context already mediated by one's interpreted experience of a tradition. Rational assessment of the historical Jesus operates within a web of beliefs about the relation of God to the world. Belief in divine revelation arises within a particular social context and is conditioned by particular linguistic conventions. Instead of asking whether we should begin with rational proofs and *add* faith when we hit a mystery, or whether we should begin with our fideistic commitments and then *add* reasonable arguments only when pressed, theologians can begin within the relationality in which "faith" and "reason" are mutually constituted.

The appeal to contextuality can help us escape the horns of this dilemma by exposing the bull beneath it: we cannot abstract ourselves from our christological inquiry and find an Archimedean point from which to observe the relation between an alleged "above" and "below" and choose between them. Christology is articulated "from within" one's interpreted experience of being related to God (cf. Shults, 1999, 166–77, 252). If one presupposes a dichotomy between faith and reason, such a claim will appear to fall on one side of the dilemma. Beginning with(in) the relationality that constitutes the dialectical relation between faith and reason can help us see that the intellectual efforts of every discipline (including Christology) operate in a dynamic tension between dwelling within our interpreted experience of being bound in relation and seeking ever more adequate interpretations of those experienced relations.

This brings us to the growing appeal for *interdisciplinarity*, the third development in the philosophy of science that bears on the task of reforming Christology today. We will have many opportunities to explore examples of this development in the following chapters, but our purpose at this stage is simply to show how the opening up of conceptual space for the kind of dialogue in which this book participates is closely connected to the late modern emphasis on relationality and contextuality.

One of the characteristics of the scientific method is the careful analysis of discrete phenomena, and this quite naturally led to specialization among and within the sciences. However, attention to specificity has sometimes led to a disciplinary myopia, turning the methodological reduction appropriate to a particular field into a material reductionism that fails to see the insights of other disciplines. Although one still finds this tendency in some circles (cf. Stenmark, 2001), the broader recognition of the relational complexity of the world and the contextual limitations of each field of inquiry has contributed to an increased openness toward interdisciplinary engagement.

This is particularly clear in the burgeoning global conversation among theologians and scientists. To use Ian Barbour's well-known taxonomy, more and more participants in this interdisciplinary field are moving beyond models of conflict, independence and even dialogue, and embracing the more complex task of integration (cf. Barbour, 1990; 2000). Much of this interaction has focused on the methodological and theoretical dimensions of the integrative process. As Mikael Stenmark points out in *How to Relate Science and Religion* (2004), we should also pay attention to the social and teleological dimensions of these disciplines. In other words, healthy mediation between the fields will require closer attention to their different social practices as well as the different goals that guide these practices. As theologians we can enhance our interdisciplinary dexterity by making explicit the way in which these dimensions operate in our own contexts.

This transgressing of boundaries between disciplines does not mean the erasure of differentiation between fields of inquiry. Each discipline has its own domain of expertise, which requires methods of analysis that are appropriate to the phenomena. During the early modern period, it was often assumed that the kind of mathematical analysis associated with disciplines like physics was the most "scientific," and other sciences struggled to accommodate themselves to this ideal. However, this form of deduction alone is not sufficient for understanding (for example) biological organisms or human cultures. A fuller and more adequate interpretation of our experience of the cosmos requires the integration of insights from a variety of disciplines. The growing appeal for interdisciplinarity will make it easier to integrate our explication of concepts like space and time with our understanding of concepts like person and community – all of which impact Christology.

We cannot explore the connection between the disciplines as though we were outside of them looking in, objectively considering the possibility of relating them. This is not simply because we are (usually) trained in only one discipline, or even because our participation with a traditioned field of inquiry affects the way we "look." There is an even deeper reason why no such neutral vantage point exists: the relations among disciplines are always and already mediated by their mutual differentiation. This differentiation is not something that is "accidental" to the "substance" of the discipline. Every mode of organized human inquiry is constituted by its differentiated relations to other modes of inquiry, and every participant in any one of these modes is inextricably caught up within that discipline's distinctive way of differentiating itself. As we develop the capacity to accept differences while acknowledging appropriate attachment relations, we can participate in healthier forms of interdisciplinary engagement (cf. Shults and Sandage, 2006, 13–36).

Christology is interdisciplinary whether we like it or not. The question is not whether science (and philosophy) will shape our interpretation of Jesus Christ, but whether we can self-critically explicate this mediation in a way that engages our own culture. As we will see, earlier christological formulations engaged the anthropological and cosmological assumptions of (for example) 4th century Neoplatonic science or 17th century mechanistic science. The context out of which and for which this book is written is early-21st century interdisciplinary dialogue. Relational categories play an important illuminative and generative role in this interdisciplinary context. Yes, this creates challenges for some traditional ways of articulating the significance of Jesus Christ. But it also provides new opportunities for *reforming* Christology in a way that recovers and refigures some of the radically relational intuitions of the biblical tradition.

Philosophy and the Science of Jesus Christ

This brings us to another dimension of the reciprocal triangular mediation of Christology, science and philosophy. If we use the term "science" to refer to organized modes of contextual inquiry operating within historical traditions, then we may think of Christology as the *science* of Jesus Christ. This mode of inquiry has its own history of methodological and material debates, which are wrapped up within the broader discipline of theology. To borrow a phrase from Thomas Aquinas, theology is the science that is interested in understanding God and all things under the aspect of their relation to God (*sub ratione Dei*).

In light of the shifts in the philosophy of science since the middle ages, we should perhaps say: understanding God and all things from within our interpreted experience of being related to all things in God. Several scholarly monographs in recent years have outlined the major developments in biblical scholarship and historical theology that have shaped the discipline of Christology (e.g., Hurtado, 2003; O'Collins, 1995; McIntyre, 1992; 1998; Schwarz, 1998; Glebe-Möller, 1989). Our focus will be on philosophical developments that have shaped the discipline.

One of the ways in which philosophy plays a role in the "science of Jesus Christ" is the *material* shaping of its formulations. We will explore several examples in more detail in the case studies below, but it is important at this stage to underline the special mediating significance of the philosophical concepts of *humanity* and *divinity* in Christology. The way in which we understand Jesus' relation to us and to God will be structured by these concepts. Under the influence of substance metaphysics, anthropology often began with a definition of a human person as an individual substance of a rational nature. The philosophical dichotomy between material substance and immaterial substance was the basis of the distinction between soul and body in the individual person. Many theologians assumed that the substance of all human souls is corrupted because of the historical "Fall" of Adam and Eve. As we will see, these anthropological assumptions play a powerful role in many traditional christological formulations. Although these categories are problematic for exegetical reasons as well, in this context we will focus primarily on the philosophical and scientific developments that have rendered them implausible.

Our concepts of God are not merely philosophical but they are at least philosophical, and these ideas shape Christology. How one interprets *divine* knowing, acting and being will shape one's understanding of the identity, agency and presence of Jesus Christ in relation to God. During the early modern period many theologians began with the concept of God as a rational causative substance. As an immaterial substance, untouched and untouchable by the material world, God was depicted as a single subject whose intellect and will are the first cause of all predetermined events. These philosophical assumptions about divine nature canalized discussions about the relation between God and the finite intellect and will of the human nature of Jesus.

Three late modern trajectories in the doctrine of God have transformed the broader theological context within which Christology may now be explicated (cf. Shults, 2005). The first is the retrieval of divine Infinity, of a way of speaking of God not as an immaterial substance (defined in differentiation from material substance) but as an intensively infinite presence from, through and to which finite creaturely differentiation is constituted. The 20th century revival of trinitarian doctrine, which begins with the constitutive relationality of the divine persons rather than the idea of God as a single subject, is a second trajectory that provides resources for resolving some of the conceptual difficulties of the christological tradition. The third is the renewal of eschatological ontology, wherein reliance on the idea of God as an efficient first cause is replaced by an understanding of creaturely temporality as absolutely dependent on the arrival of divine Futurity. In the following chapters, we will explore ways in which these trajectories have opened up new conceptual space for christological reconstruction.

Philosophical categories also play a *methodological* role in the science of Jesus Christ, shaping decisions about the organization of themes. In other words, categorical mediation is already at work in the very ordering of the loci of Christology. For example, in many early modern Protestant presentations of Christian theology the locus of Christology "proper" was limited to the doctrine of the incarnation. Explicating the significance of Jesus Christ began with a statement of who he *was*. This was then followed by a treatment of the doctrine of the atonement, which explained what Jesus *did*, typically understood as something accomplished in the past (such as a judicial decision or transaction). Exploration of the way in which that soteriological (salvific) transaction applies to us now (in the present), was usually delayed to a later locus that dealt with the "work" of the Holy Spirit.

This organizational structure is based on a distinction between the *person* (substance) and the *work* (function) of Christ. In the 19th century many theologians suggested that we ought to begin with the function of Jesus, with the way in which his activity has a redemptive effect on us. This was partially in response to the demise of substance metaphysics and partially in response to the rise of historical criticism. This "liberal" approach was met with consternation by "conservatives" who did not want Christology to be *only* about how Jesus was related to us, but about his *real* human and divine substances.

Should theology begin with the person or the work of Christ? As we saw above, the presuppositions that seem to force a choice between substantialist and functionalist Christology have been challenged by the turn to relationality. Once we recognize that functional relations are constitutive for the "substantiality" of any dynamic reality it becomes clear that this is a false dichotomy. These conceptual shifts provide us with an opportunity to develop a more integrative presentation of christological doctrine.

Another way in which philosophical categories have registered an effect on the organization of themes in Christology is less obvious. Linear concepts of absolute time and deterministic models of causality in the early modern period contributed to the exclusion of discussions of the future of Jesus from the loci of Christology (and even soteriology). While sometimes the resurrection and the "state of exaltation" were treated in proximity to the doctrines of incarnation and atonement, the way in which Christ mediates the arrival of the eschatological presence of God was usually left until the analysis of the "last things" at the end of a dogmatic treatise (cf. König, 1989). We will return to the material impact of early modern assumptions about space, time and causality on Christology in chapter 4. The main point here is that these philosophical categories had a methodological impact, splitting apart some aspects of the relation between Jesus, God and us and excluding them from the presentation of Christology (proper).

Why has Jesus' relation to the future (his "coming" or "parousia") so often been isolated from treatments of his person and work? The philosophical assumptions guiding many formulations of these latter loci are partially responsible for this segregation. The task of making sense of the experience of being confronted by a real presence that mediates the arriving reign of God has no immediate relevance for a doctrine of the incarnation that is limited to a discussion of the way in which the person of Jesus was constituted by the union of human and divine substances in the past.

In the same way, many soteriological theories focused so narrowly on a legal transaction that was accomplished on the cross (in the past) that the resurrection (ascension and coming) of Jesus played a small role (if any) in the doctrine of the atonement. This division of themes not only disintegrates what is united in the biblical witness, it also promotes an abstract Christology that has no immediate connection to a central aspect of the religious experience of practicing Christians – the real eschatological presence of Jesus Christ as the mediator of abundant life in the Spirit of God.

As a first step toward a more holistic presentation of these themes I have incorporated a treatment of the doctrine of the *parousia*, as well as the *incarnation* and the *atonement* in this book on the reciprocal mediation of Christology, philosophy and science (Fig. 1.1).

Incarnation and Evolutionary Biology (Chapter 2)	Atonement and Cultural Anthropology (Chapter 3)	Parousia and Physical Cosmology (Chapter 4)
A Shared Interest in Knowing	A Shared Interest in Acting	A Shared Interest in Being
Epistemology & Noetic Desire	Ethics & Moral Desire	Metaphysics & Aesthetic Desire
The Identity of Jesus Christ	The Agency of Jesus Christ	The Presence of Jesus Christ

Figure 1.1   A Matrix for Christological Inquiry

One of the main benefits of this way of organizing the themes is that it facilitates a concrete dialogue between christological doctrine and particular sciences, making explicit the reciprocal relation between theological presentation of the significance of Jesus Christ and scientific clarification of the dynamic structures of the world. It also provides a matrix within which we can attend to some of the philosophical interests and existential concerns shared by theologians and scientists in these fields.

One of the limitations of this thematic organization is that it does not offer an integrated presentation of these dimensions of Christology. However, as I hope to make clear in the final section of each chapter, the concepts of the identity, agency and presence of Christ commend themselves for the task of integration in the context of a broader systematic presentation of Christian doctrine (cf. the Epilogue). In the context of our current project, however, this matrix facilitates our interest in highlighting the philosophical mediation between the sciences and theological interest in Jesus' way of knowing, acting and being in the world.

Science and the Philosophy of Jesus Christ

How might the study of Jesus Christ shape inquiry in other scientific disciplines? Alongside the rise of positivism in the late 19th century there emerged a popular "warfare" reading of the history between science and religion. On this model, science has nothing to learn from theology. As historians of science have shown over the last few decades, however, theology has often had a positive influence on science, both formally through patronage and inspiration and materially through its own analysis of concepts such as space, time and causality (e.g., Brooke, 1991; Grant, 1996; Lindberg and Numbers, 1986; cf. Foster, 1934). We will have the opportunity to observe several examples of this material influence in the following chapters.

However, it is important to be clear how theology should *not* influence science. It is not the business of professional theologians to tell professional scientists how to do their empirical work. Theological symbols have no place in mathematical formulae, and religious concepts should not be inserted into gaps in scientific theories. This is why attending to the role of *philosophical* mediation is so important. Even this could easily be misunderstood. By referring to the "philosophy of Jesus Christ" in this final introductory sub-section I do not mean to imply that Jesus developed a philosophical system of propositions that can play an immediate role in, for example, explaining quantum phenomena or biological evolution.

As Figure 1.1 indicates, however, theology and science do share an interest in knowing, acting and being, and (as we shall see) they also share many of the same philosophical categories in their efforts to make sense of human life in the world. Moreover, as human persons living in the world participants in all of these disciplines share existential concerns that shape their longings for truth, goodness and beauty. In the case studies below we will observe several examples of this reciprocal mediation, but Einstein provides a particularly salient illustration. He never tried to hide his interest in theological questions, such as whether God played dice, and was straightforward about the importance of existential concerns: "the ideals which have lighted my way, and time after time have given me new courage to face life cheerfully, have been Kindness, Beauty, and Truth" (1954, 9).

Scientific inquiry that dismisses the religious longing of the human spirit produces a sterile rationality that is not worth having, and theological inquiry that evades contemporary science produces a sterile faith that is not worth having.

As we have seen, shifts in the philosophy of science have created a new milieu in which the disciplines are not forced away from each other as they were in early modernity, in which we can acknowledge our own contextual concerns and explore shared interests in the complex relations in which we find ourselves searching for more adequate explanations of our experience in the world. The exponential growth of scientific knowledge has led to technological advances that raise concerns about ecological destruction, and many scientists are becoming more interested in pursuing the truth in ways that also sponsor the flourishing of goodness and the appreciation of beauty. The science of Jesus Christ can respect the integrity of the other sciences, while also participating in a philosophical field of discourse about such things as the limitation of human reason, the importance of ethics in research and the significance of the aesthetic dimension of our life together.

In the context of the following chapters the *philosophy* of Jesus Christ refers to his way of knowing, acting and being in the world in relation to God and his neighbors. In addition to facilitating interaction with science on the field of shared existential concerns, this use of the term also serves a *theological* function. It reminds us of the New Testament emphasis on following the *way* of Jesus Christ. The book of Acts suggests that the religious movement that emerged after the resurrection of Jesus and the outpouring of the Spirit at Pentecost was initially called "the Way" (19:23, 22:4).

Theology has too often given in to the temptation to allow propositional statements about Jesus to function as idols, distracting us from what he himself taught – a way of life that rightly orients us to God and our neighbors. As we will see, this "philosophy" of life is shaped by a particular way of being related to the divine Spirit. Attending to this relationality can facilitate the integration of pneumatological concerns into a presentation of Christology. In other words, focusing on the way in which Jesus lived in relation to the Spirit, which transformed his experience of understanding, valuing and embracing others, contributes to the task of *reforming* Christology.

But what can we really know about the philosophy of the man Jesus of Nazareth? It is beyond the scope of this project to engage in detail in the findings of the ongoing quests for the historical Jesus. However, at least two developments in this arena of biblical scholarship are particularly important at this stage of the argument. First, the vast majority of participants in the more recent ("third") quest have acknowledged the extent to which earlier quests for the historical Jesus were driven by naïve hermeneutical assumptions. Across the spectrum of biblical scholars, one finds a general consensus that it is not possible (nor even desirable) to engage in the search in a wholly detached and neutral way (e.g., Crossan, 1991, xxxiv; Theissen and Merz, 1998, 13; Wright, 1992, 6–14; cf. Padgett, 2003, 137–61). We can (and should) try to offer warrants for our interpretation of the textual "objects," which may be criticized in the broader academic community, but we should (and can) also try to make explicit how we as "subjects" of the interpretation are shaped by our contexts.

In the late 19th and early 20th centuries many scholars responded to historical criticism by making a strong distinction between the Jesus of history and the Christ of faith (cf. Kähler, 1964 [1896]). In order to transgress the boundaries of this dualism, which is based on the modernist dichotomy between reason and faith discussed above, I will often use the terms "Jesus" and "Christ" interchangeably in the following case studies. This is not meant to imply that they mean exactly the same thing, nor that all christological titles should be conflated; rather, it serves the rhetorical function of underlining my argument that our theological interest should be in the whole event of the dynamic relations between this man and God (and the rest of us). We can acknowledge our passionate commitment to offering plausible explications of our experience of these redemptive relations.

A second development in the search for the historical Jesus has a more immediate material impact on our current project. Despite the variety of positions among biblical scholars, all but the most skeptical agree that, whatever else we can say about the man Jesus of Nazareth, his life was characterized by a revolutionary way of relating to his neighbors and a particularly intimate way of relating to God. Embedded within his Jewish context, under the domination of Roman occupation, Jesus actively challenged the religious segregation of the "impure" and "sinners," and the political oppression of the poor and imprisoned. Whatever term we choose to emphasize as we point to this way of relating to his social context (e.g., cynic, prophet, revolutionary, healer, sage), historical scholarship strongly suggests that what distinguished the way of Jesus was his active attempts to participate in the transformation of the powerful structures that crushed the helpless and hopeless.

The most commonly accepted authentic sayings of Jesus in the earliest layers of the New Testament suggest that this way of relating to his neighbors was reciprocally related to his sense of the intimate presence of the One he called "Father." Here too scholars use different terms to describe this way of relating to God. For our purposes, it will suffice to illustrate this briefly by pointing to the work of Marcus Borg, who refers to Jesus as a "spirit person" (1987, 25–75). The way in which Jesus functioned as a "mediator of the sacred" indicates that his self-understanding was shaped by his participation in the experiential tradition of early Jewish mysticism (Borg, 1994, 31–6).

Of course Christian systematic theology will also want to account for and incorporate the later layers of interpretation in the New Testament witness about Jesus' relation to God, but this insight from critical textual scholarship is especially relevant for our current task: exploring how Jesus' way of life (his "philosophy") plays a mediating role in theological engagement with the sciences.

Some might object at this point that bringing Jesus' *mystical* experience of the divine Spirit into the interdisciplinary dialogue is irrelevant (at best) and inappropriate (at worst). In this introductory chapter I have attempted to show how developments in the philosophy of science challenge the assumptions behind such objections, and in the chapters that follow I will attempt to demonstrate how conceptual shifts in late modern philosophy open new space for an integrative understanding of human inquiry that incorporates the passionate desire for a transformational experience of ultimate reality.

At this point, I simply remind readers that *many* of the great scientists throughout human history were mystics, *most* of the great philosophers were mystics, and *all* of the great Christian theologians were mystics. As we escape from the strictures of early modern notions of science (and philosophy) we may be able to recover the methodological humility and imaginative resources of the mystical tradition(s) as we engage contemporary science. Such an engaging recovery of the "mystical" will require *critical* appropriation; articulating Christology in a way that tends to the intensification of human desire for spiritual transformation in relation to God and other persons can utilize the dynamic and relational categories of contemporary social science without depending on particular construsals of Jesus' relation to Jewish mysticism or affirming later (especially Neoplatonic) forms of mysticism that denigrated embodiment and avoided practical communal engagement (cf. Shults and Sandage, 2006).

By way of preview, the matrix in Figure 1.1 provides an outline of the pattern that will be followed in the presentation of each case study. Each chapter begins with a brief introduction to a philosophical interest shared by the relevant disciplines (knowing, acting or being). These philosophical issues are explicitly connected to the existential desire that shapes these aspects of human life. The bulk of each chapter is an exploration of the philosophical challenges and interdisciplinary opportunities that face the task of reforming Christology in connection with particular scientific developments.

Brief overviews of the development of christological doctrine are offered in each case study, in order to illustrate the way in which material decisions in philosophy have shaped formulations throughout church history. The next step in each chapter is the identification of some key interdisciplinary proposals that have taken advantage of the opportunities provided by late modern philosophical shifts to articulate the significance of Jesus Christ in ways that engage contemporary science. The final section of each case study offers some programmatic suggestions for building on these resources as we participate in the ongoing task of reconstructing Christology.

By bracketing the chapters with treatments of the existential dimensions of our shared interdisciplinary space, I am explicitly attempting to emphasize the need for a *reformative* Christology. Christians believe that participating in Jesus' way of knowing, acting and being in the world is transformative. Like every generation before us, our task is to articulate our understanding and experience of this transformation by engaging the plausibility structures of our own context. This endeavor is sure to provoke shock and even terror among many participants of the dialogue. My hope is that it will also evoke a sense of fascination with and appreciation for the way in which weaving together insights from different disciplines can enhance our self-understanding. Embracing the trembling delight that overwhelms us in this ongoing struggle to make sense of our experience in the cosmos may also help us become better interdisciplinary lovers.

Chapter 2

Incarnation and Evolutionary Biology

Our first case study explores some of the philosophical shifts in late modern discourse that shape the contemporary conceptual landscape in which both theological explication of the doctrine of the incarnation and the sciences of evolutionary biology operate. In this context I will use the phrase "evolutionary biology" to refer generally to those sciences that deal with the continuity and discontinuity of human life with other forms of life that have emerged on earth, including Darwinian evolution, neuroscience and paleobiology. The Christian doctrine of the "incarnation" has often focused on interpreting the announcement in the prologue of John (1:14) that the Word became flesh (*logos sarx egeneto*) in the person of Jesus of Nazareth. Several scientific developments in the last two centuries have challenged the notions of embodied personhood (*sarx*) that were presupposed in many ancient and early modern formulations of this doctrine, and this provides us with a new opportunity for reforming Christology in a way that illuminates and transforms our understanding of human being and becoming.

By tending to shifts in the philosophical categories that are at work in both Christology and evolutionary science, I hope to clarify the conceptual field within which theology can articulate a reconstructive presentation of the intuitions of the biblical tradition about the identity of Jesus Christ. I will suggest that beginning with categories that highlight the dynamics of Jesus' relational identification of, by and with God can be more productive in our contemporary context than relying on the categories of substance metaphysics that shaped the contexts in which many influential traditional formulations were developed. Our first step, however, is thematizing the shared semantic (and existential) domain within which both scientists and theologians find themselves interested in the intense human desire to know and be known.

A Shared Interest in Knowing

The distinctive character of our longing to gain wisdom (*sapientia*) as we relate to one another and adapt to our ever-changing contexts, is implicit in our self-designation as *Homo sapiens*. Our species may not be the only one in which its mature members are capable of developing cognitive maps of the lived world, seeking to communicate knowledge with one other, or even achieving self-consciousness, but the *intensity* of our desire to comprehend ourselves and the world is unique. This search for wisdom is manifested in a variety of ways, from the attempt to discover more adequate ways to procure food for the long-term survival of our social groups to the struggle to render intelligible our experience of patterns within the cosmos. How are we to interpret our interpretive urges? Questions about the symbol-constructing and meaning-making dynamics of human life form an important aspect of the conceptual field within which our first concrete interdisciplinary dialogue may occur.

Understanding the human capacity for acquiring knowledge is important for both Christology and evolutionary biology, but each discipline approaches the task with its own particular methods, modes of questioning and ways of evaluating answers. *Scientists* in these fields attempt to clarify the conditions for, and dynamics of, the emergence of human cognition in relation to the broader context of the evolution of life. What were the biological and environmental conditions that contributed to the rise of self-awareness and complex linguistic functions that characterize human knowing? How are these functions related to the evolution of the human brain? *Theologians* also aim to explicate the origin, condition and goal of human knowing, but with special reference to the interpreted experience of divine revelation – the making-known of ultimate reality. How can we make sense of the claim that God is manifested (made known) in the life, death and resurrection of Jesus Christ?

This shared interest in human knowing is not merely academic. As human persons, both scientists and theologians are existentially caught up within this longing to make sense of the world and our place within it. In addition to paying attention to particular objects of knowledge that are of interest to us, the interdisciplinary dialogue may also be enhanced by exploring the deeper dynamics of *noetic* desire that structure our being-interested. During the reign of positivism, many evolutionary biologists felt compelled to try to repress their own subjective interest in the human struggle for self-understanding, to offer allegedly neutral and value-free analyses. Some still do. As the appeal for interdisciplinarity intensifies, however, more scientists are making explicit attempts to integrate the search for better understanding of the emergence of uniquely human modes of knowing with the search for wiser ways to relate to one another and our broader environment (e.g., Brown, 2000).

When theologians explore the desire among members of our species to render the world intelligible, they are interested in making sense of noetic desire in relation to particular religious conceptions of *divine* wisdom. How can we speak of the *ultimate* origin, condition and goal of this longing itself? From a theological point of view, our species needs wisdom to survive – not just in order to become the *fittest*, but in order to find out how we *fit* within the divine intention for creation. The doctrine of incarnation is an attempt to clarify this question about the coming-to-be of *Homo sapiens*. Christians interpret the life, death and resurrection of Jesus Christ as the manifestation of divine wisdom, an intentional making-known of the Creator who calls creatures to participate in the embodiment of divine grace and peace in the world.

As we saw in chapter 1, the term "Christology" has often been understood as dealing primarily with the *person* – as distinct from the *work* – of Christ. In other words, Christology "proper" has traditionally been understood as tied to the doctrine of incarnation, and has focused on attempts to work out the relation between the human and the divine natures in the one person of Jesus Christ. The term *incarnatus* emerged among patristic Latin writers as they struggled to understand the claim in the prologue of John that "the Word became flesh" (1:14). This way of articulating Jesus' relation to God was unique to John, and other New Testament authors use a variety of expressions (e.g., revealing, making-known, illuminating) to indicate the manifestation of God in the life of Jesus.

The philosophical theme most relevant to this discussion is *epistemology* – the study of the nature of human knowledge, including its limits and possibilities, as well as criteria for adjudication between conflicting claims to knowledge. As we noted briefly in chapter 1, discussions of human knowing have increasingly moved away from focusing on the rational substance of the soul toward more relational and dynamic conceptions of rationality (cf. Rescher, 1990; MacIntyre, 1999). As we will see, the sciences of evolutionary biology have demonstrated that the processes of knowing must be understood as both embodied and environmentally embedded. These epistemic shifts in the philosophy of science provide a context that is hospitable for resolving some of the traditional difficulties in the doctrine of the incarnation and articulating a radically relational understanding of the identity of Jesus Christ.

Beginning with the shared experience of noetic desire can help us refigure the questions that structure theological discourse. Much of the tradition has started by asking: how can two substances fit in one person? The turn to relationality can help us move beyond the assumptions that compel us to formulate the question in this way. We might learn to ask different kinds of questions such as: how is the life of Jesus related to the identification of God and identifiable with God? Focusing on Jesus' way of knowing and being-known, the shaping of his intentionality as he grew in wisdom, can open up new ways to speak of his life as the manifestation of the divine Logos in dialogue with contemporary science. Previous generations of theologians attempted to articulate an understanding of the incarnation in dialogue with the concepts of humanity prevalent in their contexts, a task that is passed on to us. Today our context is shaped by discoveries within the sciences of evolutionary biology. A first step toward articulating a plausible and reformative Christology is clarifying the way in which these discoveries are embedded within a new conceptual space.

Philosophical Challenges

The dialogue between evolutionary biology and Christology can be facilitated by attending to the underlying *philosophical* categories that shape formulations in both fields. As we focus on figuring out answers to particular questions, we sometimes fail to recognize the operation of categories that have configured their formulation. Three sets of philosophical categories figure largely in both christological and scientific discourse and are particularly relevant for the current case study on the incarnation and evolutionary biology:

- sameness and difference
- body and soul
- origin and goal

Examining shifts within these categories in the history of science and theology can help us come to terms with the fact that our interpreted experience of God configures our experience of interpretation, and vice versa. Exploring these philosophical factors is a first step towards articulating the intuitions of the biblical tradition in a way that allows a liberal dose of scientific insight into their formulation, precisely in order to conserve their transformative power in our contemporary context.

Sameness and Difference

As we observed briefly in chapter 1, most ancient Greek philosophers valued substance over relationality both ontologically and epistemologically. It is important to note that the category of *sameness* also received preferential treatment in comparison to the category of *difference*. The "visitor" in Plato's *Sophist* convinces Theaetetus that there are five general kinds (*genōn*): "that which is" or "being" (*to on*), "rest" (*stasis*), "change" (*kinēsis*), "the same" (*tauton*) and "the different" (*heteron*). In chapter 4 we will return to the categories of rest and change in the context of tracing philosophical shifts in the concepts of space, time, matter and causality. The key point here is that *heteron* comes last in the list, and requires more argumentation for its inclusion among the broadest genera.

A metaphysical privileging of sameness over difference is even more evident in Plato's *Timaeus*. In that context the demiurge is described as having created the world-soul by first mixing intermediate forms of being, the same and the different (i.e., a mixture of their changeless and corporeal counterparts), then mixing these three mixtures together to make a uniform mixture. This required "forcing the different, which was hard to mix, into conformity with the same" (35b). The different is linked to the unequal movement of the wandering stars (planets) and the soul's accounting of perceptible things, while the same is linked to the uniform movement of the outer fixed stars, making knowledge of rational (or intelligible) things possible.

Aristotle was more interested in classifying particular existents, and for him the definition of a thing involved naming its genus and identifying its differentiae within that genus. So, for example, human beings are a type of animal, but what differentiates them from other animals is reason. Therefore, we are "rational animals." For Aristotle, this definition of human substance is *fixed*, as is the case with all species. What it means to be human is always the *same*; the rational substance of human nature does not *differ* over time. The category of difference was further demoted in the Neoplatonic philosophy of Plotinus (3rd century AD). He accepted Plato's five kinds but linked *heteron* to quantity and relation, arguing that it applies only to the material world of existents (not to the immutable absolute One), and so does not have the same metaphysical value as the other categories.

Theology

Early patristic formulations of Christology emerged within this philosophical milieu. The classical Greek emphasis on the categories of sameness and substance clearly registered an effect on the Definition of Chalcedon (AD 451), one of the most influential traditional formulations of the doctrine of the incarnation. The term that usually gets the most attention in christological discussions of this Definition is *homoousion,* which utilizes another term (*homo*) to emphasize the sameness of substance (*ousia*). The council participants wanted to stress that the two substances that are united in the person of Jesus are exactly the same substances that constitute human nature and divine nature. The term *homoousion* is used twice, in the twin assertions that Jesus is of the same substance as the Father and of the same substance as we humans.

What often goes unnoticed, however, is that the phrase *ton auton* (the same) appears eight times within the Definition of Chalcedon, which is actually a single, albeit complex, sentence. The contractive form *tauton* used by Plato and others (see above) has an equivalent meaning. The framers of the creed confessed belief in "one and *the same* Son ... *the same* perfect in divinity ... *the same* perfect in humanity ... truly God and truly human *the same* ... consubstantial *the same* with us ... *the same* for us ... *the same* Christ ... *the same* Son..." (my translation, emphases added). The repetition of the term is so cumbersome that most English translations do not translate them all. Even Philip Schaff's classic translation, which is placed side by side with the original Greek, only translates four of the eight occurrences of *ton auton* (Schaff, 1931, 62–3). As we will see, this emphasis on the category of sameness, and the relative lack of attention to difference, placed constraints on the available options for understanding the relation between the divine and the human in the person of Jesus Christ.

The consensus during the patristic period (unanimous at Chalcedon) was that the divine substance is immutable (unchanging). Although the species of humanity was understood as fixed, individual human souls were considered mutable. This made it exceedingly difficult for theologians to make sense of the Johannine claim that the divine Logos *became* flesh. However, our interest is on a different kind of difficulty – explaining the relation between an immutable substance and a mutable substance in one individual. Divine and human substances have radically different essential attributes. How can the same person both be omniscient (an immutable divine attribute) and learn obedience through suffering (Heb. 5:8)? How can we speak of the real union of an eternal and infinite substance (divine *ousia*) with a temporal and finite substance (human *ousia*)?

Two basic ways of answering these types of questions emerged, which may be generally linked with what have come to be called the Alexandrian and Antiochene "schools" of patristic theology. Both of these approaches accepted the substance metaphysics that framed the question: how can two natures (*substances*) be truly united and yet remain *the same*? If one emphasizes the real unity, how can the distinction between these very different substances be upheld? If one stresses the distinction between the substances, how can their real unity be maintained? In their explication of the doctrine of the incarnation, Alexandrians tended to emphasize the union of the two natures, while Antiochenes preferred to stress the distinction between them. These schools represent the two logical options that are forced by this way of structuring the debate. As we will see in the next section on body and soul, these philosophical leanings may be correlated to their tendency to rely on Aristotle and Plato respectively.

The main point for our purposes here is that the philosophical tension between these two options can help to explain the crooked road that led to (and from) Chalcedon. Each approach had its share of orthodox defenders as well as heretics, who pushed the logic of their respective schools too far. In fact, an examination of the primary heretics that drew the ire of the first four ecumenical councils illustrates the back and forth dialectic between the Alexandrian and Antiochene preferences for describing the union of the two natures in the incarnation (Fig. 2.1).

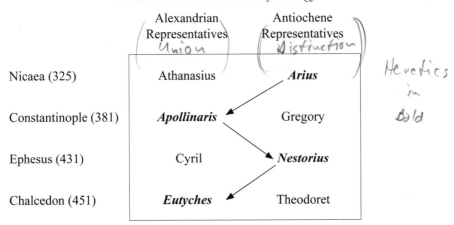

Figure 2.1 The Alexandrian/Antiochene Dialectic

I recognize that this diagram is overly simplistic and does not capture the nuances of this important phase of church history (cf. Grillmeier, 1996; Pelikan, 1971; Kelly, 1978). It is intended as a heuristic device for the non-specialist and serves only to illustrate the function of these philosophical categories in shaping the general contours of the debate.

As a theologian with Antiochene tendencies, Arius could not imagine how the man Jesus could truly be united to impassible divinity. In order to make sense of the affirmation that Jesus was indeed united to the Logos, he suggested that the substance of the Logos is similar to (*homoi*) but not identically the same as (*homo*) the immutable substance of the eternal Father. Athanasius was more Alexandrian in his approach, and his insistence that Jesus has both the same substance (*homoousion*) as the Father and as human beings, yet in such a way that the two substances are really united in one and the same person, was affirmed at the council of Nicaea.

Soon after the Nicene council the pendulum began to swing the other way. Apollinaris was a younger contemporary of Athanasius, and he too had supported the inclusion of the *homoousion* at Nicaea. However, his Alexandrian enthusiasm for emphasizing the unity of Jesus' person made it difficult for him to make sense of Jesus' being (or having) both a divine Mind and a human mind. Apollinaris argued that the divine Logos (*Nous*) took over the functions that a human mind (*nous* or *soul*) would normally serve, such as forming and enlivening the material body (*sarx*) of Jesus. This led him to speak of Christ as having "one nature" (*mia physis*), as do all humans, the difference being that his flesh was formed (in an Aristotelian sense) by the divine Logos.

In response Gregory of Nazianzus (among others) insisted that the human mind was essential to human personhood and must be assumed by the Logos if all of human nature is to be healed. Gregory's more Antiochene emphasis on the distinction of the substances led him to fight against the terminology of "one nature" and to stress the full humanity of Jesus. It appeared to him that Apollinaris' model for explaining the unity of the person of Jesus and the divine nature obliterated the human nature. The council of Constantinople (AD 381) took this into account. It affirmed the *homoousion* inherited from the original Nicene formula, but added phrases that underlined the real, fleshly life of Jesus who was "crucified under Pontius Pilate," etc.

The pendulum started to swing the other way again after Constantinople when Bishop Nestorius began to articulate this Antiochene emphasis by suggesting that in order to avoid the idea of "one nature" we should say that the two substances that constitute Jesus' person are "conjoined," forming a kind of co-operative union of the Logos and the man Jesus. Some of his followers even argued for the divisibility and separability of the two natures. Cyril of Alexandria reacted against this Nestorian formulation, insisting that the person of Christ is one nature (*mia physis*), the same phrase that had been used by Apollinaris.

At the council of Ephesus (AD 431), the convened bishops read aloud the mutual condemnations of Nestorius and Cyril, and took the side of the latter, anathematizing the former. Problems arose soon afterward, however, when Eutyches carried the Alexandrian logic to an extreme conclusion: the divine and human substances are changed when united into the one nature. Theodoret of Cyrus (among others) argued that such a formulation of the union depicts Christ as an odd mingled substance that is neither truly divine nor fully human.

The council of Chalcedon (AD 451) insisted that the union of the two natures that are united in one and the same person (and subsistence) of Jesus Christ must be acknowledged "inconfusedly, unchangeably, indivisibly, inseparably." These four negative adverbs are aimed explicitly at disallowing the Eutychean and Nestorian extremes in the debate between Alexandrian and Antiochene Christology. No one on either side doubted that to be a divine substance means to be immutable, or that the nature of the human species is fixed.

During this period several patristic theologians (especially Athanasius and Gregory) struggled to develop an understanding of *ousia* (and so *homoousion*) that was intrinsically relational, a philosophical effort we can now take up again in a fresh way. As we can see by its prevalence in the Chalcedonian Definition, however, the emphasis on *sameness* won the day in patristic theology, and it continued to dominate philosophical analysis up to the early modern period.

In late modern philosophy *difference* has made a comeback. Although Plato treated "the different" (*heteron*) last among the genera, he did argue that it actually "pervaded" all of the kinds, which "share" in the different in so far as they are in relation to the other kinds, which they are not. This intuition about the importance of differentiation from the other, which is the basis of relationality, has been recovered among several influential philosophers. For example, the categories of difference, otherness and alterity play a dominant role in Jacques Derrida's *Writing and Difference* (1978) and Emmanuel Levinas' *Otherwise than Being* (2000). This retrieval of relationality and difference had already begun in the works of earlier 19th century philosophers like Søren Kierkegaard (cf. Shults, forthcoming). Our interest in this case study, however, is on the way in which the categories of "difference" and "relation" came to play a more significant role in *science*.

The theory of evolution developed by Charles Darwin (1809–1882) challenged the notion of human nature as a substance that always remained the same. The idea of evolution itself was not new. For example, the 6th century (BC) philosopher Anaximander believed that humans had evolved from fish, but such ideas had been squelched in the ancient world by the preference for sameness. By the early 19th century, it was widely held among biologists that evolution had in some sense had occurred. Darwin clarified the process by which living organisms, including the human species, had developed over time. Darwin's 1859 *Origin of Species* outlined the theory of natural selection, which described the alteration of character traits across generations. He illustrates the mechanism for modification by pointing to the way that domestic animals are bred for particular traits, and the rest of the book is filled with examples from his work on HMS *Beagle* in the Galapagos Islands and elsewhere.

The category of *difference* serves a central function in the theory of natural selection. Darwin's logic moves from observations about overpopulation and variation to the hypothesis that competition leads to the selection of inherited traits that enhance survivability. At the end of *Origin of Species*, Darwin is quite open about the relation between his theory and belief in God. In the conclusion he speaks of the "laws impressed on matter by the Creator" and commends the "grandeur" of his view of life, "with its several powers, having been originally breathed by the Creator into a few forms or into one." The claim that human nature is not a fixed substance, however, proved a radical challenge to christological formulations that relied upon ancient theological anthropology and his theory provoked significant protest from within some parts of the Christian community.

By 1871 in *The Descent of Man,* Darwin is less concerned with placating conservative theologians. This book is more explicitly materialistic in tone and focuses on the specific phenomena of sexual selection. His thesis is that humankind, like every other species, is descended from some pre-existing form of life, and that sexual selection is the mechanism by which this descent occurs. After showing the similarities in sexual selection among other species, and especially between primates and humans, he is somewhat dismissive of the idea of belief in God and insists in the conclusion that he is "not here concerned with hopes or fears, only with the truth ... Man still bears in his bodily frame the indelible stamp of his lowly origin."

Historians of science often compare these scientific developments to the Copernican revolution; if the latter had displaced the earth from the center of the cosmos, making it merely one orbiting planet among many, Darwin threatened the human self-understanding of its special place on earth, making it simply one species descended from others. The history of the development and impact of this theory, as well as its explanatory power, have been well documented (e.g., Bowler, 1989), and its influence on Christian theology has been one of the most popular topics for interdisciplinary dialogue (cf. McMullin, 1985; Haught, 2000; Miller, 2003).

Darwin's theory of evolution itself continued (and continues) to develop. One of the problems in the original theory was that he did not have a way to make sense of the origin of the inherited variations themselves; Darwin had difficulty explaining why and how such changes arose. The mechanism for such change was elucidated in the early 20th century as biologists adopted and adapted the theory of genetics that had been developed by Gregor Mendel (1822–1884). Inherited characteristics are transmitted through the transfer of genetic information. Changes in genes were called "mutations," and these are the random source of new variations in organisms. Through the work of biologists like Theodosius Dobzhansky and Ernst Mayr these fields were brought together into what came to be called the neo-Darwinian synthesis (cf. Huxley, 1942).

The process was further clarified with the discovery of the double-stranded helical structure of deoxyribonucleic acid (DNA) by James Watson and Francis Crick in 1953. Evidence of the continuity among species as well as the process of complex genetic adaptation was further disclosed in the mapping of the human genome in the 1990s. Moreover, the question of the origin of life itself (not just human life), which had no clear answer in the 19th century, is now being illuminated by theories of emergent complexity, which suggests that what we call "life" emerged from "non-living" matter when chemical systems integrated the functions of energy transformation, information processing and self-replication (cf. chapter 4 below). Although debates over these issues still provide fuel for scientific theory-formation, the basic insights of Darwinism continue to produce positive results that ramify throughout other sciences (cf. Rue, 2000).

The findings of evolutionary biology are particularly problematic for formulations of the doctrine of the incarnation that rely on a link between

Jesus' personhood and the human nature of Adam (and Eve) before the "Fall." In this theory, which we will explore in more detail below, the first human parents were created wholly righteous and immortal. After they disobeyed God, their nature (substance) was corrupted and became susceptible to death. The soul of each newly born human being is sinful and mortal, because its very substance, which is transmitted through the sexual act, derived from the nature of the post-lapsarian pair.

On this model, Jesus escaped this diseased and guilt-ridden inheritance because his human nature was alleged to be of the same substance as that of Adam and Eve before their unfortunate lapse. This theory of the incarnation presupposes the ancient notion of a fixed (ideal) form of humanity and an historical paradise in which death did not exist, both of which have been undermined by Darwin's theory of evolution. Death has been part of the process of natural selection since the emergence of reproductive organisms; old life-forms die in order to make room for new ones.

The problem is deeper than biology. It is not simply a question of deciding between 4th century and 21st century understandings of the human organism. Our primary interest here is pointing to the way in which the *philosophical* shift from static sameness to dynamic differentiation that supported the Darwinian revolution also shapes the conceptual context within which the Christian doctrine of the incarnation must be articulated today. The idea that being truly human means being part of the ongoing adaptive differentiation of the species *Homo sapiens*, does indeed challenge some traditional christological formulations. However, late modern attention to difference may also provide new opportunities for expressing the intuition that the divine Logos is manifested in the human fleshly life of Jesus Christ. Before exploring some of these, it is important to identify two more sets of philosophical issues shared by these disciplines.

② *Body and Soul*

Theology

A second pair of categories that shapes both theological discussions of the personhood of Christ and scientific discussions of human personhood is *body* and *soul*. In this section we examine the extent to which philosophical anthropological commitments structured the christological formulations leading up to and out of the Chalcedonian Definition. This creed placed special emphasis on the way in which the relation between God and humanity in the person of Jesus Christ was *acknowledged* (inconfusedly, unchangeably, indivisibly, inseparably). As we saw in chapter 1, what it means to acknowledge something has shifted in late modern philosophy of science, and this will affect how we "hold on" to our christological assertions. The first key point for this section, however, is that all of the interlocutors of the patristic period presupposed that the soul and the body may be described as substances. Although they offered widely divergent answers, they shared the question: how can these substances be related in one and the same person?

Another methodological assumption that structured the entire christological debate was the idea that the relation between the soul and the body in an individual human person serves as an appropriate *analogy* for the relation between the divine and human natures in the person of Jesus:

Soul : Body :: Divinity : Humanity

Soul is to body (in anthropology) as divinity is to humanity (in Christology). In other words, the way in which the two natures in Christ were united was explicated in light of the way in which the two substances of body and soul are united in individual humans. We will have the opportunity to question the appropriateness of this analogy as a starting point for Christology below, but our purpose here is more narrow: pointing out the way in which Christology was shaped by anthropology. The question in each case, whether anthropological or christological, is the same: how do we explain how two radically different substances can be united in one and the same person?

The dialectic between the Alexandrian and Antiochene theological approaches is also at work here. The anthropological differences between these schools are connected to their christological differences. The Alexandrians tended toward an Aristotelian understanding of human persons, with a strong emphasis on the unity of the soul and the body. For Aristotle, the matter (*hylē*) and the form (*morphē*) of an individual person were inseparably connected; in this hylo-morphic view, the soul is the "form" of the material "body."

The Antiochenes, on the other hand, preferred a Platonic anthropology, in which the body and soul were more strongly distinguished. Plato had described souls as immortal rational substances that were trapped in material bodies; having descended from the intelligible realm they could also escape their entrapment and return. Antiochene theologians did not accept all aspects of this anthropology, but they did tend to view body and soul as separate substances that could be brought into relation and then separated again.

These philosophical intuitions influenced their understanding of the relation between the divine nature and the human nature in the person of Jesus Christ. The back and forth dialectic observed above (Fig. 2.1) may also be understood as a playing out of the tension between the Alexandrians, who emphasized the unity of the divine and human natures, and the Antiochenes, who stressed the distinction between the natures. If we start with a generic concept of substance and then try to understand how a divine substance and a human substance can be acknowledged as a real unity, we will inevitably feel pushed either toward Eutychianism (fusing the divine and human substances) or Nestorianism (merely linking the substances together by their co-operation). Chalcedon set the limits on the uses of such language (Fig. 2.2).

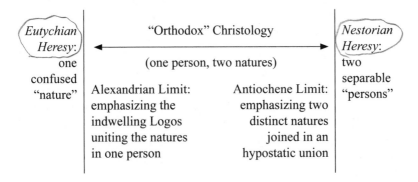

Figure 2.2 The Limits of Chalcedon

Carrying out the logic of the analogy between soul : body and divinity: humanity in either direction crosses the lines of orthodoxy. The Alexandrian limit indicates where the analogy with an Aristotelian model of the soul and body should be left behind. One must not say that the union of the divine and human substances in Jesus are changed and fused into one nature. On the other hand, one can lean toward a Platonic version of the analogy, but must stop short of saying that in the man Jesus we find two divisible or separable persons (or hypostases).

Accepting either anthropological model was permitted, as was applying it analogously to the incarnation, but following out the logic to its extreme was anathematized. If one begins with these metaphysical and anthropological assumptions as the basis for articulating Christology, these are the limits that one must accept. It remains an open question how we might conserve these intuitions in dialogue with contemporary scientific and philosophical discussions of anthropology. Although Chalcedon intended to set the limits for orthodoxy, the Definition was not universally accepted and has been hotly debated throughout church history (cf. Davis *et al.*, 2002). The important point for our immediate purposes is that the appropriateness of the anthropological analogy was widely accepted and continued to shape the conversation long after Chalcedon.

The 6th century theologian Leontius of Byzantium spelled out the options explicitly using this analogy in his *Contra Nestorianus et Eutychianos*, the title itself reflecting the poles that structured the debate. Leontius argued that just as the two substances of soul and body may subsist (be "hypostasized") in one human individual, so too may the two substances of the divine Logos and human flesh subsist in the person of Christ. Elsewhere (Shults 1996) I have challenged the historical validity of appeals to Leontius in the increasingly popular application of the terms *enhypostasis* and *anhypostasis* to the human nature of Jesus among some contemporary theologians. Reaction to that critique has tended to come from those interested in defending the use of those or similar terms by appealing to their role in the work of John of Damascus (Lang, 1998) or Thomas Aquinas (Gockel, 2000).

However, this is to miss the main point of my analysis, which I repeated at the beginning and end of the article for emphasis. It is important to distinguish between two positions: "(1) that the human nature of Jesus does not subsist except in its union with the Logos in the one person of Christ, and (2) that *enhypostasis and anhypostasis* are good terms to describe this fact about the human nature of Jesus" (Shults, 1996, 433, 446). Why should we insist on expressing the doctrine of the incarnation in ways that are tied to ancient Greek or early modern anthropological concepts of personhood, which focused on the sameness of hypostasized substances? Why not critically engage the relational and dynamic thought forms of *contemporary* anthropological discourse as we seek to articulate belief in the Word become flesh?

It is easy to understand why the turn to relationality and attention to difference is worrisome to many conservative theologians. Much of the tradition has labored under the constraints of the categories of substance and sameness in an attempt to maintain the anthropological analogy. In the middle ages Anselm, Abelard and Peter Lombard developed their Christology in proximity to the Antiochene emphasis, while Thomas Aquinas leaned toward the Alexandrian view, emphasizing a subsistence theory of the incarnation in which the body and soul in Christ are united by the Logos.

Medieval scholasticism bequeathed to the Reformation these categories and the tensions that came with them. The unity of the two natures in one person was not in dispute for Luther or Calvin, but we may think of them as portraying Alexandrian and Antiochene preferences, respectively. Luther emphasized the complete mutual interpenetration of the two substances and all their attributes. Calvin was willing to make a stronger distinction, based on his belief that even in the incarnation the Logos was not wholly contained in the man Jesus of Nazareth but present throughout the cosmos.

Both Reformers also expressed concern about the value of scholastic debates over the terminology for describing the relation of the two natures, and preferred to focus on the way in which Christ brings salvation. Calvin wished not to be "such a stickler as to battle over mere words" like *homoousios* (*Institutes* 1.13.3–5) and Luther insisted that one could refuse to subscribe to the non-biblical term *homoousios* without being heretical so long as the faith that led the writers of the creeds was upheld (Answer to Latomus, *WA*, 8, 114–20). One of the purposes of this interdisciplinary case study is to demonstrate that we are now in need of the same courage they exhibited as we engage evolutionary biology and the philosophical shifts that have reshaped the contours of the conceptual landscape of late modernity. *Philosophy*

Despite their openness to reformulation, most Reformers and early modern theologians did not challenge the underlying anthropological analogy for understanding the relation between the divinity and humanity of Christ, nor the substance metaphysical categories that saturated both sides of the analogy. Moreover, they accepted the basic contours of faculty psychology, in which the soul is understood to rule the body through the powers of the *intellect* and *will*. Plato and Aristotle had quite different ways of spelling out the number and quality of these faculties, which also ramified into theological debates over human nature (cf. Shults 2003, 165–88). The key issue here is that these ancient and medieval conceptions of the relation between the soul and the body continued to structure the options for articulating the doctrine of the incarnation through the early modern period.

The value of these philosophical categories for making sense of human rationality has been challenged by developments in a variety of sciences but especially in the field of neurobiology. Broadly speaking, neuroscientists are interested in describing and explaining the processes of the evolved human brain that give rise to what we call cognition. In early modern science the understanding of the relation between the body and the soul was deeply shaped by René Descartes, who argued for a radical dualism between the (extended) material body and the (thinking) immaterial soul. In Cartesian anthropology strong distinctions were made among the "faculties" of the soul (the intellect, the will and the affections) and between these soulish powers and the human body.

The sciences of neurobiology, however, have shown how human *Science* cognition is deeply rooted in and dependent upon the electro-chemical and neural functions of the brain. In fact, all "reasoning" (and "willing") emerges out of and is shaped by the "feeling" of the embodied brain. Higher cortical processes depend upon and are regulated by the functioning of various parts of the limbic system, which are linked through the brain stem into the whole energetic network of the body as it responds to its environment. Rationality could not have evolved, nor can it emerge within an individual, apart from the emotional responsivity of the biological organism. As neuroscientist Antonio Damasio argues:

> This is Descartes' error: the abysmal separation between body and mind, between the sizable, dimensioned, mechanically operated, infinitely divisible body stuff, on the one hand, and the unsizable, undimensioned, un-pushpullable, nondivisible mind stuff; the suggestion that reasoning, and moral judgment, and the suffering that comes from physical pain or emotional upheaval might exist separately from

the body. Specifically: the separation of the most refined operations of the mind
from the structure and operation of a biological organism. (1994, 249–50)

The main point is that what we once called the faculties of the soul are now
explained as registers of the whole human organism whose mental functioning
emerges out of brain processes embedded within a feeling body.

This is relevant to our case study because one's understanding of the relation
between human *flesh* and human *knowing* will affect one's understanding of
the embodied experience of Jesus of Nazareth. Most neuroscientists no longer
find the categories of a "soul" substance separate from a "body" substance
helpful for making sense of the phenomena they study. These concepts are no
longer adequate for articulating the complex relations that characterize the
dynamism of human knowing, nor the embodied existential intensity of what
I referred to earlier as noetic desire.

It is important to note that these neuroscientific findings do not entail a
reductionistic denial of human personhood or the rejection of the reality of
the "self." Damasio himself proposes the idea of the "neural self." What
we call subjectivity finds its basis in the neural processing and relating of
two sets of representations – the dispositional representation of key events
in our autobiography (remembered and imagined in anticipation), and the
primordial representations of our bodies. The latter includes our general
remembered body (and emotion) states. Damasio proposes a third kind of
image or representation as well: "that of an organism in the act of perceiving
and responding to an object." Subjectivity emerges when and as the brain
receives and integrates signals from object- and self-representations,
"building a *dispositional representation of the self in the process of changing
as the organism responds to an object*" (1994, 242; emphasis in original; cf.
2004).

Damasio spells out the irreducible role of the feeling body in human
consciousness in *The Feeling for What Happens*, in which he discusses
the significance of the body and emotions in the making of consciousness.
Various parts of the brain work together to trigger and execute emotional
responses, and this complex functional interaction helps the human organism
survive and adapt to its environment. Damasio describes the brain patterns
that support neural mapping, which provide the conditions for a "proto-self,"
enabling the formation of what he calls "core" and "extended" consciousness.
In other words, it is possible to develop a neuroscientific understanding of the
self that attends to the way in which the relations between neurons embrained
within a body can map both object and self *and* the relationships they hold
– the key is in the "relationship play" (1999, 20).

For our interdisciplinary case study the most important point about these
scientific developments is the way in which they challenge the categories

of substance metaphysics and faculty psychology as no longer adequate for making sense of the human experience of feeling enfleshed. They have been replaced by more relational and holistic conceptions of personhood. While this clearly threatens particular interpretations of Chalcedon, it also opens up new avenues for articulating the intuition that God was truly made known in the life of Jesus Christ, who was truly a member of our species.

In fact, these developments may also help us shake free of dependence on the anthropological analogy itself, which has wreaked havoc on theological attempts to understand the identity of Jesus Christ. Of course we have other reasons too for resisting the hegemony of this analogy. Materially, the soul–body dichotomy functioned in a way that reinforced patriarchy based on stereotypical definitions that linked male substance to reason and female substance to body. Methodologically, the way in which some theologians relied on the analogical structure of the argument sometimes led them to forget the traditional apophatic insistence that the finite and the infinite, the human and the divine, cannot be comprehended or contained within the same genus, even substance or being itself.

If one begins with ancient Greek or early modern faculty psychology, with a concept of "person" as a soul with the powers of intellect and will, and projects this onto the divine Logos (or God as *a* single subject), a familiar set of conceptual difficulties inevitably arises. How are the "faculties" of the divine Logos and the man Jesus related? Does Christ have two wills and two minds? If so, are they mingled together or do they co-operate somehow? If he has only one will and one mind, do these have divine or human attributes (or powers) or some combination of both?

The basic christological heresies flow from the logical fleshing out of a model of person that begins with the idea of an immaterial soul substance that has (or uses) faculties such as intellect and will, which act upon the material world. We can finally escape this labyrinthine confusion but it will require a theological anthropology that moves move beyond this outmoded faculty psychology and a doctrine of God that refuses to project this model onto the divine nature as a single subject.

What does this mean for the doctrine of the incarnation? Accepting these scientific insights and engaging the philosophical shifts in which they operate means that heretical options like Nestorianism and Eutychianism are no longer even live possibilities. However, this also means that we are faced afresh with the reconstructive task of articulating the claim that the divine Logos became flesh in dialogue with neurobiological insights into the evolution of human knowing. Embracing an emergent holist understanding of human persons and a robust trinitarian understanding of God opens up a different kind of conceptual space for this task. Before we explore some examples of interdisciplinary proposals that have taken advantage of this new space, we need to examine one more set of categories.

(3) *Origin and Goal*

Philosophical assumptions about the origination and orientation of *Homo sapiens* are also at work in this interdisciplinary case study, shaping both science and Christology. Evolutionary biology is quite obviously interested in the origins of the species. In the sense that it also treats the teleonomic function of natural selection, which "aims" for survival, biology is also interested in the "goals" that play a role in the process of speciation. Theology is also interested in the *origin* and *goal* of human life, and the doctrine of the incarnation claims that Jesus Christ is a hermeneutical key for understanding both. The basic philosophical challenge that we face in this section has to do with the fact that a particularly influential way of linking the doctrine of the incarnation to a literal reading of the story of Adam and Eve in the Garden of Eden has lost its plausibility in light of discoveries about the process of human evolution within the cosmos.

Much of the Christian tradition has explicitly interpreted the incarnation as a divine reaction to the failure of the first parents to obey God's command not to eat of the fruit of the tree of the knowledge of good and evil (Gen. 2–3). On this model the reason the Logos became flesh was to repair the damage done to God's creation. For example, at several points in his influential *On the Incarnation of the Word* Athanasius describes the unfortunate event of Adam's sin and its devastating effects on humanity, often repeating the phrase: "what was God to do?" The first two humans had disrupted the project of divine creation and the incarnation was necessary to salvage it. Scholars debate exactly when a literal interpretation of the story of the Garden of Eden as a historical place and Adam and Eve as historical persons took root, but it was quite dominant by the patristic period.

Augustine was the most influential theologian in the development of this model of the incarnation. In his debates with the Manichees, who believed that the bodies of the first parents had been (poorly) formed by demonic powers, Augustine went out of his way to emphasize that Adam and Eve were glorious and beautiful. In his *Literal Interpretation of Genesis*, he portrays them as having astonishing intellectual and physical capacities, as wholly righteous and in a state of beatitude. Humanity originated in the Garden of Eden, which he interpreted as a paradise free from death, disease or pain of any kind.

In *The City of God* Augustine explains that God's goal in creating Adam and Eve was the production of offspring equal to the number of predestined saints. Had they not taken of the tree of the knowledge of good and evil, they would have been able to procreate without any lust whatsoever, using their perfect wills to use "their genital organs for the procreation of offspring just as they used their other members" (XIV.11). Unfortunately the holy pair (inexplicably) willed the unholy act of disobeying God, which brought pain and death into creation. The incarnation was necessary to salvage God's goal for the divine city. Augustine was never able to explain why a righteous person in a state of blessedness would (or could) make such an evil choice, leading many to question the coherence of his proposal. The key point for our purposes here, however, is that his doctrine of the incarnation is explicitly tied to the sin of the first parents, understood as historical figures living in a paradisaic Garden in the relatively recent past.

This understanding of the origin and goal of humanity remained at the core of many traditional treatments of the doctrine of the incarnation. For example, Anselm's *Cur Deus Homo*, written in the 11th century, illustrates how such presuppositions often guided attempts to explain "why God became man." The logic behind this model begins with an assumption about God's goal for creating humanity in the first place: to fill up the places among the heavenly host that had been emptied by the "Fall" of the Devil and his minions (e.g., Book I.16, 19). Adam and Eve were immortal before their corruption (Book II.11), but became susceptible to death after dishonoring God through their disobedience. The divine plan was in jeopardy. It was not fitting, argued Anselm, for God to leave his goal unfulfilled, so it was necessary for God to become man so that the debt incurred by the first pair's disobedience could be paid off.

We will return to this theory of atonement in chapter 3, but the point here is that the logic behind it continued to dominate the doctrine of the incarnation in the work of many of the most influential Western theologians, including Thomas Aquinas and John Calvin. Like Augustine they believed that human nature was *originally* righteous and glorious but that the first parents' sin (somehow) corrupted this nature. They also believed that the *goal* of humanity, whether expressed as a beatific vision of God (Thomas) or a glorification of God (Calvin), was placed at risk by the "Fall" of Adam and Eve, which made it necessary for the Logos to become flesh.

However, there is another stream in the Christian tradition that has resisted *Irenaeus* the idea that the incarnation was logically dependent upon and a response to a "Fall." Irenaeus depicted the first parents not as perfectly righteous but as innocent children, ignorant and naïve but oriented toward knowledge of God. The origin and goal of humanity is more closely connected to Christ than to Adam for Irenaeus, who gave material and logical priority to "the Word, the Maker of all things" rather than the "first man." That which is to be saved, the first parents with their "animal" nature, is brought into existence so that they might be redeemed by the "spiritual One."

Irenaeus
E.O.

   In other words, for Irenaeus humans (with their need for salvation) are essentially oriented toward the pre-existent "saving Being" (the Word), not vice versa (cf. *Against Heresies*, III.22.3). The assumption that the *origin* of humanity is in a literal garden remained, but the *goal* of the incarnation was understood as logically prior to the failure of the first pair. This tendency prevailed in much Eastern Orthodox theology, which insisted that the goal of human creation is divinization (*theosis*) and that this cannot be abstracted from "christification" (e.g., Nellas, 1997).

   This approach was also taken up, although in quite different ways, among some medieval Franciscan theologians such as Duns Scotus as well as by Martin Luther and the Reformed supralapsarians. Some contemporary theologians have also interpreted Karl Barth's doctrine of reconciliation in this way (e.g., Jenson, 1969). As we will see below, Karl Rahner explicitly embraced this approach, which has registered an effect (especially on Roman Catholic theologians) in the theology and science dialogue. What these models of the incarnation hold in common is the insistence that the creative divine intention is inherently oriented toward inviting creatures into participation in the life of the Son in relation to the Father in the Spirit, and not a rescue effort that logically follows or is conceptually dependent upon the sin of Adam and Eve.

   Nevertheless, many of the theologians in this stream of incarnational theorizing also accepted the idea that Jesus' human flesh was not tainted by the corrupt nature inherited from Adam, but subsisted as a hypostasis of the originally righteous nature (substance) of humanity before the "Fall." Expressions of this belief were influenced by the prevailing understanding of sexual procreation. The most popular view in the patristic period was that male semen contains *logos* (or *pneuma*) that gives shape to the matter of human flesh, which is provided by the female. On this model, it made sense to interpret the incarnation in the following way: like all other humans, Jesus had real flesh, which he got from Mary, but in his case this flesh was shaped (formed, enlivened) by the divine Logos (cf. Minns, 1998, 152–3). *Ex hypothesi* in order for the flesh of Christ to be "unfallen" flesh, his mother would have had to be exempt from inheriting the corrupt material flesh of the first parents; this contributed to the rise of the doctrine of the immaculate conception of Mary.

   During the middle ages Thomas accepted Aristotle's view that a woman receives no *physical* contribution from a man when she becomes pregnant; on this biological model, it was still plausible to claim that Jesus was fully human even though he had no physical father. During the Reformation John Calvin was caught up in debates with Menno Simons and others about the nature of the "woman's seed" and the passivity of women in the process of procreation, but his main concern seems to be defending the purity of Jesus' human nature, which was exempted from common corruption. He attributed this to the sanctifying presence of the Spirit during the generation of Jesus (*Institutes* II.13.4). Specific *scientific* (and philosophical) presuppositions about human biology made it possible to argue that the substance of the flesh assumed by the Logos in the incarnation was not the sinful flesh passed on materially through the procreative process, but the original righteous and glorious flesh that existed before the "Fall." *Science*

These ways of understanding the origin of human life, and the process of procreation, are no longer plausible in light of the sciences of evolutionary biology. Augustine argued that only after the "Fall" of an historical pair living in paradise in the recent historical past did human life become susceptible to mortality and characterized by lust (and concupiscence in general). The incarnation aims at remediating this corruption of (predestined) human souls. However, contemporary genetics paints a very different picture of human "flesh." The sciences of evolutionary biology have shown that death has always been a natural part of the emergence and development of life, and that the main engine that drives the whole reproductive process (at least among mammals) is a passionate desire for copulation with a member of the opposite sex.

Among the sciences of evolutionary biology, paleobiology stands out as particularly relevant for understanding the *origin* of humanity. This discipline incorporates the general findings of Darwinian evolution and the specific insights of neuroscience, but applies them to the narrower issue of the role of developments in the brain (and body) of *Homo sapiens* that contributed to the characteristics that distinguish it from other hominid species. For our purposes, the most interesting thing about these sciences is the way in which they shed light on the emergence of religious behavior, on the intense human desire to understand our place in the cosmos. While the category of origin is clearly central here, paleobiologists are usually more hesitant to use the notion of the *goal* of human evolution. Nevertheless, one typically finds an openness to the idea of purposiveness itself; in some sense goal-oriented behavior has been endemic to the species from its nascency.

Paleobiological research indicates that religion appeared alongside toolmaking and artistic expression relatively suddenly in the upper Paleolithic period. In *The Prehistory of the Mind: The Cognitive Origins of Art, Religion and Science* (1996) Steven Mithen points to the cognitive fluidity of the mental processes of modern humans that enabled them to move from a specialized use of particular modes of intelligence to a new kind of generalized mentality that could integrate them. He argues that this capacity gave rise to the emergence of what we would now generally consider art, religion and science virtually simultaneously. This suggests that a religious interpretation of experience is in some sense a natural characteristic of our species, that the differentiation of *Homo sapiens* from other hominids between 100,000 and 60,000 years ago is connected to the capacity to construct symbols for making sense of one's place within a broader context and to thematize ultimate meaning.

In *The Symbolic Species* (1997), Terrence Deacon spells out the issue of the relation between the brain and language in more detail. Human communication is characterized by what he calls "symbolic reference," so much so that he is led to refer to our species as *Homo symbolicus*. Deacon borrows the categories of icon, index and symbol from philosopher C.S. Peirce in order to clarify this differentiation. In Deacon's use of the terms, "iconic" indicates a relation of resemblance. When something is linked to another either causally or associated with it spatially or temporally, that relation is called "indexical." For one thing to function as a "symbol" in relation to an "object" requires some shared social convention or code that links them together. In other words, symbolical relationships are composed of indexical relationships (relations between sets of indices), and indexical relationships are composed of iconic relationships (relations between sets of icons). Many other animals seem to make iconic connections between things, and some can use indexical relations, but Deacon argues that symbolic reference, which supervenes upon these others, involves a more complex kind of interpretive representation.

The origin of modern *Homo sapiens* involved the crossing of a "symbolic threshold." The conditions for the emergence of this capacity are clearly related to changes in the human brain. It has often been assumed that human brains got bigger, and then language developed. Deacon argues that the most plausible explanation for the selection pressure that led to the prefrontalization of the brain in hominid evolution is that the brain and language "co-evolved." Changes in the brain were a direct consequence of the use of words. "The first use of symbolic reference by some distant ancestors changed how natural selection process have affected hominid brain evolution ever since. So in a very real sense I mean that the physical changes that make us human are the *incarnations*, so to speak, of the process of using words" (1997, 322; emphasis added).

Elsewhere Deacon suggests that developments of this kind involve information (e.g., memory) that has a "teleodynamic" and recursive causality upon the less complex (e.g., merely organic) systems out of which they emerge (2006, 137). We will return to emergence theory in chapter 4, but the important point here is that evolutionary scientists are increasingly open to more relational and non-linear conceptions of the origin and goal(s) of human intentionality and noetic desire.

The science and religion dialogue around paleobiological and paleoanthropological issues continues to grow (cf. van Huyssteen, 2006; Shults, 2006), and one of the tasks of Christian theology in this context will be to explore ways in which the doctrine of the incarnation itself can be freshly articulated in relation to this new evolutionary understanding of human "flesh." However, we must face squarely the extent to which bringing evolutionary biology and Christology into serious dialogue will require radical reconstruction. Darwinian evolution, neuroscience and paleobiology all create profound challenges to aspects of traditional formulations of the doctrine of the incarnation that are dependent on ancient or early modern biology.

It is important to note that there are also exegetical reasons to loosen Christology from a literal reading of Genesis and a particular biological understanding of the virgin birth. There is no reference to Adam and Eve anywhere else in the Hebrew Bible, which has led most scholars to the conclusion that the story was added relatively late in Israel's history in response to the creation myths of its ancient Near Eastern neighbors.

A similar argument is made with reference to the virgin birth. The story does not appear in the earliest Gospel (Mark), and appears to register no effect on Jesus' self-identity or teaching. Moreover, it seems strange that neither Paul nor John make any appeal to Jesus' unique biological origin in their defense of the Gospel. Clearly it is *possible* to articulate the doctrine of the incarnation without depictions of Jesus' ontogeny that require a "virgin birth" or models of human phylogenesis that presuppose a historical "Fall." Systematic theology will have to engage more fully the findings of biblical scholarship that illuminate the origin and redaction of these stories (e.g., Lüdemann, 1998, 139; Brueggemann, 2003, 38), but our focus in this case study is on facing the *scientific* challenges to (and opportunities for) formulating the doctrine of the incarnation today, which are embedded within the *philosophical* shifts we have been discussing.

Theological presentations of this doctrine should aim to uphold the intuition that Jesus Christ reveals the origin and goal of the human experience of knowing God, which is wholly dependent on the creative initiative of divine grace and cannot be achieved by human effort alone. We can accept these *theological* points of the early parts of the books of Genesis and Matthew without accepting the ancient *scientific* cosmogony and gynecology of the original authors and redactors. Accepting the task of reconstructively articulating the doctrine of the incarnation in dialogue with evolutionary biology will mean more than repairing the Augustinian model or even simply opting for a more Irenean model. Nor will it suffice simply to take the theory of evolution and fit it into an ancient or early modern system, for these theological frameworks operated with radically different understandings of the meaning of the terms "*Logos*," "*flesh*" and even "*becoming*."

Clearly the sciences of evolutionary biology and the philosophical shifts of late modernity create challenges for Christian theology. So did the Copernican revolution. It took the church over four hundred years to adjust to that new cosmology. In our information age, concepts change too quickly to wait this long. Theology (and so Christology) must increase its philosophical dexterity as it engages contemporary science. This new context is frightening. But it is can also be delightful. The developments outlined about provide us with new opportunities to articulate our understanding of the incarnation by expanding the discussion beyond a focus on the Johannine concept of the divine Logos, broadening our christological discourse in a way that engages the ongoing human struggle to make sense of the noetic desire that shapes the religious (and artistic and scientific) dimensions of human becoming. We now turn to some examples of proposals that have attempted to move forward in this new conceptual space.

Interdisciplinary Opportunities

As we noted above, the themes raised by the disciplines of evolutionary biology have been among the most popular in the broader dialogue between science and religion. However, detailed attempts to relate the specific issues of christological doctrine to these sciences are relatively rare. The lack of treatment here is partially due to the difficulties (and dangers) surrounding the task of bringing the particularity of these doctrines into the dialogue with science. However, as we saw in chapter 1, developments in the philosophy of science have opened up new conceptual space for this kind of contextual engagement. In this section we explore some of the most significant proposals that have emerged in the last few decades, beginning with two scholars whose efforts illustrate particularly well the possibility and promise of using dynamic and relational categories in the reconstructive presentation of the doctrine of the incarnation in dialogue with late modern science.

Arthur Peacocke

Widely recognized as one of the founders of the contemporary theology and science dialogue, Arthur Peacocke was trained as a molecular biologist and later became ordained as an Anglican priest. In *Creation and the World of Science* (1979, 228) he observed that participants in the debates that had raged over John Hick's *The Myth of God Incarnate* (1977) often failed to attend to a prior problem: how does the theory of evolution shape our understanding of God's action and presence in the world in general? In the context of a chapter called "Evolved Man and God Incarnate" Peacocke argued that we can no longer rely on the categories of outmoded cosmologies for articulating the doctrine of the incarnation. Yet he suggested that we can still maintain Jesus' oneness with the God he called "Abba" as the unveiling of God's intention (meaning) for creation. All of creation is open-ended and "in God," and in Jesus that open-endedness becomes identified "with the God who is the source of the future – and so with the future that is God's intention for men and the world" (1979, 232). Over several decades Peacocke struggled with the question of divine action in an evolving cosmos and often explicitly treated the doctrine of the incarnation in light of these broader philosophical issues.

Acknowledging the critique of static and mechanical conceptions of the cosmos, Peacocke urged theologians to pay more attention to the category of *becoming*. This is reflected in the sub-title of his magnum opus: *Theology for a Scientific Age: Being and Becoming – Natural, Divine and Human* (1993). Observing that doctrine has for centuries been presented in terms of static images, Peacocke suggests that expressing Christian faith in more dynamic terms is not only possible but actually closer to the biblical attitude.

For Peacocke the incarnation is the self-communication of God, disclosing the ultimate purpose of the divine creative process – persons embodying the values exemplified in the life of Jesus. As the One "in whom" the world exists, God has all along been instantiating, "incarnating" God's own "personalness" in that world. Peacocke argues that this has been made supremely and explicitly manifest in Jesus the Christ. His particular embodiment of values unveils the consummation of the creative and creating evolutionary process (1993, 305–6).

As a molecular biologist, Peacock was particularly critical of many traditional interpretations of the "virgin birth." In light of our current understanding of the procreative process, accepting the traditional interpretation would leave us with two options for explaining the conception of Jesus: either the sperm was created by God *de novo* (to provide a Y chromosome), or the whole fertilized ovum was implanted into Mary who served as a surrogate mother. Peacocke's objections are not merely biological but also theological: either of these options would mean that Jesus' humanity was not in *continuity* with the emergence of *Homo sapiens*. He argues that this would undercut the point of the incarnation, which is that God's immanent care for creation throughout history is fulfilled in the emergence of this man's distinctive relation to God (1993, 274, 301). Peacocke wants to speak of the incarnation as a manifestation of creative divine activity, as God's self-expression in a human person.

The importance of the continuity of the processes of creation also reinforces Peacocke's resistance to the notion of an historical "Fall" of Adam and Eve from paradise (cf. 1993, 223; 1979, 190–1). He insists that we must think of human beings as "rising beasts rather than fallen angels!" (1998, 373). Humans are not made of different "stuff" than the rest of creation. In fact as a molecular biologist Peacocke argues that in the light of discoveries such as DNA, we may conclude that all "living matter" is ultimately built up from the inorganic atomic constituents of the physical world.

The increase in forms of complexity in the cosmos suggests that what we call "matter" has the ability to display functions and properties for which we use special terms such as "personal." This insight is connected to theories of emergent complexity, to which we will return in chapter 4. The key issue here is that biological evolution suggests that species do not represent different "kinds" of substance, but the coming into existence of new modes of structural organization. We may still speak of the uniqueness of *Homo sapiens*, with its particular "mental" and even "spiritual" capacities, but these emerged out of a continuous process of evolution (1986, 53, 123). If this does not apply to Jesus, then he is not truly human.

Augustine's literal reading of the Genesis myth cannot be made compatible with the contemporary understanding of the intrinsic role of *suffering* and *death* in the dynamics of nature's becoming, including human evolution. Peacocke argues that the process of creation is costly: new forms of life emerge only as old forms die out. Pain and risk are part of the evolution of new species. For Peacocke, the incarnation should not be understood as an exception to this process, but as the communication of a new possibility that emerges out of this experience. Rather than a "descent" of a transcendent God from "outside," Peacocke prefers to think of Jesus as the one in whom the intention or meaning of God's self-communication within creation is ultimately manifested. "By virtue of his human response and openness to God, [Jesus the Christ is] the locus where there is unveiled that which or, rather the One Who, is present continuously creating and bringing his purpose to fruition in the order of energy–matter–space–time" (1979, 241).

Already in his early *Science and the Christian Experiment* (1971), he had written of "God-becoming-man" as revealing the "self-limiting love of God" in the life of Jesus the Christ, who was transformed by being drawn up into the "very life of God himself." This "trans-mutation" was the act of God precisely as the consummation of the evolutionary process in which the rise of human persons succeeded the general biological sequence. As "truly God-made-man and the only proper Man," Jesus opens up to humanity the possibility of a new level of existence in relation to God and one another (1971, 165–70).

Peacocke spelled this out in several later essays. In "Biological Evolution – a Positive Theological Appraisal," he argued that the suffering and death of Jesus is the "suffering, self-offering love of *God* in action … actually 'in the flesh'." Jesus' openness and obedience to God "enabled him, as *the* God-informed human person, to be a manifest self-expression of this history, within the confines of human personhood, of God as creative self-expressing Word/*Logos*/'Son'" (1998, 375–6).

In his essay "The Incarnation of the Informing Self-expressive Word of God" (1996) he adapted the idea of "informing" from information theory as a way of interpreting the theological concept of "revelation." Peacocke explicitly aims to accommodate the intuitions of Chalcedon about the belief that the "Word became flesh", but to express the intelligibility of this belief by thinking of the Word (Logos) as the self-communication of God. The Creator is always informing the world, continuously creating new forms of life. God "informs" the human personhood of Jesus in a distinctive way that expresses the ultimate "Meaning" (Logos) of creation: self-offering Love that intends to welcome creatures into eternal life. Reflecting on the significance of the early believers' testimony about Jesus, Peacocke argues that we must emphasize "both the *continuity* of Jesus with the rest of humanity, and so with the rest of nature within which *Homo sapiens* evolved, and at the same time, the *discontinuity* constituted by what is distinctive in his relation to God and what, through him (his teaching, life, death and Resurrection), the early witnesses experienced of God" (1996, 330).

Peacocke argues that what the Christian tradition has meant by "incarnation" may be understood as the fulfillment of the "transcendence-in-immanence" of human religious experience that "raises the hope and conjecture that in man [*sic*], in *a* human person adequate for the purpose, immanence might be able to display in a uniquely emergent mode a transcendent dimension to a degree which could unveil, without distortion, the transcendent Creator" (1986, 132). Peacocke himself is even willing to say that God accepts "The Cost of New Life" (2001), and that *God* suffers "in, with and under" the creative processes of the world, and that Jesus the Christ is the true self-expression of God's self-giving or self-offering love in relation to the suffering cosmos. We do not have to accept his particular version of "pan-en-theism" or his construal of divine immanence to appreciate and appropriate Peacocke's broader insights into the significance of relational and dynamic categories for Christology.

Denis Edwards

Denis Edwards also recognizes that evolutionary biology challenges some traditional formulations of Christian theology, including and even especially the doctrine of the incarnation. However, he too views these developments as providing an opportunity for retrieving resources from the biblical tradition that emphasize relationality, communion, immanence, process, empathy and solidarity – themes that can facilitate a theological response to contemporary political and ecological crises. Like Peacocke he attends to the broader philosophical issue of the God–world relation, which shapes and is shaped by our conceptions of the Creator and the creation, and therefore impacts our articulation of the claim that the "Word became flesh."

In one of his earliest forays into the dialogue, Edwards explored the relation between *Jesus and the Cosmos* (1991), relying heavily on insights from Karl Rahner, who had also tried to articulate Christology in light of evolution (see below). Edwards developed three principles for understanding the incarnation in dialogue with contemporary science. First, Jesus represents "the self-transcendence of the cosmos toward God." This underlines the continuity of his humanity with ours, and indeed with the whole of creation. Second, Edwards suggests that "there is an intrinsic inter-relationship between God's communication in grace to all people and God's action in Jesus of Nazareth." The grace of the incarnation is intimately connected to God's gracious self-communication to all of creation and humanity. Third, Jesus can be understood "from God's side, as God's self-communication to the cosmos."

The first principle in particular requires some explanation. Edwards argues that if to be human is to be part of a long process of development in the universe – if we are "made of stardust" – then this must also be true of Jesus if indeed he is truly human. "Jesus is part of the climax of that long development whereby the world becomes aware of itself, and comes into the direct presence of God ... In this one product of evolutionary history, the cosmos accepts God in a definitive and absolute way ... Yet the universe could not reach this goal of itself. It occurs through God's grace" (1991, 66). As a human being Jesus is part of the creaturely universe's reaching out (self-transcendence) toward God.

The second principle points to the relation between the universal self-communication of divine grace in and to the world and the particular reality of Jesus Christ. On the one hand, God's grace is present to all creatures; this means that the incarnation is "an inner moment in the universal bestowal of grace." But can we speak of a "union" of God and humanity in the person of Jesus? Edwards argues we can and should: God's self-offering grace and human acceptance occur in an "absolute" way in the life of Jesus, and so "we can say that this is not only something God accomplishes, but it is God ... In Jesus there is such a union between a human reality and God that ... this human proclamation and offer is a reality of God ... In Jesus grace functions in such a way that this one human being is identified with God's self-offering to the universe" (1991, 69–70).

Edward's third principle also has immediate implications for his understanding of the incarnation. He follows Rahner in adopting the "Scotist" stream of the tradition, which does not see the incarnation as a reaction to the failure of a first attempt (as Plan B), but as ingredient to the eternal intentionality of God for creation. God's self-communication is expressed throughout creation, but through Jesus' response and the movement he started, it is expressed concretely and definitively. In his person Jesus embodies both God's definitive self-communication and the definitive human response to grace. In Jesus we find God giving God's self irreversibly to the world, but we also find "a part of the world, a human being, the product of evolutionary history, accepting the self-giving God without reservation" (1991, 74).

These principles lead Edwards to express the intuitions of Chalcedon in this way: "In God's self-bestowal in Jesus of Nazareth, first, *God accepts the cosmos definitively and irrevocably*, and second, *the cosmos accepts God definitively and irrevocably*, and third, these two acceptances are manifested in our history *as constituting a real unity in the one Jesus of Nazareth*" (1991, 75, emphases in original).

In his *Jesus the Wisdom of God: An Ecological Theology* (1995) Edwards outlines the importance of the Hebrew understanding of divine Wisdom for understanding both the relation between God and the world (creation) in general and the incarnation in particular. He provides a detailed account of the Wisdom literature in the Hebrew Bible, noting especially the way in which divine Wisdom is understood as intimately connected to the creation as well as the upholding and ongoing formation of the cosmos (Prov. 8). Wisdom is also personified as a woman, who mediates the relation between God and seekers of knowledge (Prov. 9). She is also described in The Wisdom of Solomon (6:12 – 11:1) in relation to the "image" and "glory" of God, pervading and penetrating, ordering and renewing all things. The book of *Sirach* speaks of her (Wisdom) as "with" God for ever (1:1), as coming forth from the mouth of God (24:3). In discussing God's relation to creation, it asserts that "by his word all things hold together" (*Sir.* 43:26).

Edwards shows how this Hebraic understanding of the Wisdom of God is identified with Jesus Christ in the New Testament. This is somewhat obvious in some explicit statements by Paul, such as 1 Cor. 1:30 – Jesus "became for us wisdom from God." However, Edwards also illustrates the implicit use of Wisdom terminology in the christological hymn of Col. 1:15–20, as well as in the Gospels, where Jesus exhibits the characteristics of Wisdom, such as inviting others to a banquet. He observes that linking Christ to the Hebrew idea of divine Wisdom comes much earlier in the New Testament written tradition than the Johannine utilization of the Greek Logos concept (cf. Dunn, 2003).

He also observes that the *Tome of Leo*, which played an important background role in the debates leading up to the formulation of the Definition of Chalcedon, explicitly linked Prov. 9:1 to Jn 1:14 – "Wisdom building a house for herself" and "the Word became flesh" (1995, 55). Edwards suggests that in our contemporary context, the concept of Wisdom may complement the Western emphasis on the titles of "Son" and "Logos." Perhaps most importantly, articulating the personhood of Jesus in relation to the Wisdom of God, which is always and already creatively and evocatively present in the cosmos, supports a view of the incarnation not as a reaction to a "Fall," but as flowing from God's free love for creatures, a view that, as Edwards points out again, has been championed by a stream of the tradition from Irenaeus through Duns Scotus to Karl Rahner (1995, 71).

Edwards also contributed two essays to the Scientific Perspectives on Divine Action series sponsored by the Center for Theology and Natural Science. In "The Discovery of Chaos and the Retrieval of the Trinity" (1997) he argues that we should think of the triune God's interaction with creatures as characterized by vulnerability. Like Peacocke, he understands the suffering of the world as a natural part of the creative process. In order to avoid a dichotomy between the doctrines of creation and redemption, he argues that God works *through* natural selection. God's love is "infinitely creative and powerful," but it is the kind of power "revealed in the death and resurrection of Jesus," respecting the structure of creation and opening it up to the "radically new" (1997, 175).

In his essay on "Original Sin and Saving Grace in Evolutionary Context" Edwards again resists the tendency to set up an opposition between natural selection and the Gospel of Jesus. He argues that God creates in and through a process that involves suffering, death and loss. The incarnation points to a vulnerable, self-limiting God, who suffers with creation, but also to the way in which creatures may participate in the life of the triune God. "The God of natural selection is the liberating, healing, and inclusive God of Jesus" (1998, 391).

As part of a broader project on *The God of Evolution: A Trinitarian Theology* (1999), Edwards provides a concise summary of his proposal for reconstructing Christology by relating "Evolution and Jesus, the Wisdom of God" (chapter 6). His overall goal is outlining a radically relational ontology grounded in an understanding of the trinitarian God as dynamic being-in-relation, who makes "space within the divine relations for a dynamically unfolding universe and for the evolution of life in all its diversity and interconnectedness" (1999, 126). This is the setting for his development of an "evolutionary Wisdom Christology" that holds together creation and incarnation. He begins by demonstrating how the early Christian community proclaimed that Sophia, the Wisdom of God, God's companion in creating all things, had made her home among them in Jesus of Nazareth.

This is expressed most radically, argues Edwards, in Paul's identification of divine wisdom with the crucified Christ. In light of the resurrection, the early church would come to claim that all things are created "in" Jesus the Wisdom of God. Speaking of "Jesus-Wisdom" as a power of transformation for the whole of creation provides us with a Christology that supports an ecological theology. Edwards encourages us to think of the diversity of life as interconnected and interdependent: each creature is a self-expression of divine Wisdom, making creation a sacrament of God's presence.

In his more recent work on Pneumatology – *Breath of Life: A Theology of the Creator Spirit* (2004) – Edwards aims to complement this Wisdom Christology with a Spirit Christology. The Spirit "breathes life" into the whole universe, "enfolds" human beings in grace and ultimately "brings about" the Christ event. Building on Ambrose's comment that the Holy Spirit is "the author of the Lord's incarnation," Edwards argues that "it is by the action of the Spirit that Jesus of Nazareth is constituted as the Son of God and the eternal Wisdom of God in our midst" (2004, 66). In this context he provides an exegetical analysis of the Gospels' testimony about Jesus' relation to the Spirit as constitutive for his identity. Christ is the one on whom the Spirit descends as a dove (Mark), who is conceived from the Holy Spirit (Matthew), who is anointed with the Holy Spirit (Luke-Acts), and the one on whom the Spirit rests (John).

Edwards provides a summary of several recent Spirit-Christologies, critically appropriating them for his own proposal that we view Jesus as "the Spirit-Anointed Wisdom of God." The Nicene-Constantinopolitan creed states that the incarnation occurred by the "power of the Holy Spirit," and Edwards sees this as occurring throughout the history of Jesus. His "Spirit-transformed humanity" becomes the receptacle for God's self-communication. The Spirit enables Jesus to give his life in love, which leads to his ugly death, but the Spirit transforms the negativity of the cross into an event of liberation through the resurrection. He emphasizes that it is the same Spirit who empowers the emergence of creation and enfolds human beings in grace who anoints and rests upon Jesus of Nazareth. "Because Jesus is a human being who is fully receptive to the Spirit, he is human in the fullest sense. Because he is totally open to the Spirit of God, he is one with God in such a way that we can say that he is the Wisdom of God, the Son of God" (2004, 83).

For Edwards, this means that the incarnation must be understood in light of the *twofold* structure of Jesus' relationship with God: not only as Son of the Father but also as the one anointed of and led by the Spirit. "Jesus has a relationship with the Spirit that enables another relation to exist – his filial relationship with the one he called *Abba*" (2004, 84). Edwards' broader interest in a relational ontology and his willingness to articulate the doctrine of the incarnation in more dynamic (or developmental) terms enhance his ability to engage contemporary evolutionary biology. Conversely, his engagement with science has led him to retrieve resources in the Christian tradition that have sometimes been eclipsed by the dominant emphasis on substance metaphysics, especially in the West. Before exploring some of the implications for articulating the identity of Jesus Christ in late modernity, let us examine some other proposals that have sought to take advantage of the opportunities for interdisciplinary dialogue opened up by these conceptual shifts.

Other Proposals

Many of the most significant theological proposals for engaging evolutionary biology in the 20th century came from Roman Catholic theologians, especially after Vatican II (cf. Korsmeyer, 1998). Much of the Protestant discussion, at least in the United States, was caught up in debates over young earth creationism or so-called Intelligent Design, which are problematic for theological as well as scientific reasons (cf. Shults, 2005, 226–30). Nevertheless, across denominations and traditions we can find creative proposals for discussing the revelation of the Word (or Logos, Wisdom) of God in the flesh of Jesus Christ, where "flesh" is understood in light of the sciences of evolutionary biology.

Certainly one of the most influential and controversial contributors to this interdisciplinary endeavor was Pierre Teilhard de Chardin (1881–1955), a paleobiologist and Roman Catholic priest. The final entry to his journal, three days before his death, is recorded at the end of the English translation of *The Future of Man*. In that entry, he summarized the "two articles" of his credo, which were: that "the Universe is centrated – Evolutively" and that "Christ is its Centre" (1964, 309). For him the doctrine of the incarnation was the key to understanding the whole of creation, including human evolution in the world and participation in the life of God.

Teilhard develops a theory of "creative union" that is meant to make sense of the genesis (and consummation) of the world. A review of the essays found in *Science and Christ* (1968) shows that he explicitly regards this as "a philosophical extension of faith in the Incarnation" (1968, 53). What he calls the first act of the incarnation is "the first appearance of the Cross," which is "marked by the plunging of the divine Unity into the ultimate depths of the Multiple" (1968, 61). Taking "physically and literally" the boldest claims of St Paul, that Christ is the plenitude who fills all things, consummates all things, and holds all things together, Teilhard speaks of Christ as "the Evolver" who "animates and gathers up all the biological and spiritual energies developed by the universe" (1968, 167).

Karl Rahner, whose influence on Edwards we noted briefly above, was another Roman Catholic theologian who explicitly tried to articulate Christology in dialogue with contemporary conceptions of anthropology and cosmology. In an essay on "Christology within an Evolutionary View of the World" (1966) he appeals explicitly to the value of the "Scotist" school for this interdisciplinary engagement. This stream of the tradition has always stressed that the basic "motive" for the incarnation was not "the blotting-out of sin," and insisted that the incarnation was the inner goal and "most original act" of divine creation (1966, 184).

For Rahner, creation and incarnation are not two separate divine initiatives but two moments in the one (intrinsically differentiated) process of God's self-giving and self-communication. In his *Foundations of Christian Faith* (1978) Rahner accepts the task of expositing the incarnation in dialogue with "today's evolutionary view of the world." He affirms the uniqueness of the hypostatic union of divine and human in the person of Christ, but argues that this is "nevertheless an intrinsic moment within the whole process by which grace is bestowed upon all spiritual creatures ... Grace in all of us and hypostatic union in the one Jesus Christ can only be understood together, and as a unity they signify the one free decision of God for ... self-communication" (1978, 201).

Process Theology

Several theologians have attempted to utilize A.N. Whitehead's process philosophy as a means for connecting the insights of evolutionary biology with the doctrine of the incarnation. For example, John Cobb, Jr. adopts process categories for linking Christ to the "transcendent Logos." Yet he interprets the latter not in substantialist terms but as "immanent in all things as the initial phase of their subjective aim, that is, as their fundamental impulse toward actualization" (1975, 76). For Cobb the term "Christ" refers to the process of God's creative transformation in and of the world, especially of human beings. He recognizes that one of the main reasons for the impasse between the Antiochenes and the Alexandrians leading up to the Definition of Chalcedon was the fact that both sides were reliant on substance categories.

Cobb also argues that moving beyond these categories can help us express the intent of the creed more intelligibly. All human persons are constituted in part by the presence of the creative lure of the Logos toward the fullest possible human realization. Jesus represents the optimum realization of this response – human existence constituting itself in unity with the lure. "This perfect incarnation of the Logos is at the same time the highest embodiment of humanity" (1975, 171).

A growing number of biblical scholars are also engaging the sciences of evolutionary biology in their interpretations of the New Testament witness to Christ. For example, Gerd Theissen's overall project in *Biblical Faith: An Evolutionary Approach* (1985) is to develop a plausible understanding of Jesus in light of both critical biblical scholarship and contemporary developments in the philosophy of science. He interprets Jesus as an "adaptation" to "the central reality," a "mutation" that introduces a new form of humanity that exceeds all previous possibilities. This new form of human existence is characterized by love, not love as a subjective emotional bond, but love as solidarity with the weak in a way that contradicts the pressures of natural selection. "In this love God reveals himself" (1985, 87).

As a participant in the movement that has come to be called "liberation" theology, Juan Luis Segundo offers another example of an attempt to speak of Jesus in a way that responds to the new context of world Christianity. In *An Evolutionary Approach to Jesus of Nazareth* (1988) he endeavors to understand Jesus from the standpoint of the primordial and the primordial from the standpoint of Jesus. For Segundo, the resurrection of Jesus must be the starting point for understanding his life as the recapitulation of the universe. He argues that too much of the debate over the incarnation in church history has focused on the question: what would have happened if Adam had not sinned? Besides its irrelevance for us today, Segundo points out that this question also obscures what he takes to be the main *eschatological* focus of Paul and the whole New Testament (1988, 111–14). All of creation may be incomplete and still groaning, but through the experience of new hope in the risen Christ, we no longer need despair in the face of suffering and death – believers no longer have any reason to fear the future, and so may give themselves over (as Christ did) to solidarity with others.

Several recent theological proposals have emphasized the importance of the concept of "symbol" for articulating Christology in a late modern context. In *Symbols of Jesus* (2001) Robert Neville explicitly utilizes Peirce's theory of symbols as the basis for his own engagement of several traditional images of Jesus. For him the symbol "Logos" indicates the transcendental form of all creation, "that in and by which all things are made that are made, and the mediator of the Creator to the human condition" (2001, 157). In a similar way, although relying on different philosophical resources, Roger Haight's controversial *Jesus: The Symbol of God* (1999) argues that Jesus is the mediation of God in human history.

Unfortunately neither of these proposals incorporates a discussion of the impact of the sciences of evolutionary biology on our understanding of "flesh." As we noted above in our discussion of the shifts in philosophical categories that underlie the challenges to particular formulations of Christology, the process of symbolization plays an increasingly important role in understanding the distinctive evolution of human consciousness. Here is an opportunity at the intersection of the disciplines: exploring the possibilities for reforming the doctrine of the incarnation in a way that explicitly engages the emerging philosophical and scientific emphasis on the mediating role of symbols and symbolization in human interpreted experience.

George Murphy engages evolutionary theory explicitly in his book *The Cosmos in Light of the Cross* (2003b). His broader concern is to develop a "chiasmic cosmology," in which all of creation is interpreted through a theology of the Crucified God. He argues that natural selection is an expression of this chiasmic interpretation: privation, competition, suffering and even death are part of the process of God's creating. Murphy's treatment of the incarnation is relatively brief. He wants to maintain both the full divinity and the full humanity of Jesus: it is "as a member of this species [*Homo sapiens*] that had become conscious and open to God but that had turned away from God and toward spiritual death that Jesus is born" (2003b, 127).

In an essay on "Christology, Evolution and the Cross" (2003a) Murphy adopts the patristic axiom that only that which is "assumed" is "healed" and suggests that in the incarnation the Logos assumes the whole of human nature in all its evolved relations. This "assumption" should be understood, he argues, as a "kenosis," a self-emptying for the sake of creation. "God does not simply stand above the evolutionary process and make it happen. In the incarnation God becomes a participant in that process, taking a place on the side of the losers in the 'struggle for survival' ... and the resurrection of the crucified means that natural selection ... is not God's last word" (2003a, 375).

In addition to these proposals, we might also point to some of the many other examples of theological engagement with the sciences of evolutionary biology that only indirectly (or briefly) deal with the doctrine of the incarnation. For example, in the context of his broader treatment of the implications of evolution for understanding culture and religion in *The Human Factor*, Phil Hefner depicts Jesus the Christ as "a proposal for the future evolution on the planet," as the "paradigm, the model of what it means to be human in the image of God" (1993, 50, 243). The biblical, philosophical and scientific problems with maintaining a literal interpretation of our first parents in paradise, which is the basis for many formulations of the doctrine of incarnation, are carefully outlined in Patricia Williams' *Doing Without Adam and Eve* (2001).

These are just a few of the resources available to us as we engage in the ongoing task of reconstructing Christology. The hermeneutical importance of the categories of becoming and relationality continues to grow in the interdisciplinary dialogue between scientists and theologians about the nature of humanity, the cosmos and God. Many of the proposals we reviewed go out of their way to offer an understanding of the God–world relation that stresses divine immanence as well as transcendence. Whether or not we agree with the use of this terminology or with specific ways in which this relation is construed, we can appreciate the fact that these proposals engage late modern conceptual space and indicate new directions for reforming the doctrine of the incarnation in this contemporary context.

The Identity of Jesus Christ

The purpose of this interdisciplinary case study has been to clarify the challenges and opportunities in the ongoing task of reconstructing the doctrine of the incarnation in the context of dialogue with the sciences of evolutionary biology. Our focus has been on the shared existential concerns and philosophical categories that shape the conceptual space within which this dialogue occurs. A fuller theological presentation of the doctrine of the incarnation would also require more careful exegetical attention to and historical analysis of the biblical tradition.

It suffices here to remind ourselves that the authors of the New Testament were able to say what they wanted to say about the identity of Jesus Christ as the one who made God known without any recourse to the idea of "two natures," and that reformers throughout the Christian tradition in both the East and the West have explored a variety of ways to formulate this doctrine without slavishly adhering to the terminology of Chalcedon.

It is important to make explicit here that the philosophical challenges explored above will require us to engage in *reforming* christological questions. It is not enough simply to figure out a new answer to an old question: how can two substances be united into one and the same person? We must refigure the task itself. The issue is not simply how the substance of the man Jesus could be identical (*idem*) with the substance of God, but how the constitutive relations in which Jesus came to find his identity as a self (*ipse*) could manifest the real relations of the trinitarian life into which creatures are called to share.

In our late modern context, we may be able better to conserve the intuitions of the biblical tradition about the revelation of God in Christ by liberating them for illuminative and transformative dialogue in response to different kinds of questions: how does Jesus' way of knowing in the world manifest the creative intentionality of divine wisdom? How is the active presence of God identified in and made known through the embodied life of Christ in a way that opens up human creatures for the transformation of noetic desire?

Attending to and participating in the transformation of philosophical categories within the conceptual space shared by theology and science is an important part of the ongoing task of reconstructing this doctrine in our contemporary context. The category of difference will be as important as the category of *sameness* in the articulation of the identity of Jesus Christ. The history of Jesus' embodied coming-to-personhood in relation to the "Father" and the "Spirit" reveals something about differentiation within God, differentiation between God and the world, and the agony and ecstasy of human differentiation.

Furthermore, the doctrine of the incarnation can break free of the constraints of the analogy between *soul* and *body* in an individual, and divinity and humanity in the person of Christ. The delightfully mysterious intimacy of the fully divine knowing and being-known among the trinitarian persons is manifested in the history of this man's fully human experience of coming-to-participate in that life as he learned to rely on the life-giving Spirit and entrust himself to the Father.

Finally, understanding Jesus' relation to the *origin* and *goal* of the human longing for wisdom no longer needs to be conceptually tied to the failure of Adam and Eve in paradise. The coming-to-be of Jesus' identification of and with divine intentionality discloses that the noetic desire of *Homo sapiens* is ultimately conditioned by the originating and orienting presence of the eternal trinitarian life of God.

We begin by emphasizing that Jesus' identity is constituted through his identification of God, his identification by God and his identification with God. The doctrine of the incarnation is about this mutual identification, in which other human persons are invited to participate. Jesus' identity was mediated to him over time as he grew in wisdom and grace (Lk. 2:52) in relation to God and his neighbors. In this sense, Jesus is like the rest of us. In the natural process of human development, a person is identified by others and comes to learn to identify himself or herself and to identify others. To be a human person is to find oneself in relation to others in mutual identification. This ongoing mediation of one's *ipseity* is characterized by anxiety because our longing to know is threatened by our fear of alienation from or absorption by the other. The difference is that Jesus' identity came-to-be graciously constituted by his dependence on the life-giving Spirit, through whom he offered himself (Heb. 9:14) to the One he called "Father." He did not grasp after equality (sameness) with God but accepted his difference, entrusting his identity to the Giver, humbling himself even to the point of death (1 Pet. 2:23; Phil. 2:6–8). After his resurrection early believers would identify him as the "Son" of God (Rom. 1:4).

Was Jesus both fully human and fully divine? Answering this question requires us to pay attention to the difference between human and divine fullness (*pleroma*). The "fullness of deity dwells bodily" in Christ (Col. 2:9) and by knowing the love of Christ believers too "may be filled with all the fullness of God" (Eph. 3:19). Jesus' relation to God – into which we are invited in the Spirit – reveals that divinity is not a substance that "fills" other things by fitting into their boundaries and that humanity is not a substance whose boundaries are threatened by such "filling."

In other words, the incarnation clarifies the truly infinite difference between God and the world. This is not like the difference between finite things, which are defined by the extension of their boundaries in relation to others. In the union of any two finite things, one or the other (or both) are threatened with the dissolution of their boundaries. The experience of God's identification of and by and with Jesus (and us) reveals that divine knowing is intensively infinite, the ultimate ground of all differentiation (and unification) whatsoever.

The life of Jesus manifests the fullness of divine *and* human knowing and being-known. Jesus' way of knowing in the world discloses the real relation of the eternal "Son" (Logos, Wisdom) to the Father and the Spirit, an eternal knowing and being known (cf. Mt. 11:27; 1 Cor. 2:11). This differentiated knowing is not an accidental property of the divine substance, but the infinite reality of the mutual identification of the trinitarian persons. The incarnation is the *making-known* of this intimately shared faithfulness, this mysterious fellowship that is the divine life, into which creatures are invited.

In his fully embodied, neurologically nested and socially mediated coming-to-personhood, Jesus manifests the Christian understanding of the ultimate origin, condition and goal of *human* knowing – sharing in the eternal Son's differentiation from and union with the Father in the Spirit. Claiming that the incarnation is a "mystery" should not come at the end of an incoherent argument about incompatible substances, but in the midst of testimony to the experience of being encountered by a delightfully uncontrollable presence that welcomes us into relation. The New Testament authors insisted that the mystery of God is *made known*, and that this mystery is precisely the relation between Christ and God into which we have access through the Spirit (e.g., Col. 1:27; 2:2; Rom. 16:25–26).

The identification of Jesus Christ is the manifestation of divine *wisdom*. Christ "became for us wisdom from God" (1 Cor. 1:24, 30). Traditional Johannine Logos Christology can be complemented by an emphasis on the relation of Jesus to divine Wisdom, a connection that arose more quickly in the consciousness of early followers of the Way of Christ. As we noted above, the Hebrew poets had personified divine Wisdom (*sophia*) as a feminine figure who creatively forms and providentially informs the whole cosmos, calling human persons into intimate relation with God (e.g., Prov. 8:30–31).

In the apocryphal Wisdom of Solomon, she is described as pervading and penetrating all things, calling all things to renewal as the image of God (7:24). The famous Colossians hymn (1:15–20) applies this imagery to Christ, in whom all things "were created" and "hold together." In the historical (trans)formation of the identity of Jesus, the all-pervading incursive and evocative presence of God appears so intensely that the New Testament authors came to identify him with and as the ultimate manifestation of divine Wisdom.

The prologue of John itself begins not with a claim about the sameness of the divine substance, but with the idea of a differentiated unity that is the source of all differentiation whatsoever. The Word was *with* God and *was* God from the beginning (1:1). John evokes the Hebrew imagery of divine Wisdom as the ruach (spirit) or light of God that orders and pervades all things (e.g., *Wis.* 7:25–27) but refigures it by linking it to the Greek concept of Logos (Word). Through the divine Logos "all things came into being" (1:3). It is precisely "life" that came into being "in him" (1:4). The divine light that enlightens all people is understood as both "in the world" and "coming" into the world (1:9–10). The differentiated relational unity of the "Father" and the "Son" who receives the "Spirit" came-to-be manifested in the relationality displayed in the fleshly life of Christ (1:14, 18, 32–34).

The Letter to the Ephesians also illustrates the appropriation of the Hebrew wisdom literature for articulating the identity of Christ. This epistle depicts the creative divine intention for human creatures as coming to *know* God more intensely within a community that is bound together in the "promised Holy Spirit." The intention of the "Father of glory" has been *made known* *in* "our Lord Jesus Christ," namely, the reception of a "Spirit of wisdom and revelation" that enlightens and enlivens the people of God (Eph. 1:9; 3:3; 6:19). In other words, Jesus' own reception of and union with divine Wisdom – his way of knowing in the world in dependence on the Father and immersed in the Spirit – revealed both the gracious faithfulness of the trinitarian God and the transformation of human noetic desire.

The coming-to-be of Jesus' relation to the divine Logos (Word, Wisdom) reveals not only the differentiation between God and the world, and trinitarian differentiation within God, but also the way in which this differentiation is experienced by creatures as a call to union with God. The New Testament authors testified to an experience of being identified with and "in" Christ (e.g., Rom. 6:23; 2 Cor. 5:17; Phil. 4:7; Jn 17:21–23) as they participated in his identification of God as a faithful Father who graciously gives the Spirit, transforming human knowing and being-known in community.

As we identify with Christ in our own longing for wisdom, we come to see his way of life (into which we are invited) as the ultimate manifestation of the Logos, the embodiment of divine Wisdom. The claim that the "Word" of God appears in Jesus' fleshly coming-to-be (*egeneto*) could only be (mis)construed as a heretical form of "adoptionism" if one assumes that the relational union of Creator and creature must be articulated under the constraints of *substance* metaphysics and a container notion of absolute space and time (cf. chapter 4).

The appearance of the divine Logos is not simply one more apparition among many, but the ground of all *phaneirōsis* whatsoever, that in and through which all things come-to-be. Precisely in the relational becoming of the personal identity of Jesus of Nazareth we are confronted with the real manifestation of God, who always and already relates to the world incarnationally (and pentecostally). All of creation is already "in" the Logos and the Logos is already "in" all of creation.

Divine Wisdom is always incarnating, granting and upholding the conditions for creaturely coming-to-be. This is experienced by human persons as an intensification of the longing to know and be-known. The divine Logos that orders and orients all things is revealed in the history of the man Jesus of Nazareth and is present to human creatures calling them to share in the way opened by his dependence on the Spirit and his reception of eternal life from the Father. In the life of Christ we encounter a divine manifesto, not as a set of propositions but as the setting-forth of an infinite welcome to trust in the omniscient faithfulness of God.

This way of articulating the doctrine of the incarnation allows us to affirm that Jesus' coming-to-be was wholly embedded within the evolution of our species and wholly embodied in the natural emergence of consciousness nested in the neural processes of a human brain. It also helps us make sense of the claim that Jesus is really united with the divine Logos, who is eternally "prior" in God. The gracious presence of the Logos (or Wisdom) of God faithfully tends to creatures, who are naturally dependent on the arriving presence of absolute divine Futurity for any and all becoming.

For human persons this coming-to-be is intensified in the consciousness of one's relation to others (and one's self), and takes shape as a longing to know and be-known beyond the threat of death, to find oneself identified in eternal faithful relations. The incarnation is not an emergency response to the sin of a primeval privileged pair, but a display of the eternal creative intentionality of God in whose presence our responsibility emerges. The relational union of Christ with the divine Logos disclosed an eternal (perichoretic) interdependence in the life of God that the biblical tradition refers to as the relation of the Son to the Father in the Spirit.

The emergence of the symbolic capacity of our species may be understood theologically as a creaturely response to the gracious presence of divine Wisdom, calling us into the intimacy of knowing and being-known that is the life of the triune God. The absolute priority of the Logos is disclosed precisely in Jesus' identification with(in) this differentiating divine presence, as his identity was formed through his response to and "mystical" union with the Father in the Spirit. This coming-to-be-united was wholly implicated within the differentiated and differentiating processes of an evolving creation. The creaturely longing for noetic union with the Unknown was infinitely intensified in Jesus' coming (in)to intimate knowledge of God. The life of Christ may thus be understood as both the manifestation of the infinitely gracious faithfulness of the divine Logos and the fulfillment of the natural noetic desire of human personhood.

We identify Jesus by identifying with him in his way of being identified by God. Pilate's famous question "What is truth?" was a response to Jesus' claim that those who listen to him "*belong* to the truth" (Jn 18:37–38). Pilate was trying to figure out the identity of this man who had been accused of claiming to be the Son of God. His question is not answered with propositions about the relation between two substances, but by Jesus' wholly entrusting himself to the life-giving Spirit of the Father even in the face of those who desired to kill him.

Here and throughout Jesus' ministry, teaching and responsiveness to others we are confronted with an understanding of truth that is not severed from truthfulness – faithful adherence to the mysterious presence of divine Wisdom that overcomes violence and death. Jesus' way of knowing in the world can be correlated to the traditional idea of his *prophetic* "office," refigured as his revelatory calling of others to participate in the ongoing incarnating intentionality of the Creator. "Anointed" by the Spirit, the Christ mediates the divine address, which calls human persons into new trustworthy relations to God and their neighbors.

The idea that we are called to *participate* in the incarnation will seem blasphemous if we hold onto the categories of substance metaphysics, which would seem to exclude us from any such "hypostatic union." However, if we take seriously the claim that the "Logos" also dwells in us richly (Col. 3:16), and that we are the "body" of Christ (1 Cor. 12:27), then we can begin to incorporate the Christian experience of identifying with Jesus, receiving the Spirit of wisdom and finding a new identity in relation to God, immediately into a presentation of the doctrine of the incarnation.

Participating in the incarnating wisdom of God always takes shape – as it did for Jesus – in fellowship with one's neighbors. The divine Logos which is always present, informing our lives and calling us toward transformed relations to God and one another, was made apparent in Jesus' way of faithfully tending to these relations. The Christian community is called to share in this truthful way of living, inviting others into the intimate embrace of knowing and being-known by God.

The shifts in the conceptual space within which the doctrine of the incarnation may now be brought into dialogue with the sciences of evolutionary biology provide a fresh opportunity for theology to articulate the *Gospel* of the identity of Jesus Christ. In our late modern context christological formulations that rely on substance metaphysics and a literal reading of the Garden of Eden no longer serve a reformative function, but foster confusion and repression within and consternation and incredulity without the walls of the church.

Articulating a truly *reforming* Christology will require breaking down the barriers that hinder a broader transformative conversation about the human longing to know and be known, a conversation that should include representatives from other religious traditions as well as other scientific disciplines. Questions about the self-identification of *Homo sapiens* in relation to God cannot be isolated from questions about the human longing for goodness and beauty. This means that we should also attempt to incorporate soteriological and eschatological concerns into the task of reconstructing Christology in our context.

Chapter 3

Atonement and Cultural Anthropology

Our second case study explores the challenges and opportunities that emerge as we attempt to articulate the intuitions of the biblical tradition about the atoning work of Jesus Christ in dialogue with contemporary scientific insights into the social and cultural dimensions of human life. Although the phrase "cultural anthropology" often refers to a specific academic field, I will be using it in this context to indicate a broader array of sciences that study humanity (*anthropos*) by attending to the mutual mediation of individual human action and interpersonal structural dynamics (including sciences such as sociology, jurisprudence and social theory). The English word "atonement" was used in the King James Version (1611) to translate the Greek term *katallagēn* in Rom. 5:11, which is now more commonly rendered as "reconciliation." Today the doctrine of atonement typically refers to the theological explication of the Christian experience of salvation – covering a broad range of biblical themes such as forgiveness, healing and redemption – all of which relate to the action of God in and through Jesus Christ that brings us into right relation with one another.

The overall purpose of this chapter is to identify promising directions for the reconstructive articulation of the Christian understanding and experience of this agency. Throughout Scripture and church history a variety of images and metaphors have been utilized to depict the way in which the events of Jesus' passion relate to the transformation of other human agents. Atonement "theories" have always been developed in conjunction with particular ways of construing the good life and the proper ordering of human action. In order to clarify the texture of the conceptual space in which this theological task operates today we will trace shifts in some of the philosophical categories that have shaped both atonement doctrine and cultural anthropology and trends in some of the recent theological proposals that have explored opportunities for reconstruction in this interdisciplinary context. Critically appropriating these resources can facilitate our articulation of the claim that Jesus Christ manifests the omnipotent justifying agency of God, calling us to participate with our neighbors in the redemptive power of divine love. First, however, let us briefly outline one of the basic conceptual concerns around which these disciplines can be brought into dialogue.

A Shared Interest in Acting

Questions about the nature of human agency are significant in both the
disciplines of cultural anthropology (broadly understood) and in Christology,
especially in relation to the doctrine of the atonement. To act (intentionally)
is to use one's power in order to secure an object or bring about a state of
affairs that one desires. While other species also exhibit such behavior, the
complexity of the social and cultural construction of mores that guide human
agency and the intensity of human anxiety about justice and the good life
are unique. As persons we use our power to secure that which we desire.
Our choice about which particular goods to acquire, as well as our decisions
about which persons are worth relating to, are shaped by our culture(s), by
the values that are mediated to us within the shared symbol systems of our
social group(s). In this sense a person's interpretation of what is good (and
evil) emerges within the context of the experience of the complex interactions
and practices of his or her communities.

While both disciplines are interested in human acting, they study these
phenomena for different reasons and with distinct methodologies. Social
scientists attempt to clarify the characteristic structures and functions of
human agency as it is mediated by and within cultures. The importance of the
concept of acting is evident even from a cursory review of influential texts in
these fields, from Talcott Parsons' *Structure of Social Action* (1968 [1937])
to Jürgen Habermas' *The Theory of Communicative Action* (vol. 1 1984;
vol. 2 1987). The sciences of cultural anthropology (in general) analyze the
origination and regulation of social structures within (and across) particular
cultures in order to understand the way in which ethical systems (broadly
conceived) condition and guide human agency. Theologians are interested
in the ultimate origin, condition and goal of human acting vis-à-vis the
interpreted experience of divine action. The practical navigation of our social
worlds is anxiety producing, because we are unsure of the sufficiency of our
power or the power of others to provide us with the goods we need, much
less with a cohesive interpersonal field within which we love and are loved
without threat of being crushed or abandoned. Atonement theory outlines
the Christian claim that this redemptive interpersonal space is graciously
provided in and through Jesus Christ, whose agency manifests the omnipotent
justifying love of God.

Our interest in human acting is not merely academic, for as scientists
and theologians we too are existentially caught up in the fear and desire of
intentional agency. Cultural anthropologists qua scientists do not typically
ask which objects really are good; they focus on the intentional and
social structures of human agency, aiming to interpret and understand the
distribution of limited goods among diverse cultures. As the late modern

appeal for interdisciplinarity intensifies, however, more scientists are open to entering into the philosophical space shared with theology and ethics, exploring possibilities for transforming (not merely interpreting) structures that unjustly divide societies by race, class and gender. This requires reflection not only on criteria for adjudicating between particular social mores, but also on the underlying longing for the good life that structures human agency. *moral*

This longing itself is what I call *moral* desire. However well we master *desire* social rules, however many goods we acquire, our deep longing for loving and just relations with others never seems to be satiated. We are still haunted by the fear of being banished from or suffocated by the social structures of our communities, and so we live in this ambiguous tension that is moral desiring. No matter how well we live, no matter how morally we behave, we will all die. Social structures, institutional regulations and cultural systems will ultimately fail to overcome the ultimate enemy of the good life – death itself. Here we are absolutely dependent on a gracious gift that can free us from the ethical anxiety that arises in the face of this final threat.

Theologians are interested in understanding this aspect of the human condition in relation to a particular conception of *divine* justice. In other words, we aim to explicate the *ultimate* origin, condition and goal of human acting. Why do we long to be united (at one) with an absolute source of goodness? What hinders and what facilitates such a salubrious relationality? The doctrine of atonement is about the way in which divine justice is manifested in the life, death and resurrection of Jesus Christ in such a way that we are now invited to participate within the reign of divine peace precisely by sharing in the loving agency of God that overcomes sin and death.

Since early modernity these kinds of theological questions have often been treated under the general theme of *soteriology*, which derives from the *soteriology* Greek term *soteria* (salvation). As I suggested in chapter 1 the unfortunate separation of this locus on the "work" of Jesus from the locus on the "person" of Jesus (incarnation) was supported by the hard distinction between substance and accidents, the latter including properties like relation, movement and the like. As the concept of "function" came to play a more significant role in mathematics, science and philosophy some liberal theologians were tempted to reduce Christology to soteriology; what Jesus did and his influence on us overshadowed questions about who Jesus really was. On the conservative side, the temptation was to reduce Jesus' work to what happened on the cross, typically understood as some form of payment or penalty. Both forms of reductionism can be overcome as we move toward an integrated presentation of Jesus' identity, agency and presence within the relational, dynamic conceptual space opening up in late modern discourse. These case studies are a step in that direction.

ethics

Because of their shared concern with human acting, atonement doctrine and cultural anthropology may also relate through philosophical discourse on *ethics*. For much of the early social theory tradition, theoretical analysis of social structures was linked to the question of "ought" (e.g., Kant), but with the rise of positivism there emerged a sharp distinction between fact and value. Today, however, many late modern cultural theorists and ethicists are working to heal this division, in light of the shifts in the philosophy of science we explored in chapter 1. Human persons desire objects they perceive as good, which brings them into conflict with their immediate kin and neighbors. Social scientists study the way in which moral reasoning is connected to structures of human organization and grouping in ways that secure the good of (at least some members of) the community. Such discourse about morality provides an arena for theological descriptions of the good life. Conversely, Christian explications of the way in which a lovely and just life is made possible in relation to God should engage the practical concerns of contemporary society.

Beginning the conversation within the shared conceptual and existential space of moral desire can help us refigure the questions that drive the formulation of atonement theory. If atonement really is about the way in which human acting is opened up to and transformed through union (at-one-ment) with the absolute Good, then only this broad perspective will do – carefully attending to the *whole* agency of Jesus Christ (*totus Christus*), and what this manifests about moral desiring in relation to God and neighbor. A more relational and holistic approach to atonement theory may help us formulate the question differently: how does Jesus Christ's life of love manifest the justifying agency of God? Our next step is to explore and clarify the philosophical developments that have shaped the late modern conceptual space within which this ongoing reconstructive task may operate today.

Philosophical Challenges

As cultural anthropologists and theologians go about their work of making sense of our pursuit of the good life, they share several *philosophical* categories. Three pairs of concepts are especially relevant for this case study:

(1) • particular and universal
(2) • law and order
(3) • us and them

Theorizing about the experience of salvation throughout church history has been shaped in part by the ways in which theologians attended (or failed to attend) to the use of these categories within the cultural contexts in which they operated. Shifts in these categories even influenced the way in which the nature of (and need for) "theorizing" about atonement was interpreted. Moreover, the choice between biblical motifs is always guided by underlying (and often unnoticed) philosophical assumptions.

Particular and Universal

One of the most enduring issues in Western philosophy has been the nature of and relation between "particulars" (individual things) and "universals" (genera or classes). Take the assertion: "Fido is a dog." When we predicate dogness of Fido, we claim that this particular individual thing (Fido) is part of a genus or "universe" of things that share a common quality (things that are dogs). Universal "things" are predicated of particular "things." If one assumes that this predicative structure has metaphysical import, or may be imported into metaphysics, then one is led to ask: what is the ontological status of these "things?" Can generic things and particular things exist apart from each other? Do both kinds of things really exist, and if so how are they related to each other? While such questions bear on any and all *genera* (being green, being round etc.), the most significant "kinds" for our current case study are predicates like being human, being a culture and being good.

Does the genus "humanity" (or "culture") exist apart from particular humans (or cultures)? The fact that such questions seem bizarre to most of us already indicates the main point of this sub-section: the underlying philosophical categories that shaped such classical and early modern debates (and so the doctrine of atonement) no longer constrain contemporary discourse in the same way. In order to understand this new conceptual space, however, it is important to outline the contours of those debates and their influence on our disciplines. The history of atonement theory is much more complex and messy than the following overview might suggest. Theologians often held more than one theory at once, and intermingled metaphors and models. My only excuse for risking such an overview is my hope that it will suffice to clarify the following point: these philosophical categories played a significant and often overlooked role in soteriological theory choice.

The way in which particular things are related to and within these broader classes is relevant for both the doctrine of atonement and cultural anthropology. One of the basic questions in soteriology is how a particular human (Jesus) relates to and can alter the quality of a whole class of humans. How does this one person's agency register a transformative effect on other members of that genus? One of the basic questions in anthropological science is how any particular individual relates to those within his or her "universe" (kin, tribe). A related question is how (or whether) particular social groups are situated within the broader genus of "culture." Shifts in the philosophical assumptions about the nature of universals (and predication) have shaped theory formation in both of these disciplines.

The three most popular options for answering the philosophical question about the relation between particulars and universals may be traced to the ancient Greek schools of Plato, Aristotle and the Stoics. Plato answered the question by appealing to his metaphysical distinction between the realm of unchanging Forms and the realm of changing matter. The eternal Forms (or Ideas) are universal and more "real" than particular material objects, which imitate the Forms and have their being only by "participating" in them.

Aristotle rejected this separation of Form from matter, but not the reality (existence) of genera or universals. For him one can speak of a universal "form" that defines human persons, but it exists only in relation to or as it subsists within particular material things (in this case, material bodies formed by rational souls). Many of the Stoics were materialists, and believed that even thinking souls were composed of matter. They were typically less interested in defining "the human" than in discussing the way in which the dispositions of this or that particular human being was connected to the all-determining creative logos (or pneuma) of the cosmos.

Variations on these philosophical themes were deeply influential in the history of the Christian doctrine of atonement. During the patristic period, Plato's approach was by far the most popular, and we have already seen in chapter 2 that his dualism played a role in the formation of the doctrine of the incarnation. How did it influence atonement theory? One common way to speak about salvation during this period was by claiming that the divine Logos healed "humanity" by becoming united with it in the incarnation. One of the most popular expressions of this approach is Gregory of Nazianzus' well-known assertion in his letter to Cledonius: "For that which he has not assumed he has not healed; but that which is united to his Godhead is also saved." Supporting this claim is the common 4th century presupposition that there is a universal "thing" – a Form of "humanity" – that the Logos can "assume," take up into itself and heal. A similar presupposition about the nature of universals is behind Gregory of Nyssa's assertion that the Logos leavened the "whole lump" of humanity.

During the previous century, Origen's dependence on the Platonic approach to universals made it difficult for him to avoid a "universalistic" view of salvation. If the Logos has healed all flesh (humanity) through its union with the flesh of Jesus, it seems to follow that God wills all to be saved and that God will draw all things together under the headship of Christ. The majority of patristic writers during this period labored hard to avoid this conclusion, but nevertheless maintained the philosophical assumption that subtended the soteriological question: how can the individual man Jesus have a healing (salvific) effect on a general group? Most agreed that in this one person, the Logos was united to this real universal and thereby transformed the nature of humanity, thereby healing the corruption of that substance that had occurred at the "Fall" of Adam and Eve.

The Aristotelian approach to universals came into dominance in the early medieval period after his writings were made newly available to the Christian West. This new philosophical way of relating particulars to universals shifted the conceptual space within which atonement theory could be articulated. If there is no universal Form – no abstract *humanum* – to which the Logos can be united, this creates a problem for the patristic "assumption" model outlined above. Aristotelians argued that "humanity" exists but only "in" individual humans. How then can the particular man Jesus have a saving effect on a larger class (or genus) of humans? It is well known that Thomas Aquinas adopted and adapted Aristotle's philosophy for theological service, and this included "the Philosopher's" argument that universals (or secondary substances) are real but exist only in particulars (or primary substances).

This limited the range of options for Thomas' soteriological theory-choice. He preferred to articulate the atonement along the lines of the "satisfaction" model that had been developed by Anselm earlier in the middle ages (see below). Thomas' way of spelling out this theory presupposes what came to be called moderate realism, the view that universals are in fact real, but they exist only in particular things (*in re*) not before or outside of them (*ante rem*). What was the mechanism by which a particular individual (Jesus) brought salvation to a class of individuals? As a member of Adam's race, he satisfied a debt that was owed by the whole group.

As we will see in the next section, developments in legal theory from Anselm to Grotius would shape the ways in which this answer was spelled out over the centuries. The main point for our purposes here is that under the influence of the Aristotelian construal of the relation between particular and universal, Thomas accepted a different way of answering the soteriological question.

In the 14th century, William of Ockham rejected Thomas' moderate realism as well as the realism of the Platonists. Ockham argued that a universal term is merely a name (*nomen*) that we give to a group of particulars. This view came to be known as nominalism. On this model, there is no such "thing" as a generic "humanity" – that is simply a name we use that helps us refer to all individual humans. This philosophical approach reinforced theories of the atonement that focused less on the healing of the *humanum* and more on the way in which the particular man Jesus could register an effect on other particular individuals. Ockham himself wrote relatively little on the atonement, apparently content to allow the idea of God's absolute power

– God can save whomever and however God wills – to buttress theological belief in salvation.

The impact of the rise of nominalism on soteriological theory in the centuries that followed, however, is quite clear. For example, Luther's emphasis on the unity of the individual man Jesus in his doctrine of the incarnation carried over into his atonement theory. Luther tended to prefer depictions of the work of Jesus that focused on his victory over the devil. He had often been interpreted during the Enlightenment as one more example of the satisfaction view, but Gustav Aulén (1954) drew fresh attention to Luther's appropriation (and refiguration) of the patristic Christus Victor theme, which we will explore in more detail below.

Our interest at this stage is not on the biblical warrant or cosmological plausibility of his interpretation of this theme, but on the following fact: Luther's way of depicting the work (and person) of Christ does not *require* the existence of a real universal human "nature." As a particular (unique) individual Jesus defeated the devil and won over the prize of (some) human souls. As we will see below, nominalism also shaped several other formulations of atonement theory from the Protestant Scholastics to modern liberalism.

First, however, it is important to observe how these philosophical shifts shaped the social sciences. The disciplines of social theory and cultural anthropology (in the narrower sense) emerged well after nominalism had gained ground over its (moderate) realist rivals. In fact, nominalism itself had contributed to the rise of early modern science. Instead of abstract reflection on general ideas (sponsored by Platonic and to a lesser extent Aristotelian metaphysics), Ockham's method privileged a focus on particulars.

This kind of careful analysis of concrete individuals was a key ingredient in the scientific method of Galileo, Bacon and others. An emphasis on empirically observable particulars shaped the way in which social theorists began to think about the relation between individual persons within groups (and cultures). For example, riding the crest of the nominalist wave Thomas Hobbes' *Leviathan* (1651) begins with the individual human person as the basic unit of analysis. This starting point influences his prescription for the ordering of groups of individuals – the enforcement of civility by governing monarchs.

Our primary interest here is not in adjudicating between political theories but in observing the tendency among many influential thinkers in the early modern period to begin their anthropological reflections by tending to the individual. The Cartesian *cogito, ergo sum* and the Lockean emphasis on the identity and autonomy of the conscious self are perhaps the most obvious examples. In the 18th century, we can see this tendency operative in Jean Jacques Rousseau's *Social Contract* (1762) and Adam Smith's *The Wealth of*

Nations (1776), which in different ways appealed to the self-interest of the individual as the basis for a just or well-functioning society. Social theory itself emerged as part of the modernist project to make sense of the relation between the autonomy of individual subjects and moral responsibility within a broader political community.

Nominalism also shaped the development of most early modern atonement theories. Taking the particular as a starting point for soteriology produced several quite distinct approaches, all of which still had to explain how the action of Jesus affected a class of other individuals whom we nominate as "human." Virtually all the theories formulated by the Protestant Scholastics in the 17th and early 18th centuries focused on individuals. Even more than the medieval Scholastics, they tended to stress penal and judicial metaphors when explaining the efficacy of the work of Christ.

Reformed Trod.

In the Reformed tradition, this took shape in the emphasis on the way in which this single individual paid the penalty, or received the punishment, for some other individuals (the elect). On this model, the object of salvation is not "humanity" but that aggregate of predetermined individuals who will not get what they deserve. The task becomes identifying the *ordo salutis* – the order in which the individual soul is moved from one state to another. We will explore these theories in more detail below.

pietism
liberalism

We find the same focus on the individual in much of the atonement theorizing of 18th century pietism and 19th century liberalism. Although these differ from the Protestant Scholastic formulations in so many ways, they share an emphasis on the particular. Some of these theories have been characterized as belonging to the so-called "moral influence" stream of the Christian tradition. Especially among modern liberal theologians, it was common to find the assertion that Jesus had a general effect on a group of individuals (the church, or even society) by providing an example of a moral life. This particular man inspires us to love as he loved. The primary object of salvation here is also the individual; inspired by Jesus, such individuals could have a social impact by inspiring other individuals.

Moral Influence

The influence of nominalism on all of these models, can also be seen in the fact that soteriology could be (and was) separated from ecclesiology in systematic presentations of doctrine (especially among the Protestant Scholastics). In other words, the doctrine of salvation was understood first and foremost in terms of "saved" individuals, whose status in relation to the atoning work of Jesus could be explained without immediate reference to the question of how they ought to relate to one another socially. The former had implications for the latter but not vice versa. On this model of soteriological theorizing, particular saved individuals are brought into aggregates but their aggregation is only a consequence of and not ingredient to their salvation.

Late modern social theories, however, became increasingly interested in the complexity of the interplay between cultural structures, systems and human action. While theorists like Locke and Kant focused primarily on the moral conduct of the individual, most 20th century theorists were more concerned with the way in which patterns of agency were mediated through social relations. We can see this in thinkers as diverse as Max Weber, Talcott Parsons, John Dewey, George Herbert Mead and Anthony Giddens (cf. Cohen, 2000). In the 19th century Auguste Comte had founded positivist sociology in an attempt to emulate the nomological approach of sciences like physics, which aimed to identify universal laws into which all particulars could be fitted. Many late-20th century social theorists argued that the age of grand European theories, which Sir Thomas More's *Utopia* (1516) is often considered to have inaugurated, is now over and we must be content with ideographic methods that provide interpretations of particular cultural patterns in relation to particular social systems (cf. Delanty, 2000).

The ongoing debates between structuralists and post-structuralists also illustrate this philosophical tension. Herbert Spencer and Emile Durkheim had contributed to the emergence of structuralism in social theory by introducing the idea of the structural integration of the whole, whose parts are differentiated by their functions. Early-20th century theorists like Malinowski and Radcliffe-Brown called for a theoretical generality based on comparative ethnography. On this model, the individual manifestations of social life are explained by the "facts" of general structures, which have causal functions within the whole (cf. Boyne, 2000). Many of the early structuralists in cultural anthropology sought universal structures (e.g. Saussure, Levi-Strauss), and a generic definition of culture into which all particular societies could fit.

Through the efforts of anthropologists like Evans-Pritchard (e.g., 1937 [1976]) the self-understanding of the discipline increasingly moved away from the Comtean idealization of natural science and toward a model closer to other human sciences (although this distinction itself has come under criticism, as we saw in chapter 1). After Clifford Geertz's influential emphasis on the *interpretation* of cultures (1973) through depth description, the majority of practicing anthropologists no longer sought totalizing theories. This acceptance of fragmentation was further buttressed by the post-structuralist critique of the hegemony implicit in so much of the discipline's generalizations regarding other cultures, and the interrogation of the very notion that categories like "religion" could be generally applied across cultures (cf. Lovell, 2000; Asad, 1993 [1982])

One of the most common themes in postmodern social theory, however, is *community*, which often brings with it a critique of individualism. How are we to make sense of this? The turn to relationality has altered the way in which the options are framed. In the debate among the Aristotelians, Platonists and

Stoic-influenced nominalists, all the interlocutors had assumed that reality has to do primarily with substances, and that substances may be represented through the subject–predicate structure of (Western) language. After the linguistic turn, language is no longer understood as a simple referential system through which external objective realities are "represented" by internal subjective ideas.

Human ideation is always and already mediated through language, which emerges within and among persons who struggle to communicate patterns of meaning embodied in symbols. Language is embedded within (and embeds) the relations among persons, and cannot so easily be forced into the categories of substantialist logic inherited from Greek philosophy. This does not mean that the individual is ignored or unimportant in contemporary cultural anthropology, but that his or her agency can only be understood by tending to the communal relations among persons.

This philosophical shift challenges models of atonement theory that presuppose Platonic, Aristotelian or even Stoic notions of the relation between particulars and universals. This debate itself was upheld by the assumptions of substance metaphysics and a substance-based theory of predication; out of the ashes of their collapse emerged the social scientific insight that all human intentional action is embedded within and mediated by linguistically conditioned cultural contexts. Here too theology is given an opportunity. In many traditional theories of atonement the relations within which the agency of Christ was embedded before (and after) his death play little or no role in the mechanism of salvation. Whether such theories involve the healing of human nature, beating the devil or making a payment, the mediation of Jesus' coming-to-be an agent is not *directly* relevant to the way in which this particular man influences the universe of "the saved."

One of the tasks of reforming Christology is making sense of our experience of Jesus' agency as mediating our salvation in a way that conserves the intuitions of the biblical tradition by liberating them for illuminative and transformative interdisciplinary discourse. Soteriological reflection itself can contribute to more relational, dynamic ways of understanding the human linguistic urge to identify commonalities and differences. Here we could learn to worry less about the individual's *ordo salutis* and tend more to the way in which we are being made at-one, to the *salutary ordering* of our real relations in community (cf. Shults and Sandage, 2003, 156–61). Before exploring examples of proposals that make such an attempt, we need to examine some other ways in which philosophical categories have shaped atonement theory.

2) *Law and Order*

The sciences of cultural anthropology and the doctrine of atonement have also been shaped by assumptions about the nature and basis of human systems of law and the values that should guide their execution in the ordering of a just society. It is important to acknowledge the reciprocal relations among developments in theology, philosophy, law and sociology. On the one hand, we will observe below several examples of the influence of particular models of jurisprudence on a variety of soteriological theories. On the other hand, the way in which cultures understand and practice social justice is also shaped by explicitly religious beliefs and experiences. Even the distinction between individualistic and communitarian thought forms – commonly associated with West and East respectively – has religious underpinnings (cf. Stone and Stone-Romero, 2002).

The main point of this section is to demonstrate how cultural assumptions about law and order conditioned the formulation of soteriological theories at various key points throughout church history. This is clearly a challenge to those who are wedded to a particular theory which they see as the only way of articulating the manifestation of divine justice through Jesus Christ. However, we will also explore the extent to which developments in contemporary social and anthropological theories about how religion functions within cultures and the growing awareness of the incapacity of human power to fulfill moral desire might also provide an opportunity for reconstructing this doctrine in late modernity.

We begin with the observation that each of the philosophical schools we identified above has its own correlated ethical and political theory. Plato developed a complex analogy between the well-ordered soul and the well-ordered city in *The Republic*. In *The Nichomachean Ethics* Aristotle argued that through the formation of virtuous character politicians will learn to manage the city-state. In his defense of what came to be called "natural law," the Stoic philosopher Cicero insisted in *De Re Publica* that "true law" involves the universal application of "right reason," which all rational individuals (and the gods) share in common. All three of these approaches explicitly acknowledged that (in some sense) the divine is the basis (or source) of human law and that well-ordered human life involves coming into right relation with the divine. Up until the early modern period this assumption could be taken for granted in the formulation of doctrines of the atonement.

Soteriological theorizing has always been conditioned (in part) by shifts in philosophical construals of the nature of law and the practice of justice. During the patristic period the concept of the "ransom" was one of the more popular ways of explaining the work of Christ. Such theories portrayed God as offering a payment to the Devil. Certain conditions must hold for such an account to make sense. In the 3rd century it was commonly believed that the cosmos was populated with evil spirits who were at war, fighting for power over the affairs of terrestrial souls.

Surrounded by people who were constantly terrified of being bound by such spirits, Origen developed the theme of ransom in a way that promised them hope. In his theory, these spiritual principalities and powers ruled and ordered the world because the Devil had deceived Adam and Eve into disobeying God. Having won this battle, the Devil had *rightfully* taken control of humanity, made them his slaves and became the ruler of the world. Origen argued that Christ was a ransom payment to the Devil by God, who has now recovered ownership and control over (at least part of) humanity.

In the 4th century there was considerable debate over whether God tricked the Devil or paid him outright. The consensus was that trickery would be inappropriate to the divine. In his Great Catechism (XX–XXV) Gregory of Nyssa argued that there was a kind of necessity for God to accomplish deliverance of humanity in a *lawful* way. On this model the rightful owner of the slaves (the Devil) was paid all that he asked as the redemption-price of his property. However, Gregory goes on to suggest that the Devil was so eager to grab this ransom, that he failed to see that the Godhead of Christ was concealed "under the veil of our [human] nature, in order that, as happens with greedy fishes, together with the bait of the flesh the hook of the Godhead might also be swallowed." The main point for our purposes here is that a particular understanding of law and order – such as the rules by which enemy combatants may be released – subtended the development of such theories.

Conceptualizations of law and order had shifted considerably by the time of Anselm of Canterbury at the turn of the 11th century. His influential *satisfaction* theory of the atonement is one of the clearest examples of the role of these philosophical categories in the shaping of soteriology. My interest here is not in adding to the litany of complaints about Anselm's model, but using him as an illustration of a dynamic that is operative in the work of every constructive theologian. He lived in a world of knights and castles, where honor provided a kind of social glue and the codes of chivalry were the key to maintaining a well-ordered society. Teutonic law required that serfs obey their lords on whose land they were allowed to live. Those who dishonored their lords by breaking a law (for example) had to provide satisfaction to the injured party or be punished accordingly.

In his *Cur Deus Homo* (Why God Became Man) Anselm used this human theory of jurisprudence to depict the relation between creatures and God as supreme Lord of the cosmic order. Adam and Eve had sinned and injured God's honor. Just as it would be unfitting *ex hypothesi* for a human lord simply to forgive a serf, so it would be unfitting for God simply to show grace to humanity because the order of (cosmic) society depends on the fulfillment and maintenance of this law. On the other hand, it would not be fitting for God to give up the goal for which human beings were created in the first place – making up for the number of angels who fell with the Devil (I.19).

From these premises, Anselm is led to the necessary conclusion: God must either punish humanity (with death) or a satisfaction must be paid by a (representative) member of their race. The first parents' sin injured the honor of the Lord of the cosmos, so the satisfaction to be paid must equal all the universe. A human *must* pay the satisfaction but only God himself *could* pay such a price. Therefore, the death of the God-man is the only possible (and therefore necessary) solution. Such a satisfaction price outweighs the sins of humanity, earning merit which is applied to (some of) Adam's race. Not only did this theory make sense in light of the contemporary understanding of law and order, it also reinforced the medieval church's penitential system wherein one still had to pay for one's post-baptismal sins.

The basic logic of this theory came to dominate the doctrine of the atonement in the West, although its formulation varied as concepts of law and order continued to develop. The Renaissance was characterized by a renewed interest in retrieving ancient (especially Stoic) models of Roman jurisprudence and this influenced political legal theorizing especially in Europe. For example, Calvin's penal substitution model of atonement took over the basic logic of satisfaction theory, but refigured it in ways that mirrored 16th century Genevan jurisprudence. In his analysis of the uses of the law, for example, Calvin went out of his way to underline its punitive function as a way of restraining malefactors and protecting the community (*Institutes* II.7).

Despite the differences between the Reformed followers of Arminius and Gomarus in the early 17th century, they held in common the assumption that Christ's death has infinite merit and is sufficient to pay the penalty of the sins for as many people as God decides. The entire debate presupposed a particular understanding of retributive justice, which could be calculated in terms of penalties, merits and payments. The basic issue upon which they disagreed was the correct answer to the question: *for whom* did Christ pay the penalty? Only three answers are possible: all, some and none. The last option was a non-starter and so the battle was between the champions of general and limited atonement, that is, between the Remonstrants and the defenders of the synod of Dordt. Each answer had its own unique logical, biblical and existential problems, as both sides were quick to point out to their opponents.

Socinius had the nerve to object to the underlying assumption that it was necessary for a penalty to be paid: why could not God just forgive? Does not God ask us to forgive others who have injured us without demanding payment or punishment? Are we held to a higher standard than God? Respondents to this audacity were plentiful, but one is particularly interesting for our purposes. The Dutch legal theorist and theologian Hugo Grotius (1889 [1617]) seems to have accepted Socinius' basic point – that it would be "just" for God to show mercy. However, he went on to develop what came to be called the "governmental" theory of atonement in his *Defense of the Catholic Faith concerning the Satisfaction of Christ against Faustus Socinus.*

In Grotius' model, God punishes Christ with a torturous death in order to provide a weighty example for us, showing God's wrath and severity in relation to sin. Such an idea is initially offensive to most people, as Grotius himself acknowledges, but he offers the following logical argument. First, he points to cases in his own society where one person is punished for the crimes of another and this is considered just. Next, he asserts that God has supreme power and can do anything that is not unjust per se. From this it follows that God can without unfairness transfer the punishment that humanity deserves onto Christ, thereby exhibiting at the same time both divine clemency and hatred toward disobedience.

Grotius was also a key player in the incorporation of "natural law" into Protestant moral theology as a whole, and atonement theory in particular. This approach is usually traced back to the Stoics although we find elements of it in Plato, Aristotle and others as well. Cicero (106–43 BC) is often considered one of its clearest early representatives. He argued that "true law is right reason in agreement with nature," and that this law is unchanging, everlasting and universally applicable. Cicero believed that all rational individuals and the gods share in common this natural reason, and that all may be judged according to this universal law.

The influence of this view can be traced throughout the Christian natural law tradition, which begins long before Grotius. In fact, it is already present in the New Testament writings of Paul, whose engagement with Stoic philosophy is now well documented (Engberg-Pedersen, 2000). For example, Paul appeals in Romans 1 to a common sense of what is right that is naturally placed in all people. In other places in the Pauline literature it is also clear that societal assumptions about slavery, the role of women in household codes, and general middle-Platonic ethical constructs are conditioning arguments for the social ordering of believers.

Augustine's reflections on social origins (especially in Books 14 and 19 of *City of God*) show evidence of a mixture of stoic natural law and Neoplatonism, and his approach had a strong influence on Christian political theory. In the middle ages Thomas Aquinas also appropriated natural law in his moral theology, although his emphasis on the virtues of the individual as the basis for ordering the good life had more of an Aristotelian flavor. On this model, God created the world and humans in such a way that all individuals *naturally* have a universal law within them, which is the basis for legal order.

Of course for Augustine and Thomas, and most of other theologians in this stream of the tradition, this natural human moral reasoning capacity had been corrupted by the "Fall."

This raises the question of the relation between this "natural" law and God's creative (and redemptive) agency. Is the nature of the law within human individuals good because God willed it, or did God will humans to have this law because it was good? If one accepts the latter, it appears that God's creative will was conditioned by something (a criterion for goodness) outside God. This would suggest that the will of God is not the absolute origin of all that is good. This result led many moral theologians to propose versions of divine command theory: whatever God wills is good. However, coming down on this side of the dilemma can make the natural law seem arbitrary (not *essentially* good). Many Christian theologians tried to develop ways to avoid these conclusions by construing the relations among the divine essence, intellect and will in various ways (cf. Shults, 2005, 235–48).

The purpose of this section is not to adjudicate between these options, but to point to the underlying *philosophical* categories that are shaping the debate itself. First, it is important to note again the influence of faculty psychology; God is understood as a single subject with an intellect and will, and the legal relationship between God and the world is parsed in these terms. A robustly trinitarian conception of God might offer a way to overcome such conundrums and develop a more participatory understanding of the relation between the justifying love of God and the communion of moral agents. Others have pointed to the importance of emphasizing the resurrection (as well as the cross) for developing a middle way between natural law and divine command theory (cf. O'Donovan, 1994).

For our current purposes, however, the important point is that proponents of natural law tended to focus on the rational and moral *individual* which then led to the question whether the *polis* – the state of living together in an ordered society – is itself *natural* or artificial (constructed). When reflection on the moral life is rooted in reflection on the individual, the issue of social aggregation can easily become a secondary consideration – important, but secondary.

During the early modern period we find a slow divorce between theology and jurisprudence, which shaped a new conceptual space within which modern social theory emerged. Grotius was also a key player in this shift, although scholars debate over the extent to which he intended to contribute to such a dichotomy (cf. Schneewind, 1998; O'Donovan and O'Donovan, 1999). Like many others writing during (and after) the religious conflicts of the Thirty Years War, Grotius wanted to find a way to discuss human law and order that did not require immediate appeal to divine revelation. His *On the Law of War and Peace* (1625) developed a theory of human rights that was based on the natural moral quality of human persons. His goal was to establish that "even if we concede" that God does not exist, human persons would still be bound to act in ways that make social life possible. Many Protestant scholastics in the 17th century continued to understand human law and order as explicitly based in the divine; Francis Turretin, for example, argued that the "ten commandments" are part of the natural law that God has placed into all human minds.

However, the fissure in the relation between concepts of law and order and concepts of God opened up by Grotius was quickly widened in the early modern period where we find new attempts to identify a common basis for jurisprudence rooted in human reason rather than on divine command or creation. Europe had been ripped apart by the Thirty Years War, in which the competing religious convictions of Protestants and Roman Catholics played a significant part. Could law and order be liberated from religion, and if so, how can society construct its own laws and ways of adjudicating between various approaches to ordering political life? By what rules shall society be ordered, and on the basis of what kind of authority can they be enforced?

Individualism came to play an even stronger role as early modern social theorists appropriated aspects of the natural law tradition. Why and how should human individuals order their lives together? In his *Leviathan* Thomas Hobbes argued that in order to sustain their own self-interest, individuals must give political power to a sovereign, that is, make a "covenant" with a ruler, authorizing him or her to maintain social order. In this sense the state is not considered "natural" but arises as a consequence of the agreement of individuals to form a society. Hobbes believed that the law should be in the hands of an absolute and irrevocable monarchy. Later in the 17th century John Locke would argue that such a covenant can and should be revoked if a monarch breaks it (he had James II in mind). He outlined a model of social organization that could give rise to "constitutional" governance through mutual cooperation.

In the 18th century Rousseau pushed further than both of these political theorists, arguing that only republican and popular forms of self-government, in which all members participated, had real legitimacy. It is important to observe the close relation between the emergence of theoretical reflection on the very concept of the "social" and the efforts of the *philosophes* to move beyond the age of faith and into an age of enlightened reason. Modern social theory was founded on the idea that law and order is created by human individuals, and must be constructed, rather than through appeal to a natural law instilled or a command revealed by a Creator. This was particularly clear in Comte's emphasis on sociology as a "positive" science, based on neutral empirical analysis of objective data – *not* theology or metaphysics.

Postmodern social theory is also interested in law and order, but has been critical of the claims to neutrality in modern theorizing, including and especially Comtean positivism. The work of scholars like Michele Foucault, Jean Baudrillard and Jean-François Lyotard (among others) represents a response to modernist theories of society that privilege the autonomy of those in power. Some of these thinkers found inspiration in Nietzsche, whose *The Genealogy of Morals* described the "slave morality" of Christian religion as leading people to accept the rule of law under which they suffered. The judgment of "good" did not originate with those to whom "goodness" was shown (the poor, oppressed, weak), but "the noble, powerful, high-stationed and high-minded, who felt and established themselves and their actions as good" (1989 [1887], 26). Marx's critique of capitalism had similar undertones and his belief that the revolution of the proletariat would inevitably bring about a new world order presupposed that such an order would arise from the passion of the oppressed.

But the will to power did not result in utopia, and after two world wars, most 20th century cultural theorists were not as optimistic about the inevitability of progress in constructing an ideal society. The failure of the Enlightenment project to identify a universal rational law has led many ethicists to claim that reason alone cannot resolve the issues of the human moral life. For example, in *Postmodern Ethics* Zigmund Baumann argues that moral responsibility precedes all thinking about decision. It is unconditional and infinite, manifesting itself in the "constant anguish of not manifesting itself enough" (1993, 250). From the other direction, a growing number of sociologists are expressing interest in engaging theological traditions in the search for ways of making sense of social issues such as human dignity (e.g., Woodhead, 2006).

Late modern social theory is especially attentive to the role of gender, race and class in the legal ordering of societies. As feminist scholars such as Luce Irigaray and Julia Kristeva have pointed out, the long history of legal theory has most often placed the law on the side of men, supporting an economics of desire and ownership that privileges maleness (cf. Lovell, 2000). Human slavery was (and is) maintained only when the law (or at least ordering power) is securely in the hands of a particular race or group. The laws and ordering of most cultures privilege the rich and already powerful. This may be more obvious to us as we look in hindsight at Anselm's feudal society, but it is also the case in modern societies where the law works best for those who can afford lawyers, and culture is ordered in such a way that the interests of the wealthy are protected. Many late modern social theorists have argued that abstract rule-following justice too easily trumps concrete compassionate care for those on the underside of history and have tried to link ethical reflection to emancipation (cf. Smart, 2000).

Philosophical shifts in contemporary conceptions of a just society clearly challenge the adequacy of some formulations of the Christian doctrine of atonement in the context of dialogue with contemporary social science. We can understand why earlier theologians would have been tempted to articulate their understanding of the work of Christ in terms that made sense to them and their contemporaries. However, it is not plausible in our context to think that the primary threats to a well-ordered society are self-conscious demonic spirits that must be defeated (or tricked), nor that the best strategy for shaping just communities is the execution of a retributive justice that punishes those who do not uphold the honor of landowners.

The proper theological response here is *not* the facile adaptation of the political power of the church to the latest social theory. The radically redemptive reconciliation that is connected to the agency of Jesus creates a kingdom that is not "of this world" although it is transformative "in the world." Jesus' way of acting challenged the idea that human flourishing could be achieved solely by following the rules of "the law." It cannot be achieved by conformity to any particular human theory of jurisprudence.

Is this a call for anarchy or antinomianism? No, but it is a call for a different way of imagining the relation between divine atonement and the salutary ordering of human communities. For Jesus the whole of the law and the prophets, the all-encompassing force of the Hebrew experience of being called into the sphere of divine justice, could be summarized in the call to *love* God and neighbor in a way that heals even the most inimical of divisive social relations. This brings us to our final pair of categories.

③ *Us and Them*

Another basic philosophical distinction that shapes both cultural anthropology and atonement theory is the relation between *us* and *them*. These categories are so pervasive and deeply ingressed within our way of interpreting the world that their basic dialectical character often goes unnoticed. In the study of culture, this distinction plays an important role in making sense of phenomena such as the development of social structures, and the use of coercion and violence in the maintenance of communal boundaries. Many anthropologists are also interested in the broader question of how religion itself functions in these processes of differentiation.

Christian theology is *inter alia* reflection on and within a particular religious tradition, which is differentiated from other traditions. Without some sense of differentiation from "the other" the Christian religion would cease to be itself. But we may ask whether the *way* in which this differentiation between *us* and *them* functions within the self-identification of the Christian community and within the process of formulating atonement doctrine is itself salubrious. Do the institutional stability of the church and the articulation of the Gospel existentially and logically depend upon a strong line of demarcation that guarantees "they" will be eternally tormented while "we" will be eternally safe? Was the main point of Jesus' atoning work the clarification of the line between the elect and the reprobate, between those whom God (timelessly) determined would be punished for Adam's sin and those who would not? Is drawing a circular boundary around "the saved" (us) over against "the damned" (them) a redemptive way for the Christian community to differentiate itself?

This sub-section provides a brief summary of a shift in the way in which the philosophical categories of *us* and *them* function within cultural anthropology (and related sciences) and explores how this might lead to new insights about the formation of theories of the atonement. First, it is important to note that this distinction is only one of many binary oppositions that are significant for the social sciences. Discovering and discerning the role of particular oppositions within cultural structures is a crucial element of ethnography and anthropological analysis. We may think, for example, of Claude Levi-Strauss' well-known and controversial observations in *Structural Anthropology* (and elsewhere) about the role of oppositions such as male/female, light/dark, dry/wet and raw/cooked in the ordering of societies and the formulation of cultural myths (1963). Post-structuralists have been critical of his way of construing the universality of such structures, but the importance of differentiations, based on caste, race, gender, family, status, class, tribe, nation and a whole host of other factors for understanding human culture has rarely been disputed.

This binary opposition (us and them) played a particularly significant role in the early development of the discipline of sociology. One of the most important figures here is Emile Durkheim, who traced *The Elementary Forms of Religious Life* (1965 [1915]) to this differentiating process. Societies are held together by the participation of its members in what he called a "collective effervescence." Social solidarity is created and secured as individuals identify with the distinctives of the group. In many of the cultures Durkheim studied religion seemed to be connected to the collective representation of that which the group most admired (or feared). Often this was connected to a particular animal associated with this characteristic (e.g., strength, speed, wisdom). Totemic or other symbolic markers represented this collectively appreciated trait, which served a self-differentiating function in relation to neighboring societies.

What most scientists in these fields held in common through the middle of the 20th century was the idea that "a culture" could be understood as a single whole, a particular synchronically identifiable set of shared symbols for organizing social action. In other words, the lines between *us* and *them* could be identified clearly enough to mark off separate social "units" for analysis. This reification of boundaries has been challenged by many postmodern theorists of culture. Some of these challengers are especially concerned about ways in which nationalism and rigid social stratification are supported by such a facile carving of group boundaries. Some cultural structures have reified in such a way that leads to the oppression of "the other," whether this otherness is defined in terms of race, class or gender. Often these boundaries are coercively maintained and supported by those in power, who have a special interest in drawing clear lines between *us* and *them*.

But this challenge is also connected to the tendency among late modern philosophers to attend more carefully to the *relation* to "the other." This is linked to the renewed attention to the category of *difference*, which we explored in chapter 2. The process of differentiation itself always and already owes something to the "other," whose presence mediates self-identification. This does not mean that there are no differentiations, but that the processes of differentiation do not leave such simple and identifiable boundaries. Despite appearances (and the efforts of those in power) social structures do not remain the *same*; "our" being-differentiated is a fluid process that is always being shaped by and in historical, dynamic interaction with "them," and vice versa. As Kathryn Tanner observes, the distinctiveness of cultural identity is "not a product of isolation; it is not a matter of a culture's being simply self-generated, pure and unmixed; it is not a matter of 'us' vs. 'them'" (1997, 57). This overlapping complex of shared mutually generating "cultures" has become more evident as a result of globalization.

Some socio-biologists have argued that the drive to differentiate between us and them is not properly speaking an aspect of *cultural* life at all, but a phenomenon susceptible to a reductive biological explanation. E.O. Wilson, Richard Dawkins and many proponents of "evolutionary psychology" assert that instances of apparently altruistic (moral) behavior in some *Homo sapiens* and indeed even in other species, are actually driven by genes (or the genetic code). A human organism may occasionally give up the fulfillment of its immediate desires (or even its life) for the well-being of another, but *ex hypothesi* such behavior typically enhances the chance that a member of that organism's kinship group will survive in order to propagate the genes they share. In other words, the social construction of *us* over against *them* serves the selfish gene. This approach has been criticized for a variety of reasons, both methodological (McGrath, 2004) and material (Sober and Wilson, 1999), but the main point for our current purposes is that the philosophical categorization of us vs. them plays a role in determining appropriate scientific *explanandum*.

Ironically this sociobiological disciplinary reductionism is itself an illustration of the role that the categories us vs. them play in science, not only as methodological tools but as foundational disciplinary markers. These categories materially shaped the "founding" of social theory itself as we can see, for example, from Rousseau's sharp distinction between civilized and savage. But they also formally shaped the self-identification of social scientific disciplines even in the 20th century. James Faubion describes the stereotype in this way: "social theorists address themselves to the West, anthropologists to the Rest; social theorists focus on the modern, anthropologists on the primitive and traditional" (2000, 245). He is among those who argue against such a hard and fast construal of the boundaries between disciplines (or between the *West* and the *Rest*). Faubion suggests that even in the work of founding figures like Marx and Levi-Strauss one can find resources for acknowledging that alterity can only be *entre nous*; regardless of one's disciplinary location knowledge is always mediated through one's relation to the "other."

As anthropologists and social scientists have increasingly tended to this constitutive relationality among the disciplines, the antagonism toward religion (and theology) that once defined these disciplines has diminished. One example of this is the relatively recent emergence of the sub-discipline of "anthropology of religion" (cf. Lambek, 2002; Bowie, 2006). In the Introduction to his book *Anthropology of Religion*, Stephen Glazier is so bold as to say that "Religion is a universal. It has been found in all societies studied by anthropologists and is one of the hallmarks of human creativity as well as a tribute to humankind's nearly infinite resourcefulness and adaptability in coping with the problems of daily existence" (Glazier, 1999, 3).

Another development that promises a different level of integration is the emergence of the "anthropology of theology." Here anthropologists engage not only the phenomena of religion but theological reflection itself, inquiring directly into human religious questions. The anthropology of theology deals with meanings, systems of values, morality and ethical codes, focusing attention on the dynamic qualities of religion (cf. Adams and Salamone, 2000).

A growing interest in a more integrated dialogue with the discipline of theology is also evident in more traditional fields such as the sociology of religion. For example, sociologist Pål Repstad points out that the discipline itself is increasingly escaping the reductionist tendencies of many of its founders. The social sciences in general "have become less pretentious in their quest for simple, universal and exhaustive explanations of social phenomena," including the phenomenon of religion (1996, 93). This opens up new possibilities for interaction between the disciplines of theology and sociology both of which, as Repstad observes, involve reflection on the "more immediate actions and experiences" (1996, 102) associated with religion.

Sociology of religion may contribute to theological reflection by illuminating both the contextual factors that have shaped particular theological proposals in the past as well as the social contexts within which we "make theology" today. Many postmodern sociologists are more "open to the sacred" (cf. Flanagan, 1996). In this new arena of discourse, theology and sociology may find a new compatibility (cf. Furseth and Repstad, 2006, 197–208). Compatibility does not mean conflation. Sociology ought not to introduce divine action into its theories as an independent variable, and theology ought not to limit itself to social analyses of the historical structures and actions of the church.

What does this mean for our current interdisciplinary case study? The recognition that traditional atonement theories emerged within particular sociological contexts will indeed feel threatening to many theologians, who may be tempted to isolate themselves from engagement with cultural anthropology in an attempt to immunize their favorite theory. However, these philosophical shifts also provide a new opportunity for theologians to increase their own capacity for differentiated mutual engagement so that they can better perform the distinctive task of theology in their own particular contexts.

One anthropological insight that has special relevance for the Christian doctrine of atonement is the discovery of the role that violence plays in the cultural construction and control of social structures. Early anthropological theorists from Frazer to Freud suggested that religious practices such as the sacrifice and eating of a totem animal are actually the sublimated re-enactment of an original act of violence, perhaps the murder of a father figure or other member of the group, which somehow solidified the ties among the other members. As we will see below, this insight has been refigured in the work of René Girard (among others). The main point for our purposes here is that violence appears to be present in every society, and not only at its founding. The separation between races, classes and genders has been reinforced throughout history through violent enslavement, oppression of the poor and sexual exploitation. Such violence has typically been authorized by those with a vested interest in maintaining the hierarchy, often with a claim that these structures are divinely sanctioned.

In relation to atonement theory, bringing up the concept of violence often evokes images of "sacrifice." Despite its popularity in hymnology and the liturgical practices of many churches, the use of sacrificial imagery, while present in almost every era (Fiddes, 1989; Gunton, 1988), has rarely functioned as a guiding soteriological motif. The term, which is used infrequently in the New Testament with reference to Christ (1 Cor. 5:7; Eph. 5:1; Heb. 7:27), is also used in exhortations to believers to "sacrifice" or "offer" themselves to God (e.g., Rom. 12:1). This language quite obviously is derived from the

Hebrew Bible, but it is important to recognize that already in the history of ancient Israel we can trace a shift in attitude toward the value of the sacrificial system.

Later prophets were critical of the deuteronomic codes that portrayed sacrifice as the way in which the relation to God should be mediated. God desires *love* and not sacrifice (e.g., Hos. 6:6; cf. Amos 5:21–24; Is. 1:11–17; Ps. 51:13–17). The prophets also increasingly challenge Israel's self-understanding – us *versus* them – and remind the people of God that the promise to Abraham was that through him "all the families of the earth shall be blessed" (Gen. 12:3). This renewed self-understanding was carried over in the preaching of the early church (Acts 3:25; Gal. 3:8) after the outpouring of the Spirit at Pentecost.

Many of the early ethnographic analyses in anthropology focused on the way in which cultures view their relation to the divine as mediated through some form of *sacrifice*, which in turn reinforced a political (or priestly) hierarchy. More recently several anthropologists have emphasized that not all groups interpret and experience their relation to the sacred in this way. For example, Luc de Heusch (1985) has argued that there are two basic ways in which human cultures experience the mediation of divine communication: sacrifice and spirit possession. The latter takes many forms, from shamanism to ecstatic prophecy. Although this twofold taxonomy may be overly simplistic, it suggests that a hermeneutical bias may have led earlier theorists to equate religion with violence.

 Feminist sociologist Nancy Jay has pointed out a connection between sacrifice, gender and patrilinear social power (1994). Sacrificial systems are correlated with patrilinear practices, while possession – or being filled with a spirit (or the Spirit) – is an experience of the sacred that is more often open to women, and in some cultures explicitly associated with a female leader. This may partially explain why so many (predominantly male) Christian formulations of the atonement (reconciliation with God) have paid such little attention to the function of the Holy Spirit. Linking Pneumatology and Christology more closely will become increasingly important as the Pentecostal movement continues to spread and shape global theological discourse.

Unfortunately the philosophical hardening of the categories *us* and *them* has registered an effect on many traditional theories of the atonement. It is at the root of questions like: For whom did Christ pay the penalty? To whom did the infinite merits of Christ's satisfaction of Adam's sin accrue? Notice that these ways of framing the debate presuppose that the main point of the atonement was to make clear the line between us and them.

The irony is hard to miss. Here the doctrine of at-one-ment is precisely *not* about reconciliation and union, but about the violent exclusion (and in some theories the endless torture) of the other. On this soteriological hypothesis one identifies the "good" (or elect) by emphasizing their separation from the "bad" (or reprobate), and vice versa. From a sociological point of view, it would be interesting to explore the ways that ecclesiastical structures operate within religious groups for whom this way of articulating the action of God in Christ is most central.

The question here is not whether there are (or should be) differentiations but whether a harsh separation between *us* and *them* ought to be the driving force behind the Christian doctrine of the atonement. Must soteriology be rooted in a basic *negation* of the other? Must we *define* (our) salvation in a way that *requires* (their) damnation? Is violent exclusion the only way for God's justice to be manifested? As we saw above in our discussion of the categories of law and order, many traditional theories struggle to hold together divine love and divine justice, assuming that the latter must be defined in terms of retribution. As we will see below in our discussion of interdisciplinary opportunities, many contemporary theologians are arguing that justice has less to do with a divine sanctioning of violence than with a manifestation of God's reconciling love that transgresses the boundaries of exclusive social structures.

It is important to emphasize that there are resources in the Christian atonement tradition for reconstructing this doctrine in ways that are not rooted in violence. These voices are those toward which defenders of penal satisfaction models are the most belligerent. For example, Anselm's contemporary Peter Abelard argued that God's compassion toward us is manifested so powerfully in Jesus' way of living and dying that love is awakened in us for God and our neighbors. Later in the 12th century Peter Lombard took up this idea in his influential *Sentences*. Through the passion of Jesus, God's "pledge of love" is given to us in such a way that we too are moved and "kindled to love God." We are made just as charity is "excited in our hearts" and we are "loosened from our sins" (III.19.1). Opponents to this approach, which is often called the "moral influence" theory, have argued that it is merely subjective – that it does not provide an objective change in human life. Clearly some proposals within this stream of the tradition (especially in the 19th century) have insufficiently emphasized the ontological dimensions of divine reconciliation, stressing only Jesus' function as a moral exemplar.

On this side of the (re)turn to relationality (which challenges dichotomies like substance vs. function, and objective vs. subjective), we have a new opportunity to recover and refigure some of these insights for the ongoing task of reconstructing Christology. Such a process will evoke anxiety among those who have come to equate the Gospel with a particular cultural construction and whose sense of Christian identity is protected by excluding the other. Facing this fear is part of reforming Christology. Openness to theological reform is connected to openness to ecclesial reform, and both of these can be pedagogically facilitated by critical reflection on the way in which philosophical categories shape our forms of life and our formulations of doctrine.

In Galatians 3:28 Paul indicates that the community that experiences salvation "in Christ" will be salutarily ordered in such a way that the divisions between Jew and Greek, slave and free, male and female will be healed. The church is called to heal – not reinforce – the divisions between *us* and *them*. The New Testament use of the metaphors that have been used to construct ransom, sacrificial and penal models of the atonement are few and far between compared to the prevalence of the phrase "in Christ," which appears as a motif for depicting salvation well over two hundred times. The shift toward intrinsically relational categories within the broader interdisciplinary space we have been exploring provides theology with a new opportunity to articulate a reformative Christology that advocates and enacts reconciling union with others and God.

Interdisciplinary Opportunities

Many Christian theologians and scholars from other disciplines have addressed the issue of atonement theory in ways that attend to these developments, but a full review of this literature is beyond the scope of the current project. H. Richard Niebuhr's *Christ and Culture* (1951) offers an interesting (and much criticized) taxonomy of methodological approaches for relating theology and culture (opposition, agreement, synthesis, polarity and conversion), but it does not provide material suggestions for relating christological doctrine to particular theories in cultural anthropology, as the title might lead one to expect. The proposals outlined in this section were selected because they help to illustrate (directly or indirectly) the way in which soteriological discussions are increasingly taking account of the shifts in the philosophical categories explored above. I pay special attention to two interdisciplinary projects that deal explicitly with the need to reconstruct our understanding of salvation in light of social scientific insights about the role of violence and oppression in human culture.

René Girard

We begin with the controversial and influential work of cultural theorist René Girard, who has written extensively on the relation between dynamics of violence in myth and society and the Christian understanding of the atonement. For the purposes of our case study, his most important contribution is the way in which his anthropological and literary analyses have led to new insights into the role of violence in the foundation and ordering of cultures and to new interpretations of the meaning and significance of the cross of Christ.

Three interrelated themes shape Girard's interdisciplinary proposal: the dynamics of mimetic desire, the scapegoat mechanism in societies and the role of the biblical texts in clarifying both of these. Girard observes that human desire for an object (whatever that object might be) is triangular, that is, the desire is mediated in relation to others who are also related to the object of desire. An individual enters into a society by copying the behavior of others, learning to imitate others' desires. In trying to understand human action, we often focus on the relation between the agent and the object of desire, but Girard suggests that this focus itself reinforces the "illusion of autonomy."

To understand desire in its fullness, we must attend to the agent's relation to the mediator, to the one whose desire for the object is imitated. This triangulation of desire can lead to competition over that which is desired, which in turn contributes to antagonism and violence. Girard's writings are filled with analyses of particular cultures, as well as myths and novels, which illustrate the way in which violence emerges within these complex structures of desire. Based on these analyses, Girard concludes that mimesis and violence are pervasive in all cultures. A society cannot survive without mimetic desire and yet if it cannot control the violence that emerges out of this desire, it will self-destruct. Somehow it must be able to deal with the violence in a way that contains it or removes it from the group.

The second major Girardian theme that is important for our case study is his view of the scapegoat as a mechanism for dealing with the violence that has arisen out of the triangulation of mimetic desire. *Violence and the Sacred* (1977) and *The Scapegoat* (1986) deal with this issue in the most detail. Girard argues that all human cultures are founded on violence. Here he is building off the insights of Durkheim, Freud and others, but he develops a clearer explanation of the operation of the social process by which violence is violently expulsed from the community: the scapegoat mechanism. He argues that many ritual practices within cultures are an interpretive key for unveiling the original violence. In other words, the ritual re-enacts the pattern of the original founding of the community through violence, which reinforces the solidarity of the group.

The pattern typically develops as follows. The collective violence of the community continues to expand until it threatens to grow out of control. In an attempt to stop the spiral, the community selects a scapegoat – typically a vulnerable victim who is perceived to be guilty – who comes to represent the source or cause of disorder in the society. All the violence is focused on this individual, re-establishing the solidarity of the group. The order (and survival) of the society is secured by destroying or removing the alleged source of evil. The violence is not actually rooted out and soon begins to expand again; in some cases, this can be dealt with through ritual re-enactment. Sometimes a new scapegoat must be found. The surrogate victim provides a religious delusion for the community, namely, that the source of its violence has been eradicated. In fact, scapegoating is just another manifestation of violence, another instance of the outworking of mimetic desire that plagues the community.

Biblical Texts

Girard claims that all early societies were founded on the identity of violence and the sacred, on the religious authorization of the scapegoat mechanism which plays a primordial role in the establishment and ongoing order of the society. The mechanism only works, however, if it is kept hidden; if the community recognized its role in its own foundation, it would realize that violence is not truly excised in this process, but simply applied over and over to new victims. Girard argues that the New Testament Gospels, anticipated in part by the Hebrew Bible, play a unique role in unveiling the scapegoat mechanism. Girard actually credits "the presence of the biblical text in our midst" as the reason for the degeneration of sacrificial practices in human societies, and the rise of attention to victimage, oppression and persecution (1996, 17).

This third theme brings us to the most controversial and important aspect of his thought for atonement theory. The Gospels tell a story that is in many ways similar to other myths. A scapegoat (Jesus) is offered in order to expunge the violence that has arisen from the mimetic desire amongst the disciples of Jesus, the Jewish leaders and the Roman government. The story of the Passion illustrates the effects of "mimetic snowballing;" the violence of the mob is contagious once the scapegoat is identified. But the ways in which the story differs from myths are highly significant. The Gospels do not portray the victim as guilty as do other scapegoat narratives. Jesus is depicted as innocent of all charges and the resurrection is taken as verification of his innocence. Moreover, the violence inherent in the expulsion of the victim, and the way in which the mechanism is intended to protect the social and religious structures of the community, are not hidden in the Gospel stories.

Stories such as Cain's murder of Abel and Joseph's being sold to slave traders by his brothers already hint at the scapegoat mechanism, but Girard argues that it is in the Gospels that the expulsion of violence by violence, which he equates metaphorically with "Satan," is most clearly and ultimately revealed. "Only the Resurrection, because it enlightens the disciples, reveals completely the things hidden since the foundation of the world, which are the same thing as the secret of Satan, never disclosed since the origin of human culture: the founding murder and the origin of human culture" (2001, 125). Here he picks up the traditional *Christus Victor* theme.

The crucifixion and resurrection of Jesus Christ unveil the mechanisms of "Satan," the personification of all the evil that leads to scapegoating violence. These "principalities" can no longer hide and so lose their power. Once the mechanism is revealed, it is rendered useless because now we can see what we are doing; we can see that this process fails to liberate our communities from violence.

Girard notes that the death of Jesus is not interpreted as a payment or sacrifice in the Gospels. On the contrary, it reveals a non-violent God who vindicates the Christ through the resurrection. The mechanism that had controlled human culture up to that point was revealed. The message of Jesus is good news because for the first time, "people are capable of escaping from the misunderstanding and ignorance that have surrounded mankind throughout its history" (1987, 201). However, this is not simply the provision of a moral example. The way in which Christ revealed that which had been hidden since the foundation of the world leads Girard explicitly to affirm Christ as God, as "the only being capable of rising above the violence that had, up to that point, absolutely transcended mankind ... Christ is the only agent who is capable of escaping from these structures and freeing us from their dominance" (1987, 219).

As an anthropologist Girard emphasizes the way in which cultures cohere as a unified complex of differences; that is, as differential systems. If differentiation allows a culture to survive, the "disappearance of natural differences can thus bring to mind the dissolution of regulations pertaining to the individual's proper place in society – that is, can instigate a sacrificial crisis ... [w]herever differences are lacking, violence threatens" (1977, 56–7). The survival of a culture depends on the right kind of differentiation; when all is the same, crisis emerges. People react violently if they are too long forced into uniformity of behavior and the "predominance of the *same*" (1986, 14). This clarifies the rationale for the choice of scapegoats. Victims are accused of eliminating (an authorized kind) of difference, which threatens the foundation of the society, and so they must themselves be violently eliminated for the sake of the many. "We hear everywhere that 'difference' is persecuted," observes Girard, but in fact "persecutors are never obsessed by difference but rather by its unutterable contrary, the lack of difference" (1986, 22).

Several New Testament scholars have expanded upon Girard's approach (e.g., Hamerton-Kelly, 1992; 1994), but we will limit ourselves here to some examples of systematic theological engagements that explicitly deal with the doctrine of atonement in historical perspective. In *Cross Purposes: The Violent Grammar of Christian Atonement* (2001), Anthony Bartlett shows how the logic of violence has dominated the major Western doctrines of atonement, and how they have unfortunately been used to sanction violence and punishment. His own proposal critically appropriates Girard's mimetic analysis of Jesus' passion, but uses the language of his abandonment into "the abyss" as the basis for the "eruption" of redemptive compassion and forgiveness (the categorically new) within human affairs. Jesus reveals and redeems the existential "abyss," demonstrating compassionate non-violent love in its midst and manifesting the evocative power of compassion in human relations.

More recently, Mark Heim has appropriated Girard's theories in his *Saved from Sacrifice: A Theology of the Cross* (2006). Heim argues that even if one contests the universal validity and scope of his anthropological proposals, and the adequacy of his treatment of the cross, Girard's insights can and should still be appropriated for the task of articulating atonement theory in our context. Accepting the basic insights of mimetic theory and the role of the scapegoating mechanism in culture, Heim develops the implications for atonement theory in more detail.

In Part I of the book, Heim explores the Girardian theme of hidden victims with special attention to the Hebrew Bible, and in Part II he expands on his analysis of Jesus' passion and death, which produces the "visible victim." Heim is more willing than (the early) Girard to acknowledge that the cross is in some sense a "sacrifice," but the cure is not more of the same; it is a sacrifice "to end sacrifice." On the one hand, we see in Jesus' passion another example of the invisible pattern of mythic violence. However, here God's redemptive purpose and action is revealed, not as an author of more violence, but as the one who vindicates the victim and reverses the mechanism through his resurrection.

Although Heim goes beyond Girard throughout his book, Part III in particular responds to common criticisms of the latter's lack of attention to the broader theological issues necessary for a fuller understanding of the cross. He titles this section "In Remembrance of Me: The Cross that Faith Keeps Empty," and focuses on the ways in which the reversal of the sacrifice mechanism is more than merely an unveiling. Alongside the myth revealed and the sacrifice reversed we also must recognize that a new basis of personal conversion and social reconciliation is instituted and substituted.

Here Heim brings in a theological discussion of the Holy Spirit and the church. "Satan" is the accuser, but the "Advocate" (Paraklete) is the one who takes the side of the victim and "proves the world wrong." As the defender of scapegoats the Holy Spirit inspires and nurtures a new kind of community that demonstrates a new "peaceful way of overcoming the rivalry and reciprocal violence that sacrifice exists to contain" (2006, 220). We are collectively addicted to persecution. The Gospel works through the same mimetic medium, but spreads contagious peace. This is *objective* atonement, not merely *subjective* example. The cross actually does reverse our human sacrificial violence, and the forces of evil in the world are really opposed and overcome as the Spirit of Christ forms communities that are converted and reconciled without the violent exclusion of the other.

Girard's proposals are important for the reconstructive task of soteriological reflection today for several reasons. He provides a way of relating culture to the cross without a divine sanctioning of violence. Moreover, on this model, God's justice is not tied to a particular culture's legal system. Girard also illustrates the possibility of bringing the particularity and contextuality of the biblical witness into rigorous interdisciplinary dialogue. In addition, his emphasis on the importance of *desire* also reinforces the approach I have been suggesting in these case studies.

As Gil Bailie expressed it in his engagement with Girard, the *anthropological* role of the Christian church in human history might be "to understand the structures of sacred violence by making it impossible to forget how Jesus *died* and to show the world how to live without such structures by making it impossible to forget how Jesus *lived*" (1995, 274). The focus on human acting, which is natural for a cultural anthropologist, led Girard to a new way of thinking about the *agency* of Christ, which opens up new ways to think theologically about how this impacts our understanding of divine agency and the transformation of our own moral desire.

Delores Williams

As we have seen, late modern social theorists are particularly concerned with ways in which cultural structures and laws ordering communities often work against persons associated with a particular race, class or gender. All three of these modes of oppression are targeted by theologian Delores Williams, who draws our attention to the need for a doctrine of salvation that accounts for and responds to the experience of the suffering of black women. She argues that both "black" theology and "feminist" theology fail to attend to this experience in their treatments of atonement theory.

Williams adopts the label "womanist" from novelist Alice Walker, for whom "womanist is to feminist as purple is to lavender." In *Sisters in the Wilderness* (1993), Williams surveys a wide array of anthropological research on the experience of slavery on African American culture and provides some new social analysis of the plight of black women. For this reason she provides us with a particularly poignant example of a theologian who takes advantage of the opportunity for interdisciplinary dialogue opened up by the philosophical shifts in these fields.

Williams' own proposal relies heavily on the biblical story of Hagar, mother of Ishmael. As a slave woman of Egyptian ancestry, she was abused by her owners Abraham and Sarah and sent out into the wilderness.

However, God appears to Hagar and empowers her to survive and sustain her family. Williams does not hide the fact that the author of these Genesis texts presupposes a divine sanction for the overarching patriarchical system, but she observes that in chapter 16 something remarkable happens: Hagar names the One who comforted her El Roi (the One who sees). This African slave's experience of homeless exile, of being forced to be a surrogate mother, of being cast in the wilderness, of surviving and being comforted by a divine presence that she herself names – this becomes the prototype and starting point for Williams' exploration of new ways to articulate the doctrine of salvation in relation to black women's issues.

She is especially critical of traditional formulations of atonement that rely on the notion of substitution or surrogacy to explain what happened on the cross. Mainline Protestant theology, which has been particularly influential on the thought-forms of African-American Christian experience, has often described Jesus as the ultimate surrogate figure. On this model, Jesus stands in the place of someone else (sinful humanity), takes sin upon himself and bears their punishment in their place. In light of African-American women's historic experience with surrogacy, Williams argues that this way of thinking about atonement is extremely problematic because it can be used to condone abuse. "If black women accept this idea of redemption, can they not also passively accept the exploitation that surrogacy brings?" (1993, 162).

Williams argues that the way in which social oppression was authorized theologically by white slaveholders is reflected today among those who tell black women that accepting their suffering and surrogacy is what it means to "bear the cross." This theological placating strategy continues even in some black men's treatment of black women. Therefore Williams is critical of many black *men's* liberation models of atonement, who argue that black people (and others) may be reconciled to God and each other through their own cross-bearing. She suggests that most black men have not suffered under the weight of forced surrogacy, which continues today in the lives of poor black women's experience of inadequate health care, domestic violence and the structural oppression of classism, racism *and* sexism.

Williams proposes a way of thinking about redemption for black women that focuses on Jesus' whole ministerial vision, not on his role as a surrogate or substitute who stands in to suffer and be punished in the place of others. She observes that every theory of atonement has an ethical principle that guides it, and makes hers explicit: "survival and a positive quality of life for black women and their families in the presence and care of God" (1993, 175). She wants to free redemption from the cross; Jesus does not redeem humanity through his death, but through his ministry of compassion and love, through his ministerial vision of righting human relations. God is the "one who sees" oppression, and in Jesus we find a way of ministering that supports resistance and provides sustenance. Williams argues that Jesus did not conquer sin through his death on a cross, but through his life; that is, through his *resistance* to the greedy urge of monopolistic ownership (e.g., Mt. 4:1–11) and his ministry of compassion and love that promoted the *survival* of the oppressed.

Engaging the sociopolitical thought and action of the African-American woman's world, Williams insists that their salvation does not depend upon any form of surrogacy – even if it is allegedly "voluntary." God did not intend the suffering and death of Jesus as a "substitute" for others and God does not authorize the surrogacy roles that have been forced on or suggested to black women. For Williams, redemption is assured "by Jesus' life of resistance and the survival strategies he used to help people survive the death of identity caused by their exchange of inherited cultural meanings for a new identity shaped by the gospel ethics and world view" (1993, 164).

Williams observes that black women are less interested in abstract issues about the relation of Jesus' human substance to his divine substance than they are in experiencing Jesus as one who functions to support their struggle for survival (1993, 203). This sense of the inadequacy and irrelevance of substance metaphysics is also evident among other theologians in contexts of oppression. For example, as Virginia Fabella observes in "Christology from an Asian Woman's Perspective," the language of the two natures doctrines in Chalcedon "are largely unintelligible to the Asian mind" (1998, 8–9). Williams argues for a Christology that is more immediately related to concrete experience; Jesus is the one who makes present the "God who sees." For Williams, this "seeing" means acknowledging and ministering to the survival and quality-of-life needs of African-American women and their children. Like Hagar, the experience of redemption includes discovering new resources for survival and resistance while entrusting the end to God (1993, 239).

Although Williams' proposal has been widely influential among womanist (and other) theologians, several concerns have also been raised. For example, in her book *Power in the Blood? The Cross in the African American Experience* (1998), JoAnn Terrell expresses more hope that the term "sacrifice" can be refigured in a broader understanding of redemption that takes black women's suffering into account. Terrell acknowledges William's point that some forms of atonement theology have reinforced cultural and racial divisions, and even expands this critique in her analysis of the connection between North American evangelical covenant theology and the social oppression of black people.

Terrell observes the way in which American whites imbibed the motif of conquest in covenant theology and "unconscionable as this may seem in an age of pluralism, the propitiatory nature of Jesus' death affirmed in Christian tradition resonated with the penal quality of life conditions in slavery" (1998, 28). More so than Williams, Terrell engages the theme of sacrifice in the Hebrew Bible, concluding that these rites were understood as a "means given by God to wipe away sin and cope with the problem of failure to fulfill the Law" (1998, 18) not as propitiations offered to God.

She agrees with Williams that the theory of substitutionary atonement inappropriately led to an interpretation of Jesus' dying "for us" as meaning that he was punished "instead of us," but Terrell does not believe this ought to preclude *any* use of the terms "substitution" or even "surrogacy." One can acknowledge that this hermeneutics of sacrifice was used to impose the suffering of slavery, but at the same time hold out for a positive use of the cross in the theological self-understanding of contemporary African Americans. The cross originally embodied a *scandal*: "that something, anything, good could come out of such an event."

Terrell argues that Jesus' "sacrificial act" was not the objective of his mission but the tragic result of confronting evil. Jesus (and later martyrs) did not passively acquiesce to evil but were empowered "sacramental witnesses." In this sense, then, Terrell proposes an understanding of sacrifice as "holistic spirituality," and argues that contemporary black women (like Jesus) can participate in a redemptive ethic of love that includes taking surrogacy roles that care for the other in order to foster human freedom. She calls this a *sacramental* understanding of sacrifice, which is not permitting (or causing) injury on one individual for the sake of another, but witnessing to and expressing God's mercy (1998, 141–2).

Karen Baker-Fletcher also appropriates Williams' critique of traditional Anselmian atonement, and agrees that the human capacity to oppress others seems to be glorified in this and similar soteriological models. She also argues against an "ethic of sacrifice" that glorifies the suffering of the oppressed. However, she suggests that we must go beyond Williams by emphasizing the *resurrection* in our interpretation of the historical reality of the cross. This can facilitate our learning to focus on the power of God in overcoming oppression. Baker-Fletcher suggests that such a model promotes an ethic of risk that actively struggles for social justice (1997, 79). A similar critique is raised by J. Denny Weaver, who proposes an atonement model he calls "narrative Christus Victor" (2001). Weaver accepts William's point that theories of redemption should deal with the historical reality of the church's non-violent action in the world, but argues that this agency can best be understood as a participation in the victory of the reign of God that has been disclosed in the resurrection of Christ.

The discussion surrounding these proposals is important for our case study for several reasons. First, they provide examples of theological engagement with social scientific analysis and reflection. Moreover, they pay special attention to the particular experience of those who have been historically oppressed by the dominant powers who control the law and order of society, by the structures that separate *us* from *them*. These proposals also contribute by more closely integrating ethical practice and atonement theory, bringing questions of agency to the forefront: the cross cannot be understood apart from the whole ministerial agency of Jesus. Indeed, soteriology must also attend more broadly to the way in which we understand the agency of God in the world and the transformation of our own agency.

I agree with Terrell that the doctrine of the atonement ought to embrace some sense in which our being united with God and one another (at-one-ment) may be facilitated as we *bear* one another's burdens in a life-giving way and with Baker-Fletcher and Weaver that the *resurrection* must be a key ingredient of any soteriological reformulation (cf. Shults, 2003, 188–205; Shults and Sandage, 2006, 111–22). As we move forward in the reconstructive process, it will be important to continue this interdisciplinary and cultural boundary crossing as we struggle together to act in ways that promote the good life. Before exploring some new directions for talking about the agency of Jesus Christ in late modern culture, let us identify some more resources for the task.

Other Proposals

Contemporary theologians are becoming increasingly critical of satisfaction and penal substitionary theories of atonement, both because of its connection to abusive forms of social power and its lack of biblical warrant (e.g., Weaver, 2002; McKnight, 2007; Brümmer, 2005; Trelstad, 2006; Jersak and Hardin, 2007). In his review of doctrinal models in *Saving Power: Theories of Atonement and the Forms of the Church* (2005), Peter Schmiechen pays special attention to how atonement theory is related to forms of being church. He commends openness to a variety of theories, but is particularly critical of penal substitution and its quest for necessity.

Tyron L. Inbody summarizes some of the objections to this theory in *The Many Faces of Christology* (2002). The theory seems inherently unjust because an innocent person suffers so that the guilty go free, it depicts a sadistic God who delights in the sacrifice of an innocent victim, and it places a retributive model of justice over the power of divine love. Finally, it appears to be a sacralization of abuse, which requires that "abusive punishment is structurally at the core of what defines and constitutes redemption" (2002, 157). Our focus here, however, is on proposals for reconstructing atonement theory that explicitly engage cultural anthropology or related sciences, especially those that attend to the issues of race, class and gender.

James Cone argues that cultural and social analysis of the black experience is central to the theological task. His (in)famous claim that "Jesus is black" means that Jesus takes the place of the poor and oppressed and helps them struggle for liberation. Cone argues that Anselm's "rationalistic" soteriology is "meaningless for the oppressed" in so far as it "dehistoricizes the work of Christ, separating it from God's liberating act in history" (1997, 211–12). Jesus' death should be interpreted as the revelation of the freedom of God, who takes "upon himself the totality of human oppression" and his resurrection as "the disclosure that God is not defeated by oppression but transforms it into the possibility of freedom" (1990, 118). Cone insists that Christians fight for justice not because of an abstract analysis of the importance of human sympathy, but because they accept the claim that Jesus lays upon human life, which "connects the word 'Christian' with the liberation of the poor" (1990, 135). Here we have a classical example of an approach to atonement theory that self-consciously engages the methods and findings of cultural anthropology and social analysis.

Interdisciplinary engagement and attention to contextuality is prevalent in soteriological discussions outside of North America and Europe. In *The Many Faces of Jesus Christ* (2001) Volker Küster argues that the recognition of the "inculturation" of Christianity in non-European cultures is particularly important for making sense of the experience of salvation through Christ. He provides an overview of developments in Christology from a variety of cultural contexts, including Latin America, Asia and Africa. In *Jesus of Africa: Voices of Contemporary African Christology* (2004), Diane Stinton identifies four main models of contemporary African Christology, which both shape and are shaped by the identity of African Christians: Jesus Christ as life-give (Healer), as mediator (ancestor) loved one (Family/Friend) and Leader (Chief/king, or liberator). Several of the essays in *Paths of African Theology* (Gibellini, 1994) also demonstrate attention to social context in the search for ways to articulate the saving work of Christ.

In many Asian contexts, anxiety about being shamed in community is more significant than individual guilt and this naturally affects atonement theorizing among Minjung ("popular mass") theologians attempting to articulate the Gospel in such societies. In *Christology with an Asian Face* (2003) Peter Phan provides an overview of several models such as Pieris' "Jesus as the Poor Monk" and Lee's depiction of Christ as the "perfect realization of change" (yin/yang, being/becoming). Phan himself offers a proposal for new christological titles such as Jesus the "eldest Son," who is the model of filial piety, and Jesus as "ancestor," who through his death and resurrection is enthroned as the highest perfection of anscestorhood (2003, 104–15, 135–45). Choan-Seng Song's work emphasizes Jesus' solidarity with the exploited and alienated. In *Jesus, the Crucified People* (1990, 215) he insists the cross must be interpreted in light of his way of welcoming the oppressed into the story of salvation so that they may participate in the arrival of the future.

"Liberation" theology emerged in the context of Latin America, as theologians struggled with and for the poor and oppressed. How does this cultural analysis and embodied praxis within social structures affect atonement theory? In *Christology at the Crossroads* (1978), Jon Sobrino develops a model that begins with Jesus' own action in service of the reign of God, with his self-understanding as participating in the arrival of God's liberating presence in society. Sobrino argues that we must always interpret the suffering and cross of Christ in light of the resurrection, and recognize that this has implications both for our understanding of God and of human life. On the one hand, God is revealed as suffering in and with and for the world but precisely as the One who "has the power to liberate and revitalize all reality" (1978, 182). On the other hand, knowledge of this liberating reality requires orthopraxis as well as orthodoxy; it involves participating in God's liberation of the oppressed as we follow Jesus in the concrete embodiment of justice and love (1978, 389).

Several feminist theologians have brought social analyses of women's experience to bear on the contemporary articulation of the doctrine of atonement. Elizabeth Schüssler-Fiorenza notes that the rhetorical meaning-making of both early Christians and contemporary feminist discourse on the cross have the same starting point. Both begin with "the historical 'fact' of unjust oppression, the experience of struggle for a different world, and an encounter with the victimization and death of the dehumanized person" (1995, 120). We can learn from the early Christians who used a variety of formulas in order to make sense of this event, but she especially commends a sophialogical understanding of the execution of Jesus, which "was not intended or willed by Sophia-G*d but is rather the outcome of his prophetic ministry and mission" (1995, 143).

Soteriological humility is also encouraged by Carter Heyward in her *Saving Jesus from Those Who are Right* (1999), where she argues against "moralism" defined as "an ideology of rightness and a posturing of certitude that absolutizes ideas and abstractions rather than actual relationships that are loving and just ... [devaluing] mutuality as the basis of justice-loving relationships" (1999, 117).

One of the key insights among feminist theologians that has special bearing on atonement theory is the recognition that often the different experience of men and women leads to different ways of approaching the cross. Cynthia Crysdale, for example, writes of the "two sides" of the cross – the forgiveness of sins and the healing of wounds. In *Embracing Travail: Retrieving the Cross Today* (2001, 25) she notes that every person participates to varying degrees in the violent cycle of perpetrators and victims. Crysdale suggests that it makes sense for those whose agency has been characterized by prideful oppression that the first step should usually be the repentance of sin and the reception of forgiveness. On the other hand, for those whose voices have been suppressed, who have borne the brunt of evil and suffering, the first step may need to be the reception of the healing and strengthening of the self, learning how to "embrace travail" (within the embrace of God) in a way that resists and transforms violent social structures.

Radical Orthodoxy is another recent theological movement that has attracted attention for discussing the relation between theology and socio-cultural analysis. John Milbank's *Theology and Social Theory* (1990) is usually considered its seminal work. He argues there for a refigured version of Augustine's "City of God" that owes nothing to the violence of the earthly city. Modern social theory, in his view, is intrinsically atheistic and agonistic, but Christianity discloses a narrative of peace that is "beyond even the violence of legality." For Milbank, Christian theology should have nothing to do (either apologetically or argumentatively) with the agonistics of social theory. Rather, theology should reconceive itself as a kind of "Christian sociology," as the "explication of a socio-linguistic practice, or as the constant re-narration of this practice as it has historically developed" (1990, 6, 45, 381). In *Being Reconciled*, however, Milbank attacks (among other things) the medieval invention of a forensic reading of the atonement (2003, 103). Yet this soteriological model is clearly a part of the "socio-linguistic practice of the church" as "it has historically developed." When Milbank opts for (parts of) the version of the Christian story told by Augustine and Aquinas, he does not (and *can* not, if he stays consistent with his methodology) offer *reasons* for choosing this rhetoric over others.

Several theologians and sociologists of religion have criticized Milbank for failing to account for shifts in late modern social science, in which one finds less anxiety about "policing the sublime" and more openness to dialogue with theology and ethics (e.g., Flanagan, 1996, 59–60; 2001; Ayres, 1996; cf. Baumann, 1993). Some of the theologians who identify with Radical Orthodoxy are more open to social scientific insights in the ongoing reconstructive process (cf. Ward, 2005), but Milbank's proposal appears intrinsically agonistic – theology (us) *versus* social theory (them). Elsewhere he insists that "either the *entire* Christian narrative tells us how things truly are, or it does not. If it does, we have no other access to how things truly are, nor any additional means of determining the question" (1997, 250). How is this rhetoric to be distinguished *methodologically* from other forms of religious fundamentalism? While we can learn a great deal from Milbank's exposition of the tradition, this isolationist approach quite clearly fails to promote (or even allow) the kind of interdisciplinary engagement exhibited by Girard, Williams and others.

We conclude our brief survey of interdisciplinary proposals with two examples of the way in which engagement with other religions, embedded in different cultures and anthropological frames of reference, might play a role in the process of reconstruction. Muslim theologian Mahmoud Ayoub points out that the Qur'an, like the New Testament, understands Jesus' mission as mediating the "Word of God" (Q. 3:45) and bringing salvation in the original sense of that term – healing, making whole, restoring to life. He argues that the "miracle" of Jesus, like the "miracle" of the Qur'an, "is not a once-only event, but an everlasting source of blessing, guidance, and salvation" (1993, 227).

Japanese theologian Seiichi Yagi has attempted to bridge Buddhist and Christian insights in explicitly relational terms. Beginning with the New Testament emphasis on human relationships, Yagi counters the typically Western Cartesian anthropology with a different kind of claim: "I exist in relationships, therefore I am." He interprets the traditional emphasis on salvation as life "in Christ" and as Christ's agency "in me" in the context of a broader construction of relationships as fields of force in critical dialogue with Buddhist thought (cf. Küster, 2001, 104–17).

These types of interdisciplinary and inter-religious dialogue can provide new impetus for Christian theologians to develop articulations of atonement doctrine that facilitate a transformational ecclesiology as well. The ongoing task of reforming Christology requires us to face the serious criticisms of particular traditional formulations as we engage the sciences of cultural anthropology. However, insights into the deleterious effects of some social dynamics, as well as philosophical shifts in this field of discourse, also open up new possibilities for reconstruction as we reflect on our experience of moral desire in the world. Attending to our shared interest in human acting can help us develop new presentations of atonement theory in our context that make sense of God's agency in Christ and facilitate the transformation of our own agency as we work together for the ordering of just communities.

The Agency of Jesus Christ

My goal in this brief case study has been to examine the challenges and opportunities in the ongoing task of reconstructing the Christian doctrine of atonement as it engages in dialogue with the sciences of cultural anthropology. I have suggested that this task can be facilitated by attending to some of the existential concerns and philosophical categories that these disciplines hold in common. This is only one moment within a broader task; a fuller systematic theological presentation would also require more detailed attention to debates among biblical exegetes and interpreters of church history.

My focus here has been on demonstrating the contextuality of previous formulations of the doctrine of atonement, illustrating how interpretations of Scripture and preferences for (and within) traditions are shaped by (often hidden) philosophical assumptions. This chapter has been an attempt to render explicit the categories that structure our late modern context for interdisciplinary dialogue. Can we self-critically demonstrate the illuminative power of the biblical tradition in our generation in a way that facilitates the emergence of communities that promote social reconciliation?

As with the doctrine of the incarnation, it is important here to face the need for *reforming* christological questions. We cannot simply go on searching for better ways to answer questions like: How did the Logos heal universal human nature? Did God's transaction with the devil involve trickery or was it fair? For whom did Jesus pay the penalty? The philosophical, cosmological and legal categories that subtend the questions themselves no longer have purchase in contemporary discourse about the human condition.

We have explored some of the conceptual shifts that have refigured the way in which our moral desire is interpreted and experienced in the late modern context of interdisciplinary dialogue. In order to conserve the liberating intuitions of the biblical tradition in a way that illuminates the problems and facilitates the transformation of human enculturation, we may need to begin by asking different kinds of questions: How does Jesus' way of *acting* in the world manifest the justifying relations of divine love? How is creaturely participation in the love of the trinitarian God opened up by the just *agency* of Jesus Christ?

As we move forward in this interdisciplinary task it will be important to pay attention to the ways in which philosophical categories are figuring our dialogue and our formulations. We are still interested in explaining how the agency of the *particular* person Jesus Christ empowers creaturely participation in the *universal* love of God. Moving beyond theories of predication and metaphysics that privilege substance, however, we might focus on construing the dynamics of atoning agency in terms of the infinite relational field of the omnipotent justifying love of God within which the moral desire of finite creatures is transformed.

We have good reason to resist merely forensic interpretations of the cross that presuppose that it is necessary for an abstract *law* to be satisfied before God can restore an allegedly ideal prehistoric social *order*. Jesus' way of ordering his life came-to-be immersed ever more intensely in the Spirit of justice, empowering him to show compassion even to his enemies, thereby disclosing the love of the One whom he intimately called "Father."

Through concrete acts of self-giving love Jesus' agency transgressed the boundaries between *us* and *them* that shaped his culture. Challenging social structures that divided people by race, class and gender, Jesus took the place of those who were oppressed and invited them into social relations transformed by the atoning presence of divine grace.

One way to liberate the doctrine of the atonement from the early modern dichotomy between substance and function, which solidified the dualism between the person and work of Christ, is to focus on Jesus' personal *agency*. This concept is more easily linked to the identity (and presence) of a person than is the idea of "work." It also helps to broaden the scope of atonement theory, which includes but is not limited to what happened on the cross. Like other human agents Jesus' very personhood was mediated in relation to the linguistic and social structures of his own culture. Human acting emerges within this interpersonal space and is characterized by an ethical anxiety that searches for the good life within a particular community. Personal agency is both gift and task; it is constituted in relation to other agents whose intentionality mediates its formation.

Jesus' agency is distinguished, first of all, by the way in which it came to be mediated as a reception of, and dependence on, divine grace rather than on his own power to manipulate social structures. He recognized that God alone is good (Mk 10:18), and that a truly righteous life is dependent on the liberating agency of this evocative presence. He received his agency as gift and task in relation to the Father, mediated through his immersion in the Spirit, in such a way that his moral desire and use of power came to be united (at-one) with God's love for the world.

However, the Christian tradition has always tried to maintain that in some sense *God* was in Christ reconciling the world (2 Cor. 5:19). In other words, the events surrounding Jesus of Nazareth are also and ultimately an expression of *divine* agency. The way in which we conceive of God and the God–world relation will inform our presentation of this claim. In our context we can move beyond the idea of God as an immaterial rational substance, and articulate this intuition by beginning with the particularity of the relationality disclosed in the life, death and resurrection of Jesus.

In other words, here we have an opportunity to take seriously the idea that what happened to, with, in and for Jesus was really the manifestation of the eternal love of God. The atoning agency of the triune God, whose life is the infinitely intense loving and being-loved among the persons of the Trinity, is actually disclosed in the intensification of this man's filial relation to the Father in the Spirit. The differentiation from and unification of the eternal "Son" (Logos, Word) with the eternal Father in the shared love of the eternal Spirit is enacted in and mediated to creation through Jesus' differentiating, self-giving agency, which so unites him to the love of the Father for the world that he is declared the "Son" of God by his resurrection through the Spirit (Rom. 1:4).

So how does the agency of the particular man Jesus mediate reconciliation between God and the rest of humanity? By manifesting the justifying omnipotence of the infinite trinitarian God as the ultimate origin, condition and goal of the human moral desire to participate in the good life of loving and being-loved in right relations. The incursive presence of the differentiating and uniting love of the triune Creator conditions the emergence of creaturely longing by calling it into being and toward well-being. This absolute originating presence of divine Futurity appears to creatures as an all-embracing invitation to grope after goodness.

Jesus' agency manifests a way of life in which human moral desire, which is always and already originated, organized and oriented by God, is transformed through union with divine love. His way of acting in the world discloses the power of infinite love to salutarily order creaturely desire by calling persons to participate in the arrival of the reign of God, which liberates them from the threat of death and empowers them to act justly. Through the resurrection Jesus' agency was vindicated (justified) by the Spirit (1 Tim. 3:16), and through the outpouring of the Spirit others are empowered to follow his way of transforming communion.

We should emphasize that Jesus' way of acting in relation to God and others is indeed the display of divine *justice*. His agency was formed in utter reliance on the Spirit of justice, whose liberating presence breaks the cycle of mimetic violence that is rooted in human anxiety over the power to secure finite goods. The justifying agency of God came-to-be manifested in the agency of Jesus as he powerfully exhibited a self-giving love that welcomes the other into a fellowship that is grounded in the infinite goodness of divine life. He challenged uses of the law that ordered society in ways that divided *us* from *them*, Jew from Gentile, clean from unclean, men from women.

Jesus disclosed a form of human agency that participates in the healing of social and cultural structures through a radical love that recognizes we are all absolutely dependent on the justifying grace of God. His way of acting (and way of responding to being acted-upon) took the form of receiving and sharing divine grace, which enabled him to enact and promise peace in relation to others. This is not peace "as the world gives" (Jn 14:27), that is, peace that is merely the opposite of war, a "peace" secured by the violent coercion, incarceration or annihilation of the other. The reign of divine justice is not simply non-violent, it is peace-full, full of the peaceable transformation of moral desire itself.

Attending to the whole agency of Jesus in relation to God and others does not mean that we ignore or downplay the significance of the cross. Many forensic formulations of atonement theory focus so narrowly on the "transaction" at the cross that they miss the fact that even in Romans Paul understands Jesus' dying "for us" in light of his being raised "for us," and understands both in light of Jesus' reception and sharing of the Spirit in community (e.g., Rom. 5:6; 8:34; 14:9). This suggests that atonement theory should be articulated in a way that acknowledges its embeddedness within broader pneumatological and ecclesiological considerations. Anointed by and immersed in the Spirit of justice the agency of Jesus was formed and transformed as he laid down his desire to secure finite goods with his own power, as he took his place among those who were afflicted and actively provided for them a merciful place for interpersonal healing.

This place-taking made present (re-presented) the grace of God that redeems the agonistic interpersonal relations (sin) that threaten the well-being of human sociality by bearing up human agency within divine love so that it works for relations of justice. This way of acting tends to elicit a violent response from those with social power. Jesus' crucifixion is a crucial moment of intensification within his way of living in dependence on the life-giving Spirit of the Father, demonstrating his active union with the infinitely vulnerable self-giving power of divine love.

In chapter 1 we noted the importance of Jesus' "mysticism," and this bears directly on our understanding of his becoming at-one with the agency of divine love. Proponents of "objective" models of the atonement will worry that this is merely another example of a "subjective" moral influence theory. However, this dichotomist taxonomification of soteriological models itself presupposes an early modern bifurcation between metaphysics and ethics: either Jesus' death metaphysically alters our *status* or it only provides an external exemplar for us to *mimic*.

The conceptual space of late modern discourse after the turn to relationality offers us a new opportunity to move beyond this impasse. Morality and ontology are not so easily separated. Mimetic desire is a robustly metaphysical force; our *being* as personal *agents* is wholly embedded within our longing for goodness. The testimony of the mystics throughout the Christian tradition is that the experience of transforming union with divine love is more "objective" than any other reality. If the omnipotent Creator *is* love, then our being brought into union with God will involve the *real* redemption of our personal agency.

On this model Jesus' way of acting does not have to be insulated from cultural anthropological analysis. His agency was mediated by and emerged within the complex kinship structures and social systems of his 1st century Palestinian culture. Like the rest of us his moral desire for the good life was also genetically and biologically conditioned. However, from a theological point of view all of these conditions are always and already held in being by God, who calls creatures toward transformative participation in divine love. Jesus discloses a creaturely way of acting that becomes one with the Creator's self-giving and welcoming agency.

Theologians can learn from the scientific analysis of culture, acknowledging that human agents are social animals, whose desire for the good life is expressed through a pluriformity of religious practices aimed at mediating the sacred. The role of Christ as mediator of the reconciliation between God and humanity has traditionally been linked to his *priestly* role (or office), and often depicted as dependent on a moment of sacrificial violence. If we broaden our scope we may be able to articulate this mediating function more holistically. In Jesus' way of loving others we are confronted with a transforming reality: a form of altruism that is not grounded in the need to propagate one's genes or protect one's kinship structures, but in the gracious embrace of an absolute Other in relation to whom one is liberated for true love.

"And who is my neighbor? (Lk. 10:29). This was the follow-up question posed by a lawyer who had tried to test Jesus' understanding of the law. They came to an agreement that the way to inherit eternal life is to love God with all one's heart, strength and mind, and to love one's neighbor as oneself. "Do this," Jesus says, "and you will live." But the lawyer wants to "justify" himself and asks another question: who is my neighbor? Toward which persons should I direct my loving action? Jesus deconstructs the question by telling the well-known story of the Good Samaritan. He then asked the lawyer which of the characters in the story was a neighbor to the wounded man.

Once again, the lawyer gives the "right" answer: the one who showed him mercy. Once again, Jesus tells the lawyer "go and do likewise." The way of acting depicted in Jesus' ministry and message is not primarily about following rules, any more than it is about being punished in the place of others. The right (atoning) question is: how can my moral desire be transformed so that I can become a loving neighbor? The answer is by ordering our finite goods in a way that comforts the afflicted and bears their burdens.

However, this is possible only by sharing in divine grace. Only as we find our own agency mediated in the infinite buoyancy of the absolute mercy of God are we able to mediate the reconciling power of divine compassion to others. In this way we follow Jesus by *participating* in divine atonement. This will sound heretical for those whose understanding of the relation between God and humanity remains embedded within substance metaphysics and forensic categories. Yet the New Testament calls believers to become like Jesus in his death (Phil. 3:10), to share in his "suffering" (cf. 1 Pet. 4:1; 2 Tim. 1:8), to function as ministers of reconciliation and even to become the righteousness of God (2 Cor. 5:18–21).

How can we understand the agency of Jesus Christ in a way that makes sense of our being called to participate in the reconciling love of God? This has nothing to do with being absorbed into the divine substance or contributing something to the satisfaction God demands. It has to do with sharing in the arriving reign of divine peace, like Jesus, by welcoming others into redemptive relationship. In other words, it has to do with becoming just in community. Participating in the atoning power of God means sharing in the gracious presence of divine love that releases us from anxious dependence on finite social structures to secure the good life and for self-giving compassionate care of others.

This approach to reconstructing the doctrine of the atonement helps to clarify why Christians believe that the agency of Jesus Christ is good news. A *reforming* Christology should articulate the saving power of God in a way that actually facilitates reformation. Continuing to depend on ancient and early modern philosophical and legal categories for explaining the Christian experience of salvation in our late modern context obscures the Gospel and alienates our disciplinary neighbors.

As we struggle in our attempts to pursue the good life together within our overlapping and often conflicting cultures and religious traditions, presentations of the doctrine of the atonement may contribute by re-presenting other-regarding forms of agency that testify to and demonstrate Jesus' way of acting in the world. The power of this transformed moral desire is not grounded in its ability to get whatever it wants, but in its participation within the incursive omnipotent love of God, whose infinite goodness so embraces and pervades our being that we are liberated to share our goods with others. In so far as this is the power of "resurrected" life, our understanding of this agency (and identity) should incorporate an interpretation of our experience of the presence and coming of the risen Christ.

Chapter 4

Parousia and Physical Cosmology

This chapter explores the possibility and promise of bringing Christian intuitions about the eschatological experience of Jesus Christ into explicit dialogue with the sciences of "physical cosmology." As in the other case studies I am using a rather broad phrase to designate the sciences with which we are bringing christological doctrine into dialogue. In this context we will be engaging not only the field of physics as it applies to cosmology, but also developments such as quantum theory and the sciences of emergent complexity, which also have something to say about the nature (*physis*) of the dynamic *cosmos*. In the New Testament, the Greek word "parousia" itself can mean either (or both) "presence" and "coming." The early church experienced the resurrected Christ as being-with (par-ousia) them in a way that mediated the arrival of new life and the reign of divine peace. The *doctrine* of the parousia attends to the variety of ways in which the biblical tradition witnesses to the experience of being confronted with the advent of God through Christ (for example, the coming of the "Son of Man"), and the relation of this arrival to the consummation of the whole created cosmos.

Here too it will be important to identify some of the key philosophical shifts that have shaped (and to some extent have been shaped by) recent developments in these disciplines. Frank Tipler has suggested that theological research in the 21st century will require a PhD in particle physics, encompassing (at least) the fields of general relativity and physical cosmology. Whether or not an actual degree is required, his point is well taken. Many medieval students of theology and the best of the early modern Protestant Scholastics mastered and even contributed to the explanatory frameworks of cosmological science in their culture. As Tipler poignantly observes, "the central problem with contemporary theology and indeed most of late-twentieth century religion is not that it is separated from science but that it is separated from *modern* [contemporary] science" (1994, 329). As we will see below, a growing number of cosmologists are interested in this dialogue but understandably skeptical about popular religious eschatological speculation about a "rapture" and other literal interpretations of apocalyptic imagery.

Changes in the plausibility structures of contemporary discourse about the nature of the world make it difficult to maintain formulations about the coming of the risen Christ that are saturated by ancient or early modern cosmological assumptions. Here too, however, we will discover that such philosophical challenges also bring with them a fresh opportunity to articulate the intuitions of the biblical tradition about Jesus' mediation of the divine transformation of *reality* in our own late modern culture. Our first step will be outlining the contours of one of the broad conceptual fields within which intercourse between the sciences of physical cosmology and the doctrine of the parousia can quite naturally occur.

A Shared Interest in Being

All living organisms struggle to find their place within a broader whole as they relate to one other in a particular environment. The future of an organism depends on its ability to "feel" its way into relations that promote its well-being. This *aesthesis* is intensified in the feeling for life among human organisms whose personhood comes-to-be as they thematize their possible future being in relation to other persons. We long to *be* within the pleasurable presence of persons or aesthetic experiences that intensify the feeling that our existence is safely secured within a broader harmoniously ordered whole (cosmos). This desire for relational well-being in the future is threatened by our sense of being constrained with(in) space and time, of being caught up in a causal nexus of energetic forces that we cannot control. On the other hand, the coming to be of persons is also characterized by a more or less hopeful sense of *freedom* in relation to an open future. How are we to understand the conditions for this experience?

The philosophical field of metaphysics has traditionally dealt with "that which is" (or "being"), which has often been understood primarily in static terms. During the rise of early modern science, the objectively *real* was often reduced to that which could be measured and analyzed quantitatively; the qualitative experience of human feeling for freedom was considered merely subjective. Just as late modern ontological reflection has been liberated from the hegemony of the category of substance, so physics has been freed from the notion of absolute "rest," which has made possible more dynamic interpretations of reality, as we will see. This allows for a retrieval of the classical philosophical intuition that the experience of being oriented toward the beautiful is irreducibly real, and even a key to understanding the nature of reality (as it was even with Plato and Aristotle). In other words, *metaphysics* and *aesthetics* belong together, for our longing for beauty has to do with our longing for *being* in relation.

Students of both Christology and physical cosmology are interested in the human experience of being (and becoming) in the world, but they approach these phenomena in different ways and for different reasons. Most scientists (qua *scientists*) do not focus on the metaphysical dimensions of these issues, but on exploring the physical *reality* of the universe and explaining the causal principles that characterize the complex dynamics of space–time–matter–energy throughout the cosmos. Feeling organisms have in fact emerged in the universe, and this bears on discussions about the necessary and sufficient physical conditions for such life forms. For *theologians* these issues are important not only because they bear on an understanding of the creation and consummation of the world but also because they raise issues about the ultimate origin, condition and goal of the human experience of coming-to-be in the cosmos. The intuition that guides the doctrine of the parousia is that the resurrected Christ mediates the advent of the promising presence of the reign of divine peace in which human becoming is liberated from death and to eternal pleasure.

As human beings who share existential concerns about our coming to be in the cosmos, scientists and theologians can work together to make sense of our appetite for beauty. We may disagree about which particular things are most pleasurable, or most worthy of our longing, but we hold in common this underlying *aesthetic* desire that pervades our experience of personal liveliness and being in the world. Since the perception of beauty involves identifying patterns, sensing the relation between parts and wholes, it is not surprising that scientists often speak with awe of the beauty of the cosmos (or even the beauty of mathematical equations). Expressions of delight in the experience of belonging within the universe are increasingly common among physical cosmologists and other scientists (cf. Richardson, *et al.*, 2002; Barbour, 1999; Goodenough, 2000). Beauty is not just "there" – it confronts us with a real presence that evocatively opens us up in hope. This aesthetic desire that manifests itself in a seemingly limitless variety of longings is an expression of hope for a new experience of our *being* in relation, in which our coming-to-be is peacefully held in relational harmony.

We tend to the advent of that which promises us well-being. Theology attends to the intensification of this hopeful aesthesis in relation to the interpreted human experience of the presence of *divine* freedom, upon which the renewal of all things is absolutely dependent. Our experience of being environed evokes both anxiety about our belonging in the future and hope for a way of being pleasurably and peacefully related to others. Feeling free in relation to our environment and especially in relation to personal others requires space and time in which we do not experience the causality of others in ways that lead to the destruction or dissipation of our energy. The final threat to our freedom is death, which absolutely crushes all hope for belonging.

The doctrine of the parousia involves the interpretation of the biblical concepts of the "resurrection," "ascension" and "coming" of Jesus Christ in a way that makes sense of the Christian experience of a *presence* that mediates new life beyond the threat of death. Christians believe that Jesus of Nazareth's way of being in the world mediates the liberating presence of God in a radical way, manifesting the ultimate origin, condition and goal of human being in relation to the infinite Beauty of eternal life. Christology may articulate and interpret this experience in light of Jesus' way of being-present, which the early church and Christians of every generation have experienced as a real comforting and convicting presence. This case study is an attempt to contribute to the process of reconstructing and articulating a Christian understanding of the parousia in dynamic, relational terms, by interpreting the experience of Jesus' resurrection-ascension-coming in dialogue with contemporary models of physical cosmology.

The sciences of physical cosmology and theological treatments of eschatological hope can meet around (or within) this shared existential concern about being in the world. Reforming the doctrine of the parousia of Christ will indeed challenge popular ways of answering questions like "When is Jesus coming back?" It will even require criticizing the assumptions behind this way of framing the question. However, interdisciplinary engagement may also help us develop new conceptual tools for articulating our experience of this presence and coming in ways that invite late modern persons to attend more carefully to the shaping of their aesthetic desire within the cosmos. Our first step is to explore the *philosophical* categories shared by both disciplines in order to clarify the context within which the refiguring of christological discourse may occur today.

Philosophical Challenges

As in the other case studies, we can identify three pairs of philosophical concepts that are particularly important for both theology and science in the ongoing attempt to make sense of the human experience of being in the cosmos:

- space and time
- cause and effect
- matter and spirit

Throughout the history of the development of the doctrine of the parousia these categories have been at work, even when they were not made explicit. Talking about the experience of God's presence mediated through the presence of Christ always occurs within a particular contextual engagement embedded within a developing cosmological view of the world and its supporting philosophical framework. Understanding the (often hidden) role of these categories is an important first step as we move toward interdisciplinary reconstruction of the doctrine of the parousia.

Space and Time

The categories of space and time have played a significant role in philosophical debates from the Presocratics to the post-moderns, but they also shape our perception and interpretation of our everyday experience of ourselves and others in the world. We should not be surprised therefore that reflection upon the spatial and temporal dimensions of human experience is a theme common to both Christology and physical cosmology. The impact of the Copernican revolution and the rise of classical Newtonian mechanics on the scientific understanding of the universe is well known, and the majority of us simply assume that plausible reflection on space and time cannot ignore these developments.

However, we are still trying to get used to the conceptual revolutions introduced by relativity theory and quantum physics. This is the context within which we must make judgments about the basic questions that have guided many traditional eschatological formulations of this doctrine: *Where* do we go *after* we die? *Where* is Jesus' body *now*? Not only the answers but the questions themselves presuppose particular conceptions of space and time.

We can begin by observing how concepts of space and time structured eschatological expectation in the Hebrew Bible. The hope of the ancient Israelites was dependent on the promising presence of YHWH, whom they experienced as calling them toward new forms of life together, but the way in which this expectation was formulated changed over the centuries. These shifts were due in part to their interaction with the cosmological assumptions of their ancient Near Eastern neighbors. For much of its history, Israel imagined that regardless of their actions in life, after death all persons went down to "Sheol," a shadowy world of darkness under the earth. The "heavens" generally referred to the great open expanse above the earth, but this was often considered the place where God dwells and from which God rules. Whether one "digs" to Sheol or "climbs" to heaven (Amos 9:2), there is no *space* to hide in this three-tiered cosmos from God's presence.

During the exile, however, the Israelites encountered the Medes and Persians whose eschatological vision was influenced by the Zoroastrian religion, and we find a marked shift away from the idea of Sheol to which everyone goes (e.g., Eccl. 9:10), toward an expectation of a heavenly savior, and an awakening in which some receive everlasting life and others everlasting contempt (e.g., Dan. 12:2). The Priestly account of creation in Genesis 1 also shows evidence of an engagement with some of the more complex cosmological assumptions of the Babylonians (cf. Schwarz, 2000), but the basic tiered structure of the cosmos remains intact. The Israelites' understanding of *time* was also altered as they moved from a cyclical experience of the seasons in the agrarian culture of Egypt to a nomadic existence; this eventually led them away from a mythic-cyclic view of time and toward an interpretation of human time itself as dependent on the opening up of the future by God (cf. Achtner *et al.*, 2002).

Jewish anticipation of a coming Messiah, hope for a renewal of peace in "the land," and fascination with apocalyptic visions of the end of the world, all formed an important part of the background of the disciples' interpretation of their experience of Jesus Christ. The New Testament authors refigured imagery from the Hebrew Bible and applied it to the "ascension" and "coming" of Jesus. Christ was interpreted using the imagery of Daniel's "Son of Man," who brings about a transformation of the cosmos, and of Isaiah's "Servant of YHWH," who brings about the transformation of human society (cf., Hill, 2002; Wright, 2003). The idea of the parousia of Jesus in early Christianity continued to be interpreted within the context of broader cosmological assumptions (cf. Carrol, 2000; Ladd, 2000 [1974]; Robinson, 1979).

Aspects of Greek notions of the underworld, which had been taken over into Jewish thought, are also at work in the New Testament. For example, the Lucan Jesus tells a story in which a rich man looks up from Hades and sees Lazarus "far away" with Abraham (16:19–31). The Matthean idea that the Son of Man would spend three days "in the heart of the earth" (12:40), the Markan assertion that Jesus was "taken up" into heaven and sat down at the right hand of God (16:19), as well as the general pattern of descending and ascending that characterizes other depictions of the mission of Christ, all presuppose a tiered hierarchical cosmology. The observation that the writers may have been using other-worldly images to depict this-worldly events is not relevant for our point: they used *these* images of space (and time) to express their experience and expectation of the coming Christ and his relation to the presence of God because *this* was the cosmological frame of reference they shared with their ancient neighbors.

It is important to remember that Christianity emerged during an era that was heavily influenced by what has now come to be called "Middle Platonism" (c. 130 BC to AD 200). This eclectic philosophical approach followed Plato for the most part, but adopted and adapted aspects of Aristotelian as well as Atomistic cosmology. The tendency during this period was to begin with a notion of space as a kind of receptacle for matter, and then to interpret time as the measurement of the movement of bodies through or "in" space. Already in the earlier Atomists, such as Democritus, we find that space was conceived as an empty container extended throughout the universe, a receptacle that had no impact on the movement of material atoms through it. Plato also accepted a container notion of space (*chōra*), but he applied it only to the sensible realm, not the realm of the Forms. Space, then, was a category that properly referred to that medium in which the sensible copies moved, in which they were differentiated as they imitated the intelligible realm.

Time was also limited to the sensible realm for Plato. Understood as a measure of the movement (change) of sensible things through space, temporality could not be applied to the intelligible realm, which was considered eternal (unchanging). The Neoplatonist Plotinus would later express this by depicting time itself as the life of the world-soul, which arose along with the very process of differentiation from the intelligible. However, the fact that Plato had posited a separation (*chōrismos*) of the realms already implied spatial difference between them, placing the eternal in its own kind of space apart from the temporal. The conceptual and existential difficulties of dualistic metaphysics have always plagued Christian theologians who took Platonic cosmology as their starting point.

Aristotle thought of space in even more explicitly quantitative terms, which fit his interest in measuring the movement of particular bodies. Time was understood as the measure of motion and rest, which meant that it too functioned primarily as a quantitative category. Both the movement of time and the extension of space in this model were considered continuous and homogenous. *Ex hypothesi* bodies are contained within (occupy) particular spaces, and can move from one space (or "place," *topos*) to another. From this Aristotle deduced that the place of a thing was not part of the thing, but separable from it. Place is the inner boundary of each containing receptacle, the content of which may be changed.

Aristotle also contributed significantly to solidifying the dominant view that the earth was at absolute rest at the center of the universe. The seven "planets" (the Moon, the Sun, Mercury, Venus, Mars, Jupiter and Saturn) rotated around the earth in perfect circular motion, creating the harmony of the concentric spheres of the heavens. In fact, the rotation of the spheres did not appear to be perfectly circular and so Aristotle postulated the existence of 55 intermediary spheres rotating in various directions to maintain this ideal. Aristotle also argued that each terrestrial element (earth, water, fire, air) has its own "proper" place in the cosmos, and moves upward or downward (relative to the earth) toward its special place. Furthermore, the movements of all elemental bodies in the terrestrial sphere ("under" the moon) are directly influenced by the movements of the heavenly bodies, which are composed of a fifth (quintessential) element.

This geocentric, astrological and elemental understanding of the cosmos was maintained and even solidified in much Christian theology from the patristic period into the middle ages and in some cases even into early modernity (cf. Wildiers, 1982). This was the cosmological air in which the New Testament authors breathed, and so it is not surprising to find traces of this world-view in their writings; for example, Paul speaks of the "third heaven" (2 Cor. 12:2), Matthew of astrologers who observe a star that foretells where Jesus will be born (2:1), and James of God as the "father of lights" (1:17). In the Gospel accounts of the post-resurrection Jesus, his ascension is understood as a going *up* into the heavens, and his coming again as a coming *down* from the heavens. The New Testament authors may have been using this language metaphorically, as many scholars argue, but (as we have already noted) this should not obscure the fact that they were using *these* metaphors because of their cosmological assumptions.

These presuppositions are even more explicit in the eschatology of patristic theologians like Origen (cf. Lyman, 1993). Noting Jesus' prayer for the disciples – "I will that where I am, these may be also" (Jn 17:24) – Origen explained that Jesus passed "into" the heavens (or globes), and suggests that this also applies to the resurrection of believers. In *On First Principles* he argued that when "the saints shall have reached the celestial abodes, they will clearly see the nature of the stars one by one, and [will come to understand] why that star was placed in that particular quarter of the sky, and why it was separated from another by so great an intervening space [and ...] what would have been the consequence if it had been nearer or more remote" (II.11.7). The link between Jesus and "the saints" here has relevance beyond the question of life "after" death. Eschatology, cosmology and *ecclesiology* were all woven together in the patristic debates over the "ascension" of Christ (cf. Farrow, 1999). In other words, cosmological assumptions about the risen Jesus also ramified into the way in which believers interpreted their present experience of one another in space and time.

In his *Almagest* Ptolemy compiled and combined the dominant cosmologies of his era, relying most heavily on Aristotle. Although it was written in the 2nd century AD it was not made widely available to the broader Latin-speaking theological world until the medieval period. In the *Summa Theologiae* Thomas Aquinas accepted Aristotle's notion that the heavenly bodies were moved by spiritual "intelligences" (angels), and that these movements were causally related to the movements of bodies on earth. He acknowledged three heavens beyond the spheres of the planets: "the first is the empyrean, which is wholly luminous; the second is the aqueous or crystalline, wholly transparent and the third is called the starry heaven" (*SumTh*. I.69.1). Like Origen, his discussion of the ascension focuses on explaining Jesus' movement through and beyond the heavenly spheres, but his description is shaped more explicitly by Aristotelian cosmology (*SumTh.* III.57).

Under the pressure of the Copernican revolution the logic behind the idea of Jesus' ascent and descent, of a movement "up" and "down" through the cosmos, which had been presupposed in the New Testament as well as many of the early creeds, began to erode. The important point for our purposes here is to observe the philosophical battles shaping the scientific shifts. Mediated through Thomas, Aristotle's philosophy had become embedded within Roman Catholic doctrine. Alongside the rise of early modern science we find a growing interest in the philosophy (and cosmology) of the Atomists and Epicureans, and by the 17th century aspects of Plato's cosmology had come back into favor among several philosophers (e.g., the Cambridge Platonists).

Much of the resistance to the astronomical proposals of scientists like Kepler and Galileo .was philosophically based; their findings challenged the deepest assumptions of Aristotelian cosmology, which had become intertwined with formulations of Christian eschatology. The perfect harmony of the celestial spheres was disturbed by Kepler's demonstration of the non-circular (elliptical) movements of the planets and imperfections on their surfaces. Galileo was bothersome to many theologians not simply because he embraced a heliocentric understanding of the cosmos, but because his way of interpreting and measuring the relation between bodies in space was closer to the Atomists than to Aristotle. The whole Galileo affair, which has often been simplistically presented as a prime example of the warfare between science and theology, in fact illustrates the significance of philosophical mediation in the ongoing dialogue.

Isaac Newton preferred Atomism, and not only for "scientific" reasons: he believed that Moses himself had been an Atomist and that this cosmology supported monotheism. Newton's *Principia Mathematica* (1687) formulated laws of motion and force that applied to the movement of material bodies throughout the universe. This homogenizing of the terrestrial and celestial spheres further undermined Aristotelian cosmology. However, Newton maintained the idea of absolute space as a container and absolute time as the measurement of the movement of bodies "in" it. The interval of time between any two events could be measured unambiguously by any two observers regardless of their location. In this sense, time was independent of space, for the latter was conceived as a static receptacle that could be measured in terms of three-dimensional Euclidean geometry.

Written during the same decade as Newton's *Principia*, Francis Turretin's *Institutes of Elenctic Theology* depicts the ascension by maintaining that "Christ went up locally, visibly and bodily from the earth into the third heaven or seat of the blessed above the visible heavens ... by a true and local translation of his human nature" (XIII.18.3). Here we see evidence of the container notion of space, as well as vestiges of Aristotelian geocentrism.

In the late 19th century Charles Hodge, who relied heavily on Turretin, resists speaking of the ascension as a movement "up," but continues to insist that Jesus' risen body "takes up a definite portion of space." The ascension "was a local transfer of his person from one place to another; from earth to heaven. Heaven is therefore a place. In what part of the universe it is located is not revealed … (but) it is a definite portion of space where God specially manifests his presence" (1981 [1872], 629–30). Notice how far we have come from the Platonic flavor of Origen's view of the ascension. In *On First Principles* the latter had argued that we should not understand the risen Christ "as existing in those narrow limits in which He was once confined for our sakes, i.e., not in that circumscribed body which He occupied on earth, when dwelling among men, according to which He might be considered as enclosed in some one place" (II.11.6).

Several important aspects of Newtonian cosmology have been undercut by developments in late modern physics, leading to new conceptions of space, time and their relationship (cf. Jammer, 1993; Reichenbach, 1958). Albert Einstein pulled together insights from several of his 19th century predecessors and articulated what came to be called the special theory of relativity. Clerk Maxwell's theory of the electro-magnetic field challenged the idea of inertial space and the Michelson–Morley experiments had weakened confidence in the notion of "aether" as a medium for the movement of light.

Einstein wondered what would happen if he gave up the notion that space is constant, one great extensive co-ordinate system at absolute rest through which bodies moved. His innovation was to begin with two assumptions: that the laws of physics are the same in all inertial frames of reference, and that one of these laws is that the speed of light (in a vacuum) is constant to every observer, regardless of his or her speed in relation to the source of light.

Through a series of thought experiments, he showed that these two postulates suggest that what appear to be "simultaneous" events to one observer are not simultaneous for another observer in a different co-ordinate system. "Every reference-body (co-ordinate system) has its own particular time; unless we are told the reference-body to which the statement of time refers, there is no meaning in a statement of the time of an event" (Einstein, 1961, 26; cf. Einstein and Infeld, 1938). Instead of understanding space as a passive homogenous container independent of the material bodies that move through it, and time as the measurement of its changing content, Einstein conceived of a four-dimensional space–time continuum which itself changes and warps.

In his general theory of relativity, Einstein developed field equations that attempted to account for the effects of gravity, and which could be applied to any frame (not only inertial frames). As physicists searched for solutions to Einstein's field equations of general relativity theory and applied them to the distribution of galactic clusters, they predicted that such clusters would be moving apart from each other. This was confirmed by Edwin Hubble's telescopic observations, measuring the red shift of background radiation in the 1920s, which showed that galaxies were receding at a velocity that was proportional to their distance from us.

The realization that the universe is expanding led to what is now popularly called the "Big Bang" theory (cf. Guth, 1997). Moving beyond the limits of Euclidian geometry, Einstein had shown that the universe may be more adéquately described using relationally and dynamically complex Gaussian co-ordinates and Riemannian non-linear geometry. Light does not move through aether, but may itself be bent and even arrested (as in a black hole). Gravity warps (or is the warping of) space itself, and the measurement of time depends on the speed of the observer in relation to other objects within the space–time–matter–energy field. The Newtonian universe of absolute space and time was undone (cf., Barbour, 1999).

These cosmological developments challenge several aspects of traditional formulations in Christian eschatology, perhaps even more deeply than the rejection of empyrean spheres and elemental astrology by Newtonian mechanics. Here we have issues that go far beyond simply giving up the tiered hierarchical cosmos presupposed in some expressions of Jesus' ascension. The idea that Christ will "return" from a place in the cosmos at a particular point on a timeline, simultaneous to all observers, is itself rendered problematic in light of relativity theory.

This clearly undercuts the whole enterprise of trying to determine the date for such an event on an (absolute) "time-line," but it also opens up a whole range of new possibilities for Christian eschatology. The main point at this stage in the argument is that we must engage the cosmological assumptions of our own context, just as Origen and Thomas (and others) engaged theirs. Undoubtedly our current understanding of space and time will seem equally inadequate to future generations, but this should not keep us from embracing the ongoing theological task of reforming Christology.

Cause and Effect

A second and closely related set of philosophical categories that influences both physical cosmology and Christian eschatology is *cause* and *effect*. Scientists are interested in understanding the dynamics of motion that apply throughout the universe. The attempt to make sense of movement leads to questions like: What are the causes of change in the cosmos? Is it possible to predict what future effects will result from past (and present) causal forces? Although some philosophers have questioned the very coherence and appropriateness of the idea of causality (e.g., Hume), this pair of concepts has always played a basic role in the scientific enterprise.

Christian eschatology is also interested in cause and effect. For example, the way in which one articulates a "cosmological argument" for the existence of God as first cause ramifies into one's understanding of all effects whatsoever, including those at the "end" of the causal chain. Our interest here, however, will be on exploring how specific ways of utilizing these philosophical categories have shaped Christian formulations of the causal powers related to the resurrection and the efficacious presence of the ascended Christ.

Plato believed that things moved because they were enlivened by active principles that were endowed by the Creator. Causation is explained in this model by the presence of living forces within all sensible things that strive to participate in the intelligible Forms that they imitate. Variations of this explanation of causality were critically appropriated within most patristic doctrines of the creation and consummation of the world.

Later medieval theologians tended to follow Aristotle rather than Plato. Aristotle rejected his teacher's appeal to two separate realms (sensible and intelligible) and developed a different way to explain causal relations. His theory of causality was much more complex and lent itself more readily to scientific analysis. Aristotle identified four types of causes – material, formal, efficient and final – which all work together in every (terrestrial) movement or change. He illustrates these by asking: What is the "cause" of a bronze sculpture? Its material cause is the bronze out of which the statue is made. The pattern of the human body is the formal cause. The final cause is the *telos* or goal of the change; which in this case is aesthetic presentation. The efficient cause is the sculptor. If this fourfold typology of causes seems strange today, this is because after the rise of modern science, most of us think of causality primarily or only in terms of *efficient* causality – one thing pushing another along a timeline, from the past through the present toward the future.

For Aristotle, however, this was only one aspect of causation. The forms of material things changed because entelechies were working within and upon them, drawing them toward their particular goal (actualization). The celestial spheres were not considered to be merely efficient causes; they also provided the *telos* of the movement of the four basic elements that composed terrestrial bodies. For Aristotle, God played a role in this process as the ultimate primary cause behind all secondary (or instrumental) causes. The unmoved mover is beyond the outermost celestial spheres. As "thought thinking itself" this mover moves all things not as an efficient force but as the ultimate final cause; its non-moving perfection provides the ultimate *telos* and motivation for all movement, including the harmony of the celestial spheres.

Thomas Aquinas and most medieval theologians (and natural philosophers) accepted Aristotle's model of causality, although we find a mixture of Neoplatonic and Stoic influences as well. Thomas relied on these notions of cause and effect in his attempted proofs of the existence of God as the first cause of the universe and as the intelligent substance who provides material bodies with the final causes that move them. The Aristotelian categories of causality continue to play a role later in the *Summa Theologiae* when Thomas addresses the issue of the resurrection of Jesus.

Thomas' primary concern in this doctrine seems to be determining its causes and its effects. Jesus' resurrection is the efficient and formal (exemplary) cause of the resurrection of believers. Properly speaking it is a secondary cause, the absolute power of the Father being the primary cause. Thomas also wonders whether Christ ascended beyond the celestial spheres by his own power or by the power of the Father; the answer is both, explicated again in terms of primary and instrumental causation (*SumTh*. III.56–7). The notion of God as unmoved mover also shaped his depiction of the resurrected and ascended saints as achieving a final *state* of perfect contemplation of the rational substance of God.

During the late medieval and early modern periods, alongside the rise of classical mechanics in modern science, the vitalistic categories of Plato and the teleological categories of Aristotle slowly lost their conceptual hold on the Western mind. This is in part because of the renaissance of appreciation for Stoic and Atomistic accounts of causality, both of which are more deterministic in tone. The Stoics had only two principles for explaining movement: the passive and the active. The active principle was described in various ways (e.g., fire, pneuma and logos), but was always understood as the divine principle that determined all movement, including the movement of rational human individuals. For Atomists like Epicurus all motion in the cosmos is explained quite simply as the collision of impenetrable atoms; all that exists is material, and so there is no need for the hypothesis of living principles or entelechies. Both Stoic and Atomist models of causality seem to entail fatalism, a conclusion that many of these philosophers explicitly embraced.

The Atomist model of causality played an influential role in the formulation of Newton's idea of absolute space, in which bodies at rest and bodies in motion follow the laws of inertia. Newton himself struggled to maintain a place for final causes (and so for divine causality), even in the text of the *Principia* itself (cf. the General Scholium). The success of classical mechanics in explaining and predicting motion in the universe, however, eventually contributed to the popularity of materialism and determinism among scientists. On this model, the only place in the causal chain left for God is as the first efficient cause at the beginning of the timeline. What is left for God to do? This is the background for Laplace's legendary comment to Napoleon that he had no need for God as a hypothesis to explain the motions within the deterministic causal system of the cosmos.

It was during the rise of this philosophical understanding of cause and effect that early modern Protestant Scholastic eschatology was formulated. How were they to make sense of the idea of the consummation of creation linked to the parousia of Christ in their context? For the most part, 17th century Protestant theologians focused less on the challenges of science than they did on defending their eschatological positions in debate with Roman Catholic opponents. Many Lutheran and Reformed Scholastics met the latter on their own philosophical grounds, utilizing Aristotelian conceptions of causality in their arguments over the material, formal, efficient and final causes of the resurrection and ascension of Christ. Some embraced aspects of the new Atomism, while others brought Platonic conceptions to bear against it. For the most part eschatological reflection was focused on delineating the order and causes of the "last things" that would occur on the timeline of world history.

For most of the Reformed Scholastics, these final events were already predetermined and their primary cause was the absolute and eternal decree of the divine will. It is well known how this led to debates over the nature (or existence) of human free-will, but the important point for our purposes here is the impact of these philosophical categories of causation on Christology. Turretin devoted only two pages explicitly to the resurrection in his *Institutes*, and he was concerned with one question: "Did Christ rise by his own power?" (XIII.17). Against the Socinians (and some Lutherans), Turretin's concern was to insist that Jesus himself had causal efficacy in this regard.

Charles Hodge would later devote only six pages to the resurrection and ascension: his main concern was to identify the "efficient" agent of the resurrection (1981 [1872], 629). This way of approaching the resurrection may seem odd and even irrelevant to us today, but understanding the cosmological assumptions about cause and effect that shaped their world-view can help us understand why such questions seemed important then.

The early modern mechanistic, linear and deterministic conceptions of cause and effect that dominated science (and theology) for so long have been challenged by developments in 20th century physical cosmology. First, we can point to the role of the theory of quantum indeterminacy, which emerged in response to the problems of measurement that plagued the exploration of sub-atomic particles in the 1930s. Light itself has both particle-like and wave-like qualities, but studying the former requires disturbing the energy field of the latter.

Electrons have properties (or, properly speaking, *may* have properties) that cannot be known (or had) until they are measured. One cannot determine the locality and velocity of an electron before the experiment, because the experiment itself (observation) will alter one or the other. This strange aspect of electrons is sometimes called "superposition," which refers to the fact that an electron may be "here" and "not here" and have any number of other "states" that are superpositions of "here" and "not here" (cf. Polkinghorne, 2002; Baggott, 2004; Albert, 1992). Heisenberg called this the "uncertainty principle," and argued that it is not simply an epistemological or methodological limit; the nature of sub-atomic reality is not susceptible to deterministic prediction (cf. Heisenberg, 1971).

The dominant Copenhagen interpretation of quantum physics suggests that real possibility is inherent in the coming-to-be of the physical world. As Milič Čapek observes, this means the end of the Laplacian illusion of a static world. On deterministic models, the future loses its "futurity" and is merely an unknown part of the present reality. It is only on the assumption of a static world that indeterminism appears irrational. In a dynamic universe we may think of indetermination as "synonymous with the objective indefiniteness of the future ... with the futurity of the future" (1961, 337). Causality occurs within complex and surprising fields of relations, not in wholly deterministic linear chains in which one body collides with another in perfectly predictable ways (cf. Cushing and McMullin, 1989).

The downfall of determinism and the collapse of confidence in predictability was not solely a result of exploration of the microphysical world. Chaos theory deals with macroscopic phenomena such as "dissipative systems," which are open and draw energy from their environment (but are far from thermal equilibrium with it). In such systems a new organization of the system can spontaneously emerge; this dynamic process has been demonstrated at a variety of levels, from simple fluid convection to chemical processes to the development of organisms.

Although the new organization of the system emerges (out of apparent chaos) within a particular possibility space, sometimes graphed by what is called a Lorentzian strange attractor, the specific structure of the new patterns cannot be determined or predicted from the initial conditions (cf. Prigogine and Stengers, 1984). Chaos theory also suggests that the new patterns of behavior and emergent functions within non-equilibrium dynamical systems cannot be reduced to the linear interaction of its component parts.

Biologist John Campbell argues that, given the right sort of ultra-complex organization, causality may operate "from the future to the present." This would "transcend current axioms of scientific logic, and make the future operatically available somehow to the present. Significantly, appropriate organization can meet these two demands" (1985, 161). He recognizes that scientific distaste for "teleology" would resist this, but suggests that the abuse of this notion does not mean we should ignore the phenomena that led to teleological explanations. Although most scientists and philosophers are (understandably) unwilling to reintroduce Platonic vitalism or Aristotelian entelechies into their theories, one finds a growing recognition that the intuition behind these ancient models, which was lost in early modernity, must somehow be accommodated in light of these kinds of scientific developments (cf. Juarrero, 1999).

Even at the level of the universe as a whole, some cosmologists speak of a top-down or "reverse" causality. For example, the cosmological anthropic principle suggests that the presence of conscious human beings indicates that the rate of initial expansion of the universe after the Big Bang could not have varied by even one part in 10^{55}, or the rate would not have been at the level of criticality necessary for the relative smoothness of the galaxies in the universe, and the emergence of stars in which hydrogen and helium could be burned and form new elements (cf. Barrow and Tipler, 1986; Murphy and Ellis, 1996; Worthing, 1996). Acknowledging the irreducibility of purposiveness in the cosmos does not "prove" the existence of God as a "designer." However, it does raise philosophical questions about the relation between the future and causality that provide an opportunity for fresh theological reflection.

As with the other developments in physical cosmology, this brings both challenges and opportunities to the task of Christology. Even this brief overview demonstrates that every theological presentation of the parousia is shaped by *some* philosophical conception of cause and effect, whether self-consciously or not. Eschatological presentations that presuppose ancient or early modern cosmologies will become increasingly misleading and inappropriate in discourse about the parousia. Physicists will continue their debates on the nature of quarks and bosons, dark matter and dark energy, and on the usefulness of theories like loop quantum gravity or superstrings, and a whole host of fascinating models. Christology does not have to make judgments on the final adequacy of any of these in order to take advantage of the underlying philosophical shift in the categories we have explored.

The current conceptual milieu, in which the early modern deterministic world-view and understanding of mechanistic causation have been left behind, may actually be a gift for Christology. The cost of constructing eschatology under the reign of mechanistic determinism was the expulsion from natural philosophy (or "science") of the qualitative and existential intensity of the human experience of time, which is characterized by a hopeful and imaginative longing for the surprisingly new.

Exploring the conceptual link between futurity and causality opens new possibilities for making theological sense of the purposiveness of human aesthetic desire by interpreting it in relation to the advent of an absolute

Future that constitutes temporality itself. In light of more dynamic and holistic conceptions of causality, we now have a new opportunity to articulate the Christian experience of the cosmos interpreted in light of the reception of the liberation of aesthetic desire in response to a promising presence that cannot be controlled or predicted. Before exploring such possibilities, let us outline one more conceptual shift that shapes the way we articulate our understanding of the parousia.

Matter and Spirit

This final set of philosophical categories is closely connected to the categories of body and soul, which we explored in chapter 2, and is also shaped by some of the same considerations about the particular and the universal, which we outlined in chapter 3. The way in which Greek (Platonic) and especially early modern (Cartesian) substance dualism have structured all of these philosophical questions has had a crippling effect on Christology. Descartes made a basic metaphysical distinction between extended (material) things and thinking (immaterial or spiritual) things. On this model, science was about the mathematical measurement and mechanical explanation of the movement of material bodies.

The mind (or soul) played a central role in Descartes' philosophy, but its function in relation to the human body was always ambiguous: how could a non-extended thing have an energizing effect on an extended thing? For many scientists in the early modern period, such questions about the human "spirit" seemed to have no real bearing on explaining the material world. As we will see, developments in late modern science and philosophy have led to more holistic ways of conceptualizing the relation between matter and energy.

First, however, notice how this basic dualism (whether in its Platonic or Cartesian form) shapes the way in which we can imagine the parousia of Jesus. If being real means either being a material or an immaterial substance, what kind of reality does Jesus have now? The majority of the Christian tradition has tried to uphold the intuition that the resurrection, ascension and coming of Jesus are in some sense "*bodily*." At the same time the tradition has wanted to affirm (with Paul) that as the manifestation of eschatological humanity the risen Jesus became a life-giving *Spirit* (1 Cor. 15:45).

Under the hegemony of a metaphysical dichotomy between the philosophical categories of "material" and "spiritual" (or immaterial, ideal, etc.), attempts to articulate the parousia faced a dilemma: should we think of Christ's presence as a material substance or an immaterial substance, or some mixture or conjoining of both? Notice that this is the same conceptual problem faced by the early church in the doctrine of the incarnation.

As a first step, we should observe that the New Testament witness to the resurrection of and hope in the coming of Christ was itself ambiguous. The biblical authors struggled with the inadequacy of language to capture this new experience. The risen Jesus is not always immediately recognizable; Mary at the tomb, the men on the road to Emmaus, and the disciples in their boats are not initially sure how to identify the presence that confronts them. This new presence had some discontinuity as well as continuity with the Jesus they knew before the crucifixion. In some cases, they are urged not to touch him, in others they were invited to feel his scars.

The ambiguity of this confronting presence is also evident in the story of Saul's conversion on the road to Damascus; only he hears a voice and is blinded by the light. As N.T. Wright observes, the conflicting stories about the empty tomb all have a puzzled air about them as if the authors were saying, "I didn't understand it at the time, and I'm not sure I do now, but this is more or less how it was" (2003, 611). Theology is not forced to choose between rejecting all these reports as fictional constructions and attempting to construct a narrative that reconciles their differences. We may let the stories be what they are, and ask how we in our own context can talk about this strange and overwhelming experience of a presence that mediates new life.

The next step is to acknowledge some ways in which past theological attempts to testify to the parousia were shaped in various contexts by the philosophical categories of matter and spirit. As we have seen, Plato and Aristotle had quite different ways of using the concept of form. However, in both cases, form has to do with the energizing or movement of matter. While neither philosopher uses the term "form" in exactly the same way that they (and others) use the term "spirit," this latter term also evokes images of energetic motion and force in distinction from matter (cf. Jammer, 1999 [1957]). Our interest is less in the terms than in the role that such concepts play in philosophy, science and theology.

In eschatological formulations that are shaped by Platonic tendencies, we often see an emphasis on the need for the human spirit (or soul) to escape from the body. For the sake of simplicity, I will stick with some of the same historical examples used above in order to illustrate this point. In *On First Principles* Origen depicts the risen Christ as no longer in a circumscribed body but "passing swiftly through all things." The same holds for the "spiritual" bodies of the saints, which will not be encumbered by the carnal sense, but will have forms suitable for existence in the "celestial realms" (II.10–11).

For theologians influenced more directly by Aristotle, a different way of thinking about eschatology prevails. Thomas Aquinas' embrace of hylomorphic physics creates a conceptual problem for his understanding of resurrected bodies: he cannot dissociate human *matter* from human *psyche* as easily as the (neo)Platonists. Having accepted Aristotle's understanding of bodies as composed of the four elements, Thomas feels compelled to apply this also to the body of the risen Christ (*SumTh*. III.54.2).

Few theologians have tried to articulate eschatology under the constraints of Atomist materialism, although a great number have accepted the determinist aspects of this philosophical approach. As we have seen, this led to treatments of the doctrine of the parousia that focused on determining the final states of those individual souls who have been predestined to join Christ in heaven and the final states of those who have not.

Another way to illustrate the role of the categories of matter and spirit is by observing their influence on a closely related issue: the "real presence" of the body of Christ in the bread of the Eucharist. The differences in philosophical construals of the relation between matter and spirit (or body and soul) that constrained the options in the debates over the doctrine of the incarnation are also operative here. The Roman Catholic view (transubstantiation) insisted that Jesus is really present because the substance of the bread really becomes the substance of his (material) body.

As we saw in chapter 2, Luther tended toward Alexandrianism in his Christology and this is reflected in his doctrine of the sacrament: the fleshly body of Jesus is really present and united with the substance of the bread. Later Lutherans would prefer the concept of consubstantiation, but it relied on the same basic Aristotelian distinction that was utilized by Thomas (the "substance" of the bread and its "accidental" properties such as taste and texture).

Calvin's preference for an Antiochene approach to the incarnation registered an effect on his understanding of the Lord's Supper. The body of Christ is really present. However, he argues in his Commentary on 1 Corinthians 11 that this biblical language is figurative and symbolic. We should not say the body is actually "mixed" with the bread. As he puts it in the 1559 *Institutes*, we must not think of the presence of Christ as either fastened to or enclosed in the bread (IV. 17.19). The Zwinglians and the Anabaptists, of course, rejected the notion of a real "bodily" presence completely and were satisfied with a "spiritual" presence. The main point here is that all of these early modern debates presupposed particular philosophical ways of thinking about the difference between material and spiritual substances, and this affected their articulation of the real *presence* of Christ.

Platonic and Aristotelian conceptions of matter (and its relation to space, time and causality) have clearly been the most dominant in Christian theology. For historical and other reasons the alternative metaphysics of the Stoics was rarely appropriated for theological reconstruction. In some of their models of the cosmos the continuity between and among the material bodies of the universe was explained by appealing to an active divine principle of the cosmos. This all-pervading agency tensively held together all the parts of the cosmos, energizing their dispositional movements. The idea of a void made no sense in this metaphysic, at least inside the cosmos. Some Stoics postulated the notion of an infinite void surrounding the island (so to speak) of the continuous matter of the universe, whose coherence was secured not by the outer spheres (as in Aristotle) but by the active principle of an immanent logos or rational principle that pervaded it and held it together.

Whereas Aristotle's cosmos required a concept of absolute rest, the Stoics emphasized the active tension in all bodies. Chrysippus, for example, began not with the concept of space as a container but with the notion of the extension of bodies themselves. In other words, "bodies" are active and extend themselves by making room, or make room precisely by extending themselves. This emphasis on fields of tension rather than absolute space has more in common with contemporary physics than either the Platonic or Aristotelian models. This Stoic conception of space was closer to those developed in 20th century relativity theory and field theory. The relative lack of engagement between theological reflection on the parousia and Stoic physical cosmology leaves us with fewer traditional resources for critical appropriation in the task of contemporary reconstruction.

The very notion of *matter* itself has been refigured as a result of late modern developments in physical cosmology. As we have seen, early modern cosmology took material bodies as the basic unit of measurement, and then measured force in terms of the relation of bodies in motion. On this model, understanding the presence (or coming) of a thing required measuring its mass and calculating its velocity based on its movement in absolute space. Einstein's famous formula ($E=mc^2$), however, indicates that mass and energy are "equivalent" and inextricably linked to motion.

In this model the measurement of the mass and the energy of a "body" cannot be separated, because any such measuring requires the specification of a particular co-ordinate system in the space–time continuum. In classical mechanics, an increase in velocity (the quantity of motion) had no effect on the mass of a body, and an increase in velocity could never spring from the body itself, but must be externally caused. In relativistic physics, mass varies with velocity and kinetic energy may be converted from the "rest-mass" of photons.

When matter was understood in terms of small extended entities (atoms) that mechanically bump into each other, and spirit was conceptualized as unextended substance, it was difficult to explain how the latter could have any real relation to the former. *Spiritual* experience became divorced from scientific study of the *material* cosmos. The philosophical concept of "field" opens up a new non-dualistic way of linking energy and matter. Today even "particle" physics is not really about particles – in the traditional sense of atomic (un-cuttable) "entities" – but about excitations within a shared energy field.

What physicists call particles are what happens within a probability wave when a particular type of experiment is performed. "Atoms" are understood as fields of energy, within which we can conceptually distinguish electrons, protons and neutrons, as well as quarks (and bosons, etc.), which do not rest in an inertial state. The strong force holds quarks together and the weak force is responsible for most radioactive decay. The electromagnetic force holds broader fields of energy together. Physicists continue to search for a grand theory that will unite these three forces with gravity.

The success of this scientific venture is less important to Christology in general, and the doctrine of the parousia in particular, than the underlying shifts in philosophical categories that the venture itself presupposes. Matter has been "demoted from its central role, to be replaced by concepts such as organization, complexity and information" (Davies and Gribbin, 1992, 15). The dynamic, energetic forces that used to be explained in philosophy by postulating a different kind of substance (spiritual or immaterial) may now be understood as the complexification of fields of force in which matter is organized. This brings us to the sciences of emergent complexity.

Here we are on explicitly interdisciplinary terrain, for the leading theorists in these fields are attempting to identify principles of emergence that can make sense of all kinds of complex phenomena, from quanta to quasars. As Per Bak observes, if the same principles that govern the criticality of self-organized complexity in physics apply to the evolution of life itself, there is no need to postulate a new principle to make sense of life (1996). The basic idea here is that the appropriate organization of matter within energy fields can lead to the emergence of new properties and causal forces that cannot be reduced to the components themselves. One of the easiest examples to understand is the property of wetness, which is not a property of individual water molecules, but emerges when they are organized appropriately in sufficient quantities.

Most philosophers acknowledge this "weak" form of emergence, but the tougher philosophical question is whether a stronger claim can be made about the "reality" of phenomena such as life and consciousness (which have traditionally been linked to the category of spirit). Stuart Kauffmann addresses these issues in *At Home in the Universe* (1995; cf. 2003). He describes the way in which sufficiently complex mixtures of chemicals can spontaneously crystallize into systems of collectively autocatalytic sets, which can sustain themselves and reproduce. This tangle of chemic reactions that powers cellular life is what we call a living metabolism. "Life, in this view, is an emergent phenomenon arising as the molecular diversity of a prebiotic chemical system increases beyond a threshold of complexity ...

[it] is not located in its parts, but in the collective emergent properties of the whole they create" (1995, 24).

As Kauffman points out, this does not mean that life is not real, nor that it has no causal efficacy in the world, but it does suggest that we no longer need to postulate another metaphysical (immaterial) substance to make sense of the phenomena. Our conscious experience and feeling within the world is natural; we belong in the universe. Far from excluding religion from the dialogue, these developments invite theological reflection; Kauffman himself begins and ends his book by attending to the spiritual hunger and longing for the sacred that characterizes human life.

A growing number of philosophers are arguing for a stronger view of emergence. In *Mind and Emergence* (2004), Philip Clayton outlines and defends such a model. On his view, we may think of the world as being made out of one kind of stuff (monism), but as having become hierarchically structured, with new forms of complexity emerging over time. We may identify patterns across levels of emergence without postulating a monolithic law that explains them all.

Clayton also suggests that we accept not only the existence of emergent properties, but also emergent objects – ontologically real entities that exercise distinct causal influence on other objects as well as on the "lower" level out of which they emerged. He sees the human "mind," which emerges out of the self-organized complexity of the human body in relation to its environment, as one such object. The mind is dependent on the biological organism of the embodied brain, but is not reducible to it and is capable of influencing it through "mental causation."

The philosophical debate over the value and nature of the concept of "emergence" continues to rage (cf. Gillett, 2002), but for our purposes the main point is that most physical cosmologists no longer rely on the categories of material and immaterial substance to make sense of complexity in the organization of patterns of energy. This does indeed challenge many traditional formulations of the doctrine of the parousia.

However, it also provides new opportunities for reconstructing the way we talk about the presence of the risen Christ. On this model, interpreting one's experience of the presence and coming of another is not caught in the dilemmas forced by matter/spirit dualism. Where does this leave those of us who hope for and in the parousia of God as we struggle to feel our way in and through the cosmos?

Interdisciplinary Opportunities

Many theologians have engaged scientific developments such as relativity theory, quantum physics and Big Bang cosmology and asked about how they impact the concept of God or divine action generally. Relatively few, however, have addressed the specific implications for eschatology, and even fewer have explored how they might be brought into dialogue with the doctrine of the parousia. In this section, we will review some of those proposals that have explicitly engaged the philosophical implications of contemporary physical cosmology in their attempts to articulate the Christian understanding and experience of the resurrection, ascension and coming of Jesus Christ. As in the other chapters, I begin by highlighting two proposals that I believe provide us with particularly helpful conceptual resources for reforming Christology.

Thomas Torrance

Our first example is Scottish theologian Thomas F. Torrance. His long-term theological program has been to highlight a stream of the tradition that he believes can be traced from Athanasius through Calvin to Barth, a stream characterized by its attention to what he calls "onto-relations," or being-constituting relations. Torrance argues that this theological approach has implications for physics, suggesting that the relational intuitions of James Clerk Maxwell's Reformed tradition informed his development of a dynamical theory of the electromagnetic field (1984, 215–42), which prepared the ground for Einstein's relativity theory.

   Torrance's theology is a magisterial attempt to articulate the dynamic relation between divine (trinitarian) order and the contingent order of created reality (cf. 1981). In light of contemporary physical cosmology, he understands the universe "as a continuous integrated manifold of fields of force in which relations between bodies are just as ontologically real as the bodies themselves, for it is in their interrelations and transformations that things are found to be what and as and why they are" (1980, 28).

   Our main interest in this context, however, is Torrance's own application of relational thought forms to the Christian understanding of the presence of the risen Christ. In *Space, Time and Resurrection* (1976) Torrance argues for a *holistic* understanding of the event of the parousia. He observes that the New Testament only uses the term in the singular; the one parousia covers the "first" and the "second" advent, the whole happening of Jesus' coming-and-presence. In our everyday experience, we split apart space and time, and cannot grasp the totality of the event of the coming of Eternity into time.

From a theological point of view, however, the concept of the parousia should be understood as embracing the whole of Jesus' appearing, including his resurrection, ascension and coming. In this sense, Torrance can speak of a *"space–time parousia"* that bears upon the present throughout the history of creation, and of the whole historical Jesus as "downright *resurrection* from beginning to end" (1976, 94, 144). Torrance argues that the church exists in an "eschatological pause" in the midst of the one whole parousia of Christ. As a community it is held together as it tends to the always imminent presence of the risen Lord. The allegedly problematic "delay" of the return of Jesus, he suggests, is an invention of biblical scholars who have split the space–time of the one indivisible parousia (cf. 1976, 154).

In *Space, Time and Incarnation* (1969b), Torrance argued that many of the conceptual problems (such as the split between space and time) that plagued the modern doctrine of parousia are rooted in the static, "container" model of space, which was hardened in Western philosophy and science by Kant and Newton. If we accept the latter's notion of absolute space, in which God is conceived as the infinite Container of all things, then the entry of God into the world is no more thinkable than the idea of a box becoming one of the things it contains.

The problem goes back to the patristic era, where Torrance argues that Arius accepted the Greek idea of space as an infinite receptacle. Athanasius, on the other hand, viewed space as "the ontological and dynamic relations between God and the physical universe *established* in creation and incarnation," as a "differential concept that is essentially open-ended, for it is defined in accordance with the interaction between God and man, eternal and contingent happening" (1969b, 2–3, 18). Torrance finds remarkable similarities between Athanasius' theological understanding of creation and the "relational notions" of space–time in contemporary physics and cosmology (1976, xi, 24, 44–5).

Torrance also finds elements of this relational dynamism in the reformers, especially Calvin, but argues that Newton returned to the Aristotelian notion of an inertial system of absolute rest that had gained dominance in the middle ages. In *Christian Theology and Scientific Culture*, he observes that the anti-trinitarian Newton "threw in his lot with the heretic Arius" rather than Athanasius (1980b, 19). In light of contemporary cosmology, we now have the opportunity to recover relational concepts of space and time. These are not receptacles apart from bodies and forces, but functions of events in the universe. This allows us to think of the ascension not as a movement "in" time and "through" space, but as a moment within the whole parousia of Christ, which is the *redemption* of the contingent intelligibilities and natural structures of space–time–matter–energy, disclosing a new creaturely experience of their field of determination in relation to God (1976, 130–1).

Torrance insists that the resurrection–ascension–coming of Christ is not an infringement of the laws of the natural order, but the event of the creative presence of God that *gives* order. The (whole) parousia is the redemption of the order of space–time that constitutes "the relevant boundary conditions within the natural order where it is open to the transcendent and creative reality of God" (1976, 23). We should not abstract the historical experience of these events (including the resurrection) from the "field of force set up by God in the Incarnation, thus isolating it from the whole interrelatedness of creation and redemption ... [we should] refuse to abstract it from the field of living power disclosed in the Person of Christ ... [from] His whole space–time track in the cosmos" (1969b, 85).

Because of the infinite differentiality of the divine (trinitarian) life, human becoming is confronted by an inexhaustible and surprising source of possibility. This means that the movement of Eternity into time manifest in Jesus Christ "is not a movement that passes over into these structures or gets stuck in them, for it continues to operate livingly and creatively in space–time, travelling through it, fulfilling the divine purpose within it and pressing that fulfilment to its consummation in the new creation" (1969b, 72).

Torrance recognizes that the doctrine of the parousia must escape from the early modern conception of a predetermined timeline. He points to the resurrection as a new kind of historical happening, a real happening that not only outruns the decay of death but "comes to meet us out of the future." We are to think of the risen Christ as "more real than any of us." The resurrection is *in* space and time but precisely as the redemption *of* space and time, so that we now are "caught up in a vectorial movement that runs counter to the regressive flow of corruption and decay and carries us forward into the future to the final and full disclosure of our real being in Christ" (1976, 89–90). This way of thinking is only possible if one overcomes the fateful linking of the idea of divine immutability to an abstract notion of absolute space and time as an inertial system, which led to the early modern conceptual framework in which it was difficult (if not impossible) to make sense of the experience of the dynamic presence of God in the world.

In the closed and deterministic Newtonian system, time is irredeemable. In the open-structured and dynamic understanding of the cosmos in contemporary physics, however, order can spontaneously emerge out of disorder, as chaos theory and the sciences of emergent complexity have shown. Such transformation requires that "lower" levels, such as random fluctuations in non-equilibrium thermodynamic systems, must be indeterminate, that is, open to the boundary conditions of "higher" levels of organization. The irreversibility of this process suggests that time, as a dynamic dimension of the cosmos, is itself redeemable.

Torrance acknowledges that humanity itself is a product of spontaneous self-organizing order, but his interest is in the broader theological implications of these conceptual shifts. We can observe a convergence between this understanding of the cosmos and a theological interpretation of the resurrection as a surprising renewal and reordering of life by God (cf. 1989, 99–105; 1984, 185–8). As a resource for theological reconstruction of our understanding of the movement of the Eternal in time, Torrance points to Søren Kierkegaard, who utilized a "kinetic logic" that moves along with the truth in order to understand it rather than appealing to an abstract point of absolute rest (1984, 278).

All of this is embedded within Torrance's broader understanding of theological rationality. "Dogmatic" theology is rational, but its axioms must be fluid rather than fixed; at key points it must be correlated to mystical theology, for "it is in mystical theology that the boundary conditions of our dogmatic formalizations are kept open toward the transcendent and unlimited Rationality and Freedom of the living God" (1985, 93). Torrance credits Calvin with the reversal of the abstract medieval approach to theological analysis: instead of beginning with the question of a thing's essence (*quid sit*) we should begin our interrogation with the particular character of a thing as it discloses itself to us in relation (*quale sit*).

This has been reinforced by several late modern philosophers of science, but Torrance is partial to Polanyi, who emphasized the importance of the personal coefficient of knowledge (cf. Torrance, 1980a). The way in which God's presence in the world is mediated through Christ cannot be grasped through abstract substantial definitions. One understands the redemption of the cosmos through the parousia only by "*following* the space–time track in truth and life that is Jesus Christ" (1969b, 73).

Robert Russell

Our second major example is the research program outlined by Robert John Russell, the Ian G. Barbour Professor of Theology and Science In-Residence at the Graduate Theological Union, Berkeley, and Founder and Director of the Center for Theology and the Natural Sciences in Berkeley, California. Russell's basic academic training was in both physics and Christian theology and his attempt to bring these disciplines into dialogue with the Christian doctrine of the risen Christ is by far the most ambitious and scientifically literate proposal to date. He is well aware of the importance of philosophical categories in this dialogue, and suggests that the way in which concepts such as the origin, contingency and evolution of the universe overlap disciplines requires a "trialogue" among theology, philosophy and science (1996, 221). Unlike so many contemporary treatments of the issues surrounding the doctrine of the parousia, Russell insists that this doctrine must take into account shifts in scientific conceptions of the *cosmos* itself as it articulates the claim that "the groaning of *all* of nature will be taken up in and healed by the transfiguration of the universe which has already begun with the Resurrection of Christ" (2004, 572).

Although this belief is central to the Christian religion, Russell observes that it is surprisingly underrepresented in the interdisciplinary dialogue. This is due in part to the fact that the discipline of theology itself for the most part continues to articulate eschatological doctrine in ways that presuppose Newtonian classical mechanics and absolute space and time (at best) or ancient three-tiered cosmology (at worst).

Russell wants to link Christology to a doctrine of *creation* (and *new* creation) that engages contemporary conceptions of the universe. He recognizes that some New Testament scholars have taken an easy way out, suggesting either that the disciples' experience was merely "subjective" or that they experienced a presence that had "personal" continuity with the pre-Easter Jesus but not physical or material continuity. Russell explicitly tackles what he calls the hardest challenge for relating theology and science: the challenge posed by contemporary scientific cosmology, with its concepts of matter and its predictions about the far future of the universe, to Christian eschatology and its insistence on the idea of a *bodily* resurrection.

In this brief survey of his proposal I will follow the structure of his argument as it is laid out in one of his most comprehensive essays on the topic – "Eschatology & Physical Cosmology" (2002b) – and fill out the outline with references to some of his other works. It will be important to keep in mind a terminological difference from Torrance; Russell tends to use the term "parousia" to refer to the final eschatological consummation of creation, not to the whole event of the appearing of Jesus Christ.

Despite this difference, however, Russell (like Torrance) explicitly argues that Christology can shape our scientific understanding of the cosmos and not simply the other way around. The dialogue involves "creative mutual interaction" (2002b, 266). Russell explains that his research project aims to "give a more coherent overall view than is now possible of the history and destiny of the universe in light of the Resurrection of Jesus and its eschatological completion in the parousia" (2002b, 288). How can belief in such a consummation be possible in light of contemporary Big Bang cosmology, which seems to imply that the far future of the universe will end in one of two scenarios – "freeze" (expand forever) or "fry" (slow down and re-collapse) – neither of which is hospitable for human life as we know it?

Russell identifies four theological movements that converge on these issues surrounding resurrection, eschatology and cosmology. The first has already been mentioned above: the ongoing debates about the bodily nature of the resurrection. Russell's argues that the New Testament links the latter to God's "new creation" of the whole cosmos in a way that overcomes the world-denying tendency of Gnosticism (cf. 1994, 572). Another movement that bears on these issues is the increased theological attention to the problem of natural evil and theodicy in light of the recognition of billions of years of suffering and disease in evolutionary history.

In several places, Russell has argued that an adequate response to this problem will require a robust theology of the resurrection and an eschatology that makes sense of the transformation of this universe as a new creation (2002b, 275; cf. 2003b; 2005). He recognizes that eschatology and creation must be treated together, and he himself has explored the theological significance of the concept t=0 in Big Bang cosmology (cf. 1996). Our focus in this context, however, will be on his exploration of the implications of contemporary physics for our understanding of the "end" of the universe and its relation to the resurrection of Jesus Christ.

The third movement is what Russell calls the 19th and 20th century "discovery of the essentially eschatological dimension of the NT traditions." He is particularly interested in critically appropriating the work of Wolfhart Pannenberg and Jürgen Moltmann, both of whom we will revisit briefly in the next section. Russell observes that for these "trinitarian theologians eternity is not timeless," as Augustine and others had argued. Rather, eternity is the "fully temporal source and goal of time" (2002b, 275). Both of these theologians have engaged developments in physical cosmology to some extent, but their insistence that we must prioritize the future in our understanding of God's relation to time comes from their interpretation of the New Testament message.

Although Russell is both appreciative and critical of the way in which he deals with contingency in physics, he applauds Pannenberg's emphasis on linking God to the ontological power of the future (1988, 41; cf. 1997) and recommends his philosophical (and theological) argumentation for "duration" in nature and the "eventlike" nature of matter (1988, 33; 2002a, 28). Russell agrees with Moltmann (and others) that we need to "ontologize relationships," including temporal relations between what we call past, present and future. In light of special relativity theory, Russell suggests that we speak of the "fractal structure of time," and spells out these complex non-linear relations of its inhomogeneous ontology (2000, 53).

The fourth convergent movement is the field of "theology and science" itself. The growth of this interdisciplinary dialogue has special bearing on the question of eschatology and physical cosmology because virtually every attempt to reconstruct the doctrine of the parousia has emerged within this arena. Russell builds on the work of several pioneers in this dialogue, and outlines his own model of the complex interaction of these disciplines (2002b,

277; cf. 2002a, 12). Adopting Lakatos' concept of a "research program," he asks how scientific and theological research programs mutually interact.

Russell identifies several "paths" by which the natural sciences can influence theology. For example, theories in physics can provide direct data that place constraints on theology, or indirectly provide aesthetic resources for theological imagination. Conversely, theological theories can also influence science in various ways. They may provide some philosophical assumptions underlying the natural sciences, act as sources of inspiration in the construction of new scientific theories, and aid in theory choice by shaping criteria for selecting among theories that explain all the data in equally adequate ways.

In this "complex mutual interaction," how might scientific cosmology shape theological reflection on the resurrection of Jesus Christ? Russell insists that we must face the challenges of science to particular theological claims. This means, for example, that a doctrine of eschatological divine action should not violate the special theory of relativity, which implies that there is no simultaneous "present" shared by all observers in the cosmos. Moreover, even speculative scientific theories such as quantum gravity or multiverse cosmology bear on theology, in so far as they raise questions about the contingency of the universe.

For example, even though the existence of an initial singularity, $t=0$, which signifies the origin of the universe in standard Big Bang cosmology, becomes uncertain in inflationary and quantum cosmologies, the emergence of more complex temporal domains out of this initial singularity should lead theologians to move beyond models of creation that depict God primarily as a deterministic first cause and combine with this the idea of God as the immanent, ongoing creator of the world (*creatio continua*). He notes that theoretical constructs like the Feynman/Wheeler advanced potential (or like tachyons that would allow for backward causality) suggest the conceptual possibility that what we call the future has some impact on what we call the present. Finally, Russell suggests that interaction with contemporary science should lead theologians to correlate the transcendent act of *creatio ex nihilo* more adequately with *creation continua*, God's immanent presence to and in the emerging structures of nature (2002b, 270, 278).

According to Russell, one of the key ways in which science informs Christian eschatology is by providing certain formal conditions for the possibility of the transformation of the universe by God. In other words, assuming with many New Testament scholars that the eschatological new creation will be a transformation rather than a "junking" of the old one and starting "from scratch," Russell suggests that science can help theology understand the "elements of continuity" that must exist now in order for it to be possible for the universe to be transformed. More than this, it can provide resources to theology for thinking through the "elements of discontinuity," that is, which aspects of nature might be healed or transfigured in the new creation.

Russell argues that while the discovery of the emergence of the irreducibly new in contemporary science within the context of the basic laws of nature has suggested fruitful approaches for non-interventionist objective divine action (NIODA) and, with it, theistic evolution, we need a new avenue for theological reflection on the resurrection of Jesus Christ. Instead of focusing on the continuity within discontinuity, the relation should now be inverted. In this approach, the conditions for the continuity of Jesus' risen body are interpreted within a more radical and underlying discontinuity, which is implied by the idea of a new creation as the transformation of the universe *ex vetere* (to use John Polkinghorne's phrase for "out of the old"). This avoids what Russell sees as two inappropriate extremes: naturalistic and reductionistic views such as "physical eschatology," on the one hand, and neo-Orthodox "two-worlds" eschatology, on the other (2002b, 295–6).

However, if the interaction is mutual, then scientists can also be influenced by theology to ask new questions about nature and perhaps thereby to point to new avenues for scientific research. Russell himself provides several examples of ways in which theological reflection (via philosophy) can impact theory choice and even suggest new scientific research programs. One of his most fascinating illustrations arises out of his engagement with the Hawking–Hartle hypothesis (Russell, 1999; 1997; cf. Hawking, 1988). Their model of quantum cosmology suggests that it is logically and mathematically possible that the universe does not have a "beginning" (in a temporal sense), but that its past is nevertheless "finite." The universe is finite but not bounded or, as Hawking says, its boundary condition is precisely that it has no boundary.

But the theory leaves open how to explain the distinction between what Russell calls the "Hawking domain" of the very early universe, in which non-temporal quantum gravity applies, and the "Einstein domain" covering from a fraction of a second after the Big Bang into the far future, in which general relativity applies and conditions temporal experience. In other words, time itself is domain-dependent. Russell argues that theological reflection on the relation of God to these contingent domains can inspire scientific theorizing about the need to postulate a *transitional* domain that mediates between the very early universe with its background field of three-spaces and the current universe in which we experience four-dimensional space–time. Russell's *theological* claim in this context is that "the universe is such that in certain broad transition domains within it *God creates the transition to time and time's arrow*" (1999, 313).

Turning explicitly to the implications of physical cosmology for eschatology, Russell asks: what conditions would need to hold in the universe now for an event such as the resurrection of Jesus to have occurred, and what implications does this have for the idea of a "new creation" in which we hope also to participate in a general resurrection? On the one hand, we can acknowledge that such an experience presupposes a radical *discontinuity* between creation and new creation, including the transformation of the background conditions of space, time, matter and causality begun proleptically at Easter. However, we must also consider the preconditions for the possibility of *continuity* in the resurrection.

According to Russell, this means that our current universe should exhibit certain characteristics which will remain intact during its transformation, such as "flowing time." These qualities should be eschatologically transformable in such a way that allows for the co-presence of the past, present and future, for a proleptic understanding of the eternity–time relation, and for a causal global future. Some interpretations of special relativity theory challenge such possibilities, especially a shared global future, while general relativity allows for a variety of future topologies for the universe. A "flowing time" interpretation of the cosmos would support such an eschatological understanding of resurrection, while a "block time" interpretation would render it problematic (2002b, 301–8).

It may appear that Russell's methodology places theology in a primarily defensive position in relation to science. On the contrary, he sees both disciplines as actively engaged in understanding human experience in the world. Far from recommending retreat, Russell argues that theologians ought to take their belief that in the resurrection of Jesus the new creation has already begun into the dialogue, insisting that the universe has a more complex temporal topology than that of linear time, and that this might even be prefigured in some way by the musings of theoretical physics and cosmology. He even suggests that an "eschatological interpretation of temporality and relationality," grounded in a more complex and dynamic understanding of time in relation to the "not yet" but "already" arriving eschaton, could lead to new insights into aspects of the physical nature of the universe that cosmologists have so far overlooked (2007, 575).

We have seen that Russell takes seriously not only the eschatological dimension of the New Testament witness, but also the revival of trinitarian doctrine. We should also note that he has also participated in the retrieval of the importance of the philosophical concept of infinity for theological reflection (cf. 1997b). Although Russell has not yet set out a full systematic theological treatment of the doctrine of the parousia, his methodological and philosophical theological contributions provide us with resources as we move forward in this ongoing reconstructive process.

Other Proposals

Although the relation between the doctrine of the parousia and physical cosmology has not received as much attention as our other case studies, we are not left without additional resources. Most of the following proposals are from scholars whose primary discipline is theology. Many of them have participated in the broader renewal of eschatological ontology that played such a significant role in 20th century theology. Others are leading figures in the general theology and science dialogue. All of them have taken advantage of the opportunity provided by late modern shifts in the categories of space, time, matter, energy and causality for reforming theological interpretation of the Christian experience of the presence and coming of Christ. The following brief descriptions are not intended to offer critical appraisals, but only to provide more illustrations of the kind of resources that are available for the reconstructive task.

As in our case study on the incarnation and evolutionary biology, Pierre Teilhard de Chardin stands out as one of the early courageous voices to engage these cosmological shifts; many other proposals at the intersection of these sciences have engaged his work to some extent. As a theologian Teilhard wanted to think through the implications of the Pauline idea that Christ will incorporate all things in himself and bring them into relation to the Father so that God will be "all in all" (1 Cor. 15; cf. Eph. 1:10; Col. 1:20), and to express this in a way that illuminates our scientific understanding of an evolving universe.

In *The Phenomenon of Man*, he argues that the whole trend toward increasing complexity and consciousness in the cosmos is oriented by and toward the "Omega Point," which is the "Prime mover ahead," an energizing force of love that attracts all things toward itself. But the Omega is not just in the future, it is really present. "To be supremely active, Omega must be supremely present" (1961, 269). In *The Divine Milieu*, Teilhard connects this more explicitly to Christ. He argues that as a consequence of the incarnation, "the divine immensity has transformed itself for us into the *omnipresence* of christification" (1960, 101).

Here and in several of his other later essays, Teilhard weaves together the concepts of the presence of God, the dynamic transformation of the cosmos and the coming-to-be of Christ. In *The Activation of Energy*, he argues that God's creative and redemptive presence must be understood in a way that makes sense of the dynamic development of the cosmos. The discovery of a developing universe means that "God cannot appear as prime mover (ahead) without first becoming incarnate and without redeeming – in other words without our seeing that he becomes Christified; and in which, by way of complement, Christ can no longer 'justify' man except by that same act super-creating the entire universe" (1970, 263–4).

In some of the essays in *Science and Christ*, Theilhard makes the connection even more explicit. Christ-Omega is "the evolver" who animates and "gathers up" *all* the energies of the developing universe. "In position and function, Christ, here and now, fills for us the place of Omega Point" (1968, 165). This radical integration of the doctrine of the parousia into an all-embracing interpretation of the evolution of the universe has had its detractors, but it remains one of the most significant attempts to articulate the Christian experience of the presence of Christ in a way that coheres with big bang cosmology.

Jürgen Moltmann is well known for his insistence that the doctrine of creation must be understood in light of eschatology. He has also explicitly engaged several of the developments in contemporary physical cosmology, especially shifts in the concepts of space, time and causality, arguing for a robustly relational understanding of the mutual indwelling of God and the world. Moltmann appropriates the scientific and philosophical critique of linear notions of time, and develops a theological understanding of God's relation to the world in which the future is prioritized as the "source" of the other modes of time (e.g., 1996, 287; cf. 1985; 2003).

When he applies this to Christology, Moltmann shows the link between the doctrine of the parousia and the presence of God who was understood as the "coming One" in the Hebrew Bible. In so far as the resurrection of Jesus means that he now participates fully in the eschatological reign of God, Moltmann says that "He comes from there – from the centre of divine power – and represents that power through his coming" (1993, 332). This coming is not simply the arrival of God "from" the future, understood as a mode of time that makes things old, but the *advent* of the fullness of God, who makes all things new, calling all of creation to participate in the inexhaustible aesthetic creativity of the triune life. Jesus' resurrection is the appearance of this eternal life and his coming "draws all things in to his future, so that they may become new and participate in the feast of God's eternal joy" (1996, 336–8).

Another theologian who has attempted to articulate Christology in general, and the doctrine of the parousia in particular, in dialogue with contemporary physical cosmology is Wolfhart Pannenberg. Like Moltmann, he is well known for his emphasis on God as the power of the future and on the eschaton as the creative beginning of the cosmic process. Already in his very early writings, Pannenberg made clear that this insight derives not primarily from philosophical and scientific analysis, but from the revelation of God in Jesus Christ. The Easter appearances represent the divine confirmation of Jesus' claim to manifest the presence of the reign of God, a coming-to-appearance that does not conflict with its futurity but remains differentiated in the presentness of its appearing (1969, 133–4). In his later *Systematic Theology* (and elsewhere) Pannenberg demonstrates how the introduction of relation into the concept of substance in both philosophy and science can facilitate theological reflection on such issues (1994, 367).

Pannenberg goes out of his way to link the parousia to the working of the Spirit, who "constantly encounters the creature as its future, which embraces its origin and its possible fulfillment" (1994, 102; cf. 1993, 137). In the resurrection of Jesus from the dead by the power of the Spirit the future of creation has already come: participation in the eternal life that by the same Spirit unites the Son to the Father (1994, 396). The Easter event was the proleptic manifestation of the reality of this new, eschatological life, which under the creaturely conditions of the form of duration, creatures experience as an anticipation of the consummation of the entry of eternity into time (1998, 627).

Niels Gregersen is one of the few theologians who have explored the implications of the sciences of emergent complexity for Christian theology. He has paid particular attention to ways in which the discovery of autopoietic processes in nature impact theological articulation of the doctrines of divine providence and human freedom (e.g., 2002, 2004). In a recent article on "Emergence in Theological Perspective" he spells out the idea of God as the eternal source of emergence in explicitly trinitarian fashion. The emerging reality of creation is "always initiated by God ('the Father'), expressing God's Logos ('The Son'), and being enabled and embraced by God ('The Spirit')" (2006, 316).

Gregersen also makes some initial suggestions for how this would impact Christology. Is the human person Jesus an emergent reality, and if so how can he be the expression of God's embracing love? If we take seriously the preconditions of this emergent phenomena, argues Gregersen, then we must also insist that (one way or another) God is "pre-existing as a divine milieu of love." Such an emergentist Christology could argue that "in the radically contingent life-story of Jesus, and in his poignant parables, it is exactly the eternal life-story of God that was expressed, re-enacted or revealed" (2006, 317). Although Gregersen does not treat the concept of the parousia explicitly, he does hint that Jesus tapped the "resources of the emerging reality of the reign of God" (2006, 318) as well as the reservoir of religious traditions.

John Polkinghorne has been one of the leading figures in the growing theology and science dialogue over the last four decades. Like so many others, he argues that Christian faith in the resurrection of Jesus and hope for a new creation must be reformulated in light of our contemporary understanding of an evolving cosmos. Most of his work has focused on broader questions about divine action in creation and eschatology rather than Christology, but he does explore the implications for this doctrine in several places (e.g., 1994, 167; 1998, 104–12; 2000, 39). Polkinghorne argues for a real bodily resurrection and an empty grave, but suggests that the risen body of Jesus must be thought of as the "transmutation" and glorification of his dead body.

In this sense, Jesus already participates in the new creation, which Polkinghorne emphasizes is the divine redemption of the old creation (*creatio ex vetere*). He postulates that resurrection (both for Jesus and for us) involves the recreation of something like a mathematical pattern (or form) that will have continuity with the information-bearing patterns of this life, but will subsist within the transformed "matter" of the new creation. For Polkinghorne, the experience of and hope for participating in the resurrection of Jesus must be articulated in conjunction with a broader proposal for understanding the eschatological transformation of the whole cosmos.

We find a growing recognition among theologians that articulating the doctrine of the parousia (resurrection, ascension and coming) of Christ in late modern culture will require engagement with contemporary understandings of the cosmos. For example, C. Wessels critically examines the New Testament witness in his *Jesus and the New Universe Story* (2003), suggesting that a "triple-decker" cosmology placed constraints on the biblical authors' articulation of their experience. Moving beyond the metaphors of ascent and descent, he proposes that we think of Jesus as revealing a "new depth of consciousness" emerging in the universe.

Roger Haight's controversial *Jesus: The Symbol of God* does not explicitly engage scientific developments, but he does argue that the "symbol" of the resurrection should be interpreted today in a way that does not require a transfer of Jesus to "another space and time." His proposal is to speak of Jesus as "ontologically alive as an individual within the sphere of God" (1999, 151). In the *Future of the Universe*, Arnold Benz outlines the scientific discovery of an open universe and faces the dire predictions for its far future. However, he insists that through the eyes of faith Christians can interpret the cosmos in light of the paschal events (including Easter), which reveal the "future newness" that is already breaking into the world (2000, 155).

Even if we are critical of the methodological and metaphysical assumptions that guide some of these interdisciplinary proposals, we can appreciate the way in which they explicitly engage existential questions about our interpreted experience of human freedom and aesthetic feeling for life in the world as they search for new ways of articulating the eschatological dimensions of Christian faith. Theology can and should regain its voice in the ongoing human struggle to understand our shared experience of coming-to-be in the cosmos as we hope together for a peaceful and harmonious future. This is the task of reforming Christology.

The Presence of Jesus Christ

In this brief case study we have attempted to identify some of the challenges and opportunities that arise in the ongoing task of reconstructing the doctrine of the parousia in dialogue with the sciences of physical cosmology. Our strategy was to explore shifts in the interpretation and use of several key philosophical categories that play a role in the conceptual space shared by these disciplines. It is important to emphasize that this is only one moment within the larger task of offering a fuller theological presentation of the parousia, which would require more detailed exposition of the relevant resources in the biblical tradition.

Our more limited goal here has been to demonstrate the extent to which previous formulations have been shaped by their own contexts, which should embolden us to press forward in engaging ours as we conserve the intuitions of the biblical tradition about the experience of the parousia in a way that liberates them for transformative interdisciplinary dialogue.

Once again it is crucial that we find the courage to engage in *reforming* christological questions. It is not sufficient to come up with new answers to questions like, "When is Jesus coming back?" and "Where is the body waiting now?" These questions make no sense in light of relativity theory and quantum cosmology. The reconstructive task will require us to rethink the assumptions that have guided so many attempts to develop new timelines for Jesus' return and to depict his placement in the heavens. In light of the conceptual shifts traced in this chapter, it is no longer plausible to speak in the same way that (for example) Origen or Hodge did about Jesus' presence and coming. This is not because Jesus is not present or coming, but because the way we *interpret* our experience of being confronted by an arriving presence has been refigured.

Today, to be present means to subsist in tensive relations within a spatio-temporal field of energized material complexity. In this context theological discourse on the parousia of Jesus Christ can be more adequately guided by different kinds of questions. How is the promising *presence* of God mediated through Christ in a way that transforms human aesthetic desire? How does Jesus' way of *being* in the world manifest divine freedom in relation to creation?

It is important to attend to the ways in which philosophical categories are figuring the discourse between Christology and science. We do not have to accept ancient and early modern concepts of *space* and *time* in order to affirm Jesus' parousia. In our context we can interpret our spatio-temporal experience of coming-to-be as a being-called toward a transformation prefigured in Christ and countenanced by an omnipresent divine welcoming into new being.

Reflection on this eschatological presence does not need to be constrained by questions about the *causal* order of the "last things" or the *effects* of the "second" coming. Acknowledging more dynamic and holistic conceptions of causality, we may speak of the all-embracing evocative presence of God as constituting the infinite possibility field out of and into which creaturely desire for eternal pleasure emerges.

The demise of the dualism between *matter* and *spirit* provides us with an opportunity to move past conceptual dilemmas about the location of Jesus' body (or soul). Without de-materializing the resurrection (or ascension or coming) of Christ, we can imagine this transfigured energized presence as participating in the divine nature in a way that mediates to us God's incursive invitation into communion. Such an approach can connect the doctrine of the parousia more immediately to our experience of responsibility within our particular co-ordinate systems of space–time–matter–energy.

The doctrine of the parousia explicates the claim that Jesus Christ mediates the promising *presence* of the Creator vis-à-vis creation. Here the biblical link between the presence and the *face* of God is informative. We are not dealing here simply with a substance that is "there," but with an experience of being-appeared-to, of being-called into relation. Here too (as with identity and agency) Jesus' being-present was always and already mediated through and by his relations to other human faces. The evocative experience of the human face is important for human development, because our felt sense of being-present is mediated to us in relation to other significant faces.

We cannot control these facing presences; their confronting of us and absenting from us appear together, which is partially why we feel ourselves lured (or repulsed) by them. We come to fear that all of our energetic striving for pleasurable effects in space and time cannot satiate our longing to feel the beautiful presence of another who faces us graciously and peacefully. However, Jesus' way of being present to God and to others discloses a transformed creaturely experience of aesthetic desire beyond the threat of entropic dissolution.

It is important to emphasize that the parousia of Christ is a real mediation of the *divine* presence of the Creator to, in, with and for creation. In order to makes sense of this, we must remember that the promising presence (face) of God is not like any other presence. This is not a finite presence (or a coming) in space–time that competes with other energized material forms. It is the arriving presence of the intensively infinite Creator, whose being-there for creatures constitutes the conditions for spatio-temporal experience precisely by calling them out of non-being and orienting them toward new-being.

The parousia of Jesus should not be construed as the approach of one more substance in space–time, but as the adventitious presentation of the relational life of the triune God – the creative presence of an all-embracing welcome into pleasurable fellowship. The infinite beauty of the eternal liveliness of God was already being manifested in Jesus' earthly ministry as he faced others in a way that mediated the glorious hospitality of Eternity, precisely by liberating them into a hopeful openness to the future. His resurrection (ascension and coming) manifests the *promising* presence of the life-giving Spirit who calls the world toward renewal in union with God.

The parousia – the whole incursive and evocative Christ event – manifests the ultimate origin, condition and goal of human aesthetic desire, namely, the omnipresent welcome of the trinitarian God. We long to belong to and be longed-for in harmonious community beyond the threat of death. This desire is constituted by the intensively infinite presence of the Creator. However, this constitutive presence faces us (and all of creation) in a way that holds together and opens up our coming-to-be, which we experience as a temporal trajectory.

The all-embracing advent of Eternity creates the aesthetic desire of human creatures precisely as its conditioning goal. This countenancing of creation is the infinite "ground" of our spatio-temporal experience of being called into new forms of energized material complexity. A phenomenology of the Christian experience of the parousia of Jesus Christ intimates the appearance of this evocative grounding that conditions the human longing to participate in the pleasurable communion of God.

The "coming" of Christ that mediates the divine presence in and to creation manifests the *freedom* of God. Much of the Christian tradition has attempted to explain divine freedom with reference to the "will" of an all-powerful single subject. Instead of projecting this concept borrowed from faculty psychology onto God as an immaterial causative substance, we might begin with the relationality of the divine life disclosed in the appearance of Jesus. Divine freedom does not compete with human freedom "in" space or time, relying on its greater capacity to get what it wants.

The experience of the parousia discloses the liberating presence of the triune God as the capacious advent of Eternity that grants the conditions for human coming-to-be, calling us into being and toward new being in relation. We feel constricted within our dynamic co-ordinate systems of space–time–matter–energy and desire to find our place in the whole without being crushed or abandoned. Our "freedom" is constituted by the opening up of the trajectory of creation oriented toward Eternity, the presence of which evokes our aesthetic desire and holds it in becoming. The persons of the Trinity are freely present to and in relation to one another, eternally belonging to and being longed-for in beautiful communion. The incursive appearance of the life-giving Spirit of the Father who draws the man Jesus into a new emergent form of participation in the eternal life of God manifests the divine liberation of creation; for "where the Spirit of the Lord is there is freedom" (2 Cor. 3:17).

Christians experience that liberating presence as mediated by the parousia of Jesus Christ. "If the Son makes you free, you will be free indeed" (Jn 8:36). "For freedom Christ has set us free" (Gal. 5:1). The biblical references to Jesus as the *image* of God are particularly relevant here (cf. Col. 1:15; 2 Cor. 4:4). As the image of God he makes present to us the divine call to share in the glory of eternal life. Believers long to be transformed into his image, to experience freedom "in Christ" as we participate in his way of being-present to God and his neighbors.

Jesus' experience of the reception of the life-giving Spirit came to mediate his sense of hope in the promising divine countenance so fully that he was freed from the ontological anxiety of being crushed or abandoned by the finite energized materiality of his spatio-temporal neighbors. This mediation of the advent of Eternity overflowed the bounds of finite being, and so could not be crushed even by his death. Jesus' iconic function of making present divine grace by welcoming others into redemptive relation with the God of hope continued to be manifested after his resurrection among those who followed his way of being in the world, especially when they were gathered together in and by the Spirit (cf. Mt. 18:20; 1 Cor. 12).

We must remember that our language about the parousia, like all theological language, is finite, human language, which itself operates embedded within the creaturely field of space–time–matter–energy, and cannot escape this field in order to conceptually grasp its relation to the ultimate reality that makes conceptual grasping possible. We want to claim that Jesus *is* coming and that God *is* present. Our use of the copula "is" normally functions as part of our attempts to bind particular (more or less desirable) predicates to particular subjects. This linguistic strategy for dealing with creaturely things does not work in the same way on the Creator. *onto-theology*

We cannot even say that "God is" without apophatic qualification, because here we are confronted not simply with one more pleasurable object that is susceptible to the copulative urges of human predication, but with the ultimate ground of all desire for copulation whatsoever – the all-embracing origin, condition and goal of our natural longing to be bound in free relations of harmonious ecstasy. Even the desire for human intercourse evokes a peculiar kind of trembling that cannot wholly be captured by language, and this is part of what makes the anticipation of the coming of one's beloved so delightful. Far from outlawing discourse about that which we find alluring, these linguistic limits simply remind us of our finitude and intensify our hopeful anticipation of transformative communion – human and divine.

How then can we articulate belief in the resurrection, ascension and coming of Jesus Christ in dialogue with contemporary physical cosmology?

Christians believe that Jesus has been raised up "bodily" into a redeemed relation to God through the Spirit. However, the way in which we articulate this belief will be shaped by our understanding of what it means for a (material) body to be energized in space–time.

We are no longer required to imagine heaven as a place (near or far), where Jesus is watching and waiting for the right time to return. In light of contemporary cosmological categories, we can move beyond thinking of the "ascension" as a movement through space, away from a fixed inertial point, or of the "coming" of Christ as a return from a particular space at a fixed time. Instead, we may think of the whole parousia as the manifestation of God's incursive and evocative redemption of space–time–matter–energy, as the arriving consummation of the creaturely desire to belong to and be longed for within an infinitely redemptive field of hopeful communion.

If the experience of space–time is relative to each conscious observer, we may imagine the mediation of new life disclosed in Jesus' resurrection as already bearing upon us in each and every moment, opening up the future to us in our own particular tracks of dynamic energized materiality, freeing us to relate to one another in the presence of Eternity. This way of understanding the contemporaneity of Christ frees us from early modern attempts to prove exactly where the body was at different moments on the historical timeline between his crucifixion and the day of Pentecost (and beyond).

The disparity in the textual accounts of the empty tomb, and the variety of images used to depict his appearances to the disciples, all of which differ from Paul's encounter with a light and a voice, suggests that this was not the concern of the New Testament authors in the first place. The interpreted experience of the risen Christ must in some sense be "embodied" in so far as it registers an effect in the field of space–time–matter–energy. But we should not abstract the *felt* reality of the "presence" of Jesus, which is *really* felt ("then" and "now"), from the presence of the life-giving Spirit who mediates the arrival of Eternity to and in all creaturely temporal experience.

The Gospel of John depicts Jesus' aesthetic desire as wholly oriented in hopeful dependence on the gracious gift of being in relation to the Father in the Spirit, which he mediated to others by his way of being present with them. The disciple's anxiety about being separated from this presence by the death of Jesus is expressed in Peter's question: "Where are you going?" (Jn. 13:36). The Johannine explication of the answer has to do with the promising presence of a mutual indwelling by and in God mediated through the Spirit.

This experience of being united in, to and with God through the Spirit allowed them to interpret the risen Christ not only as "contemporary" but also as "coming." This is related to what the tradition has sometimes called Jesus' *kingly* office or role – his making present the reign of the God of peace. If all things are from, through and to God (Rom. 11:36), then all that creatures are, have been and shall be is absolutely upheld within the dynamic infinitely hospitable presence of the Creator.

Christians experience this presence as a parousia that opens up new emergent forms of relationality liberated from the threat of death and into the pleasure of Eternity. Like followers of Jesus' way of being in the world throughout history, contemporary believers also desire to *participate* in the parousia. However, this should not be construed as a waiting for a rapture that will take us up out of terrestrial and into celestial space but as a rapturous transformation of our experience of space (and time) in the cosmos as we live with(in) the advent of Eternity. To experience the presence of Jesus Christ today is to follow in his way of facing and being faced, being called into the beauty of harmonious communion. Participating in the parousia means receiving and mediating the promising presence of the God of hope in and to the world, inviting others into the experience of the glorious divine renewal of all things.

The task of reconstructing doctrine in our context requires giving an accounting for the hope that is within us (1 Pet. 3:15) in a way that engages contemporary physical cosmology. Here we also have an opportunity to articulate a *reformative* Christology that makes clear why the arriving presence of God in, to and for the world is good news. Depicting the parousia as a future point on a timeline at which some of us will escape the destruction of the planet earth is not only problematic for all of the biblical and scientific reasons outlined above; it also obscures our responsibility to face our neighbors in practical interdisciplinary and inter-religious dialogue about our shared longing for peaceful presence in communion.

Our coming to and being present with others should be characterized not by an anxious reliance on our own metaphysical weightiness to secure our aesthetic desires by energetically competing with other creatures for limited material goods in space–time, but by a hopeful welcome into the all-embracing life-giving presence of the Spirit of the One whose absolute Beauty makes all things new. Participating in Jesus' way of being in the world makes present the reformative power of the Gospel of the advent of God.

Epilogue

In chapter 1 and at several points during the presentation of these case studies I have emphasized that the primary function of the matrix of themes that guides this project is to provide us with a way of linking concrete christological issues to particular scientific developments by organizing them around shared philosophical interests in knowing, acting and being. Because our focus here has been on the reciprocal mediation of philosophy, science and Christology, exegetical and historical analysis of the biblical tradition played only a supporting role, although these concerns were always in the background. However, I have also hinted that this matrix can serve a broader theological purpose, facilitating the integration of christological themes within a more expansive systematic presentation of Christian theology. *Reforming* Christology must ultimately be interwoven within this broader reconstructive task. For those readers who are interested in such a holistic project, this epilogue provides a brief summary of my use of this theological matrix in other contexts and some suggestions for further integration of the doctrines of the incarnation, atonement and parousia.

In several places I have explored other ways in which Christian doctrine may be reconstructed in explicit dialogue with late modern developments in epistemology, ethics and metaphysics by attending to the existential dimensions of the human longing for truth, goodness and beauty. In each case, themes relevant for the task of reforming Christology were integrated into the discussion. For example, in *Reforming Theological Anthropology* (2003) I outlined some of the ways in which the philosophical turn to relationality provides new conceptual space for reconstructing the doctrines of human nature, sin and the image of God by linking them (respectively) with knowing, acting and being. I demonstrated in that context how particular ways of construing the doctrines of incarnation, atonement and parousia shaped and were shaped by interpretations of these anthropological themes.

In Part II of *The Faces of Forgiveness: Searching for Wholeness and Salvation* (Shults and Sandage, 2003), I outlined an approach to reforming soteriology that also incorporated ecclesiological and eschatological issues. My focus in that context was on reconstructing the doctrine of salvation in a way that attended to the Christian experience of knowing in sacramental community, acting in baptized community and being in eucharistic community. Tracing the themes of facing and forgiveness throughout the biblical tradition, I emphasized the importance of the motif of spiritual union with God in Christ. In that context, I analyzed the interpersonal dynamics that hinder and facilitate forgiveness in light of the theological concepts (and experiences) of faith, love and hope. In each case I connected the experience of salvation with the way of Jesus Christ, showing how participating in the manifestation of divine grace (forgiveness) can be understood in terms of finding our identity with Christ, dying to sin with Christ and being conformed to the image of Christ.

In *Reforming the Doctrine of God* (2005), I explored the conceptual space opened up by the recovery of the categories of intensive Infinity, robust Trinity and absolute Futurity in late modern theology. Moving beyond the idea of God as a rational causative substance and engaging contemporary developments in philosophy, science and biblical scholarship, I offered a reconstruction of the doctrine of God organized around the themes of omniscient faithfulness, omnipotent love and omnipresent hope. Challenging the ancient and early modern assumptions that contributed to logical impasses in the debates over foreknowledge, predestination and timelessness, I incorporated a discussion of the relation of Jesus Christ to the Holy Spirit immediately into a presentation of the Christian doctrine of *God*.

In Part I of *Transforming Spirituality* (Shults and Sandage, 2006), I argued for reconstructing Pneumatology in a way that is intrinsically linked to the reformative concerns of Christian life. I showed how some theologians' reliance on particular early modern categories of matter, person and force led to models of spirituality that focused on the causes and linear ordering of the states of the individual soul. Beginning with more relational and dynamic categories, I argued that becoming wise, becoming just and becoming free involve an intensification of faith, love and hope in the Spirit. In that context I also demonstrated how this transformational process may be spelled out as sharing in the knowledge, suffering and glory of Jesus Christ. This provided a framework for reforming the Christian understanding (and practice) of prayer, service and hospitality.

In addition to bringing theological doctrines into dialogue with contemporary philosophy, science and biblical scholarship, this way of organizing the themes also helped to display patterns and connections among doctrines that have not always been obvious. However, the matrix has its limits – philosophically, scientifically and theologically. The triadic structure of the matrix should not obscure the fact that epistemological, ethical and metaphysical commitments are inextricably interwoven. There is no epistemology that is not value-informed and oriented toward being in some sense, no ethics that does not have to do with knowing the good, which orients one's coming-to-be, and no metaphysics that is not inherently driven by our longing to know and value reality. As we saw in our case studies above, ultimately we cannot separate knowing, acting and being, even if making distinctions between them is useful for analytical purposes.

From a scientific point of view, my limitation of the case studies to particular fields of study is not at all meant to be prescriptive or proscriptive. These are simply examples of the kind of concrete dialogue that has been made possible by the late modern recognition of the permeability of academic disciplinary boundaries. Moreover, the dynamics of human knowing, acting and being should not be compartmentalized within particular sciences. In most contemporary psychological models of personhood, for example, *identity*-formation is not abstracted from the development of intentional *agency* nor the spatio-temporal and interpersonal dynamics of mutual *presence*.

In each case study I also emphasized that a fuller *theological* presentation would need to clarify the mutual mediation of the concepts of the identity, agency and presence of Jesus Christ. Such an integrative approach could weave together themes that have so often been separated in traditional formulations of the doctrines of incarnation, atonement and parousia. For example, the claim that Jesus' *agency* is not exclusively or even primarily about a transaction that occurred on the cross, but a disclosure of a way of acting in the world that transforms human life in relation to the divine, would need to be more explicitly linked to an understanding of how Jesus' *identification* of and by the Father in the Spirit manifests the *presence* of God. We might also explore a more holistic presentation of the prophetic, priestly and kingly "offices" of Christ, mentioned only briefly in our case studies.

Finally, it should be emphasized that this project on the reciprocal mediation of Christology, science and philosophy has by no means exhausted the task of presenting the significance of Jesus Christ in late modern culture. One of the greatest challenges (and opportunities) in our contemporary global context is learning to tend to religious others with greater compassion. Authentic dialogue across traditions will require (and enable) us to pay closer attention to the way in which other forms of religious experience in the world reveal the origin, condition and goal of the human longing for truth, goodness and beauty. Engaging in the ongoing task of reforming Christology might help Christian theologians learn to become better inter-religious lovers too.

References

Achtner, Wolfgang *et al.* 2002. *Dimensions of Time: The Structures of the Time of Humans, of the World, and of God.* Grand Rapids, MI: Eerdmans.

Adams, Randolph and Frank A. Salamone. 2000. *Anthropology and Theology: Gods, Icons, and God-Talk.* Lanham, MD: University Press of America.

Albert, David Z. 1992. *Quantum Mechanics and Experience.* Cambridge, MA: Harvard University Press.

Asad, Talal. 1993 [1982]. "The Construction of Religion as an Anthropological Category." In Talal Asad, *Genealogies of Religion: Discipline and Reasons of Power in Christianity and Islam.* Baltimore: Johns Hopkins University Press, 27–54.

Aulén, Gustav. 1954. *Christus Victor: A Historical Study of the Three Main Types of the idea of Atonement*, trans. A.G. Hebert. New York: Macmillan.

Ayoub, Mahmoud. 1993. "The Miracle of Jesus: Muslim Reflections on the Divine Word." In R.F. Berkey and S.A. Edwards, eds., *Christology in Dialogue.* Cleveland, OH: Pilgrim Press, 221–8.

Ayres, Lewis. 1996. "Theology, Social Science and Postmodernity: Some Theological Considerations." In Kieran Flanagan and Peter C. Jupp, eds., *Postmodernity, Sociology and Religion.* Basingstoke: Macmillan, 174–89.

Baggott, Jim. 2004. *Beyond Measure: Modern Physics, Philosophy and the Meaning of Quantum Theory.* Oxford: Oxford University Press.

Bailie, Gil. 1995. *Violence Unveiled: Humanity at the Crossroads.* New York: Crossroad.

Bak, Per. 1996. *How Nature Works: The Science of Self-Organized Criticality.* New York: Springer-Verlag.

Baker-Fletcher, Karen, and G.K. Baker-Fletcher. 1997. *My Sister, My Brother: Womanist and XODUS God-Talk.* Maryknoll, NY: Orbis.

Barbour, Ian. 1990. *Religion in an Age of Science.* San Francisco: Harper & Row.

Barbour, Ian. 2000. *When Science Meets Religion.* San Francisco: HarperSanFrancisco.

Barbour, Julian. 1999. *The End of Time.* London: Weidenfeld and Nicolson.

Barrow, John D. and Frank J. Tipler. 1986. *The Anthropic Cosmological Principle.* Oxford: Oxford University Press.

Bartlett, Anthony W. 2001. *Cross Purposes: The Violent Grammar of Christian Atonement*. Harrisburg, PA: Trinity Press International.

Baumann, Zygmunt. 1993. *Postmodern Ethics*. Oxford: Blackwell.

Benz, Arnold. 2002. *The Future of the Universe: Chance, Chaos, God?* New York: Continuum.

Bohm, David. 1981. *Wholeness and The Implicate Order* New York: Routledge.

Borg, Marcus J. 1987. *Jesus, A New Vision: Spirit, Culture and the Life of Discipleship*. New York: Harper & Row.

Borg, Marcus J. 1994. *Meeting Jesus Again for the First Time: The Historical Jesus and the Heart of Contemporary Faith*. San Francisco: HarperSanFrancisco.

Bowie, Fiona. 2006. *The Anthropology of Religion*, 2nd edn. Oxford: Blackwell.

Bowler, Peter J. 1989. *Evolution: The History of an Idea*, rev. edn. Berkeley, CA: University of California Press.

Boyne, Roy. 2000. "Structuralism." In Bryan S. Turner, ed., *The Blackwell Companion to Social Theory,* 2nd edn. Oxford: Blackwell, 160–90.

Brooke, John Hedley. 1991. *Science and Religion: Some Historical Perspectives*. Cambridge: Cambridge University Press.

Brown, Warren, ed. 2000. *Understanding Wisdom: Sources, Science and Society*. Philadelphia: Templeton Foundation Press.

Brueggemann, W. 2003. *An Introduction to the Old Testament*. Louisville, KY: Westminster John Knox.

Brümmer, Vincent. 2005. *Atonement, Christology and the Trinity*. Aldershot: Ashgate.

Campbell, John H. 1985. "An Organizational Interpretation of Evolution." In D.J. Depew and B.H. Weber, eds., *Evolution at a Crossroads: The New Biology and the New Philosophy of Science.* Cambridge, MA: MIT Press, 133–67.

Čapek, Milič. 1961. *The Philosophical Impact of Contemporary Physics*. New York: Van Nostrand Reinhold.

Carroll, John T. 2000. *The Return of Jesus in Early Christianity*. Peabody, MA: Hendrickson.

Cassirer, Ernst. 1923. *Substance and Function*, trans. William Curtis Swabey and Marie Collins Swabey. Chicago: Open Court.

Clayton, Philip. 2004. *Mind and Emergence: From Quantum to Consciousness*. Oxford: Oxford University Press.

Coakley, Sarah. 1995. *Christ Without Absolutes: A Study of the Christology of Ernst Troeltsch*. Oxford: Clarendon Press.

Cobb, John B. Jr. 1975. *Christ in a Pluralistic Age*. Philadelphia: Westminster Press.

Cohen, Ira J. 2000. "Theories of Action and Praxis." In Bryan S. Turner, ed., *The Blackwell Companion to Social Theory,* 2nd edn. Oxford: Blackwell, 73–105.

Cone, James. 1997. *God of the Oppressed.* Maryknoll, NY: Orbis.

Cone, James. 1990. *A Black Theology of Liberation*, 20th anniversary edn. Maryknoll, NY: Orbis.

Crossan, John Dominic. 1991. *The Historical Jesus.* Edinburgh: T&T Clark.

Crysdale, Cynthia S.W. 2001. *Embracing Travail: Retrieving the Cross Today.* New York: Continuum.

Cushing, James T. and Ernan McMullin, eds. 1989. *Philosophical Consequences of Quantum Theory: Reflections on Bell's Theorem.* Notre Dame, IN: University of Notre Dame Press.

Damasio, Antonio R. 1994. *Descartes' Error: Emotion, Reason and the Human Brain.* New York: Avion.

Damasio, Antonio R. 1999. *The Feeling of What Happens: Body and Emotion in the Making of Consciousness.* New York: Harcourt.

Damasio, Antonio R. 2004. *Looking for Spinoza: Joy, Sorrow and the Feeling Brain.* New York: Vintage.

Darwin, Charles. 1936 [1859]. *The Origin of Species.* New York: The Modern Library.

Darwin, Charles. 1936 [1871]. *The Descent of Man.* New York: The Modern Library.

Davies, Paul and John Gribbin. 1992. *The Matter Myth: Dramatic Discoveries that Challenge our Understanding of Physical Reality.* New York: Touchstone.

Davis, Stephen T. Daniel Kendall and Gerald O'Collins, eds. 2002. *The Incarnation.* Oxford: Oxford University Press.

Deacon, Terrence W. 1997. *The Symbolic Species: The Co-Evolution of Language and the Brain.* New York: W.W. Norton.

Deacon, Terrence W. 2006. "Emergence: The Hole at the Wheel's Hub." In Philip Clayton and Paul Davies, eds., *The Re-Emergence of Emergence: The Emergent Hypothesis from Science to Religion.* Oxford: Oxford University Press, 111–50.

de Heusch, Luc. 1985. *Sacrifice in Africa.* Bloomington: Indiana University Press.

Delanty, Gerard, 2000. "The Foundations of Social Theory: Origins and Trajectories." In Bryan S. Turner, ed., *The Blackwell Companion to Social Theory*, 2nd edn. Oxford: Blackwell, 21–46.

Derrida, Jacques. 1978. *Writing and Difference*, trans. Alan Bass. Chicago: University of Chicago Press.

Dunn, James D.G. 2003. *Jesus Remembered: Christianity in the Making, Volume 1*. Grand Rapids, MI: Eerdmans.

Durkheim, Emile. 1965 [1915]. *The Elementary Forms of the Religious Life*, trans. J.W. Swain. New York: Free Press.

Edwards, Denis. 1991. *Jesus and the Cosmos*. New York: Paulist Press.

Edwards, Denis. 1995. *Jesus and the Wisdom of God: An Ecological Theology*. Maryknoll, NY.

Edwards, Denis. 1997. "The Discovery of Chaos and the Retrieval of the Trinity." In R.J. Russell *et al.*, eds., 2nd edn, *Chaos and Complexity*. Berkeley, CA: Center for Theology and the Natural Sciences, 157–75.

Edwards, Denis. 1998. "Original Sin and Saving Grace in Evolutionary Context." In R.J. Russell *et al.*, eds., *Evolutionary and Molecular Biology*. Berkeley, CA: Center for Theology and the Natural Sciences, 377–92.

Edwards, Denis. 1999. *The God of Evolution: A Trinitarian Theology*. New York: Paulist Press.

Edwards, Denis. 2004. *Breath of Life: A Theology of the Creator Spirit*. Maryknoll, NY: Orbis.

Einstein, Albert. 1954. *Ideas and Opinions*, New York: Bonanza Books.

Einstein, Albert. 1961. *Relativity: The Special and the General Theory*. New York: Crown.

Einstein, Albert and Leopold Infeld. 1938. *The Evolution of Physics*. New York: Clarion.

Engberg-Pedersen, Troels. 2002. *Paul and the Stoics*. Louisville, KY: Westminster John Knox.

Evans-Pritchard, E.E. 1937 [1976]. *Witchcraft, Oracles and Magic among the Azande*. Oxford: Clarendon Press.

Fabella, Virginia. 1998. "Christology from an Asian Woman's Perspective." In Virginia Fabella and Sun Ai Lee Par, eds., *We Dare to Dream: Doing Theology as Asian Women*. Hong Kong: Asian Women's Resource Centre for Culture and Theology, 3–14.

Farrow, Douglas. 1999. *Ascension and Ecclesia: On the Significance of the Doctrine of the Ascension for Ecclesiology and Christian Cosmology*. Grand Rapids, MI: Eerdmans.

Faubion, James D. 2000. "Anthropology and Social Theory." In Bryan S. Turner, ed., *The Blackwell Companion to Social Theory*, 2nd edn. Oxford: Blackwell, 245–69.

Fiddes, Paul. 1989. *Past Event and Present Salvation*. Louisville, KY: Westminster John Knox.

Flanagan, Kieran. 1996. *The Enchantment of Sociology*. London: Macmillan.

Flanagan, Kieran. 2001. "The Return of Theology: Sociology's Distant Relative." In Richard Fenn, ed., *The Blackwell Companion to Sociology of Religion*. Oxford: Blackwell, 432–44.

Foster, M.B. 1934. "The Christian Doctrine of Creation and the Rise of Modern Natural Science," *Mind*, NS 43.172: 446–68.

Furseth, Inger and Pål Repstad. 2006. *An Introduction to the Sociology of Religion: Classical and Contemporary Perspectives*. Aldershot: Ashgate.

Geertz, Clifford. 1973. *The Interpretation of Cultures*. New York: Basic Books.

Gibellini, Rosino, ed. 1994. *Paths of African Theology*. Maryknoll, NY: Orbis.

Gillett, Carl. 2002. "The Varieties of Emergence: Their Purposes, Obligations and Importance," *Grazer Philosophische Studien*, 65: 89–115.

Girard, René. 1977. *Violence and the Sacred*, trans. Patrick Gregory. Baltimore: Johns Hopkins Universtiy Press.

Girard, René. 1986. *The Scapegoat*, trans. Yvonne Freccero. Baltimore: Johns Hopkins University Press.

Girard, René. 1987. *Things Hidden Since the Foundation of the World*, trans. Stephen Bann and Michael Metteer. Stanford, CA: Stanford University Press.

Girard, René. 1996. *The Girard Reader*, ed. James G. Williams. New York: Crossroad.

Girard, René. 2001. *I See Satan Falling Like Lightning*. New York: Orbis.

Glazier, Stephen D. 1999. *Anthropology of Religion*. New York: Praeger.

Glebe-Möller, Jens. 1989. *Jesus and Theology: Critique of a Tradition*, trans. Thor Hall. Minneapolis: Augsburg.

Gockel, Mattias. 2000. "A Dubious Christological Formula? Leontius of Byzantium and the *Anhypostasis-Enhyopstasis* Theory," *Journal of Theological Studies*, NS 51.2: 515–32.

Goodenough, Ursula. 2000. *The Sacred Depths of Nature*. Oxford: Oxford University Press.

Grant, Edward. 1996. *The Foundations of Modern Science in the Middle Ages*. Cambridge: Cambridge University Press.

Gregersen, N.H. 2002. "Beyond the Balance: Theology in a Self-Organizing World." In Niels Gregersen and Ulf Gorman, eds., *Design and Disorder: Perspectives from Science and Theology*. Edinburgh: T&T Clark, 53–92.

Gregersen, N.H. 2004. "Complexity: What is at Stake for Religious Reflection?" In Kees van Kooten Niekerk and Hans Buhl, eds., *The Significance of Complexity*. Aldershot: Ashgate, 135–6.

Gregersen, N.H. 2006. "Emergence in Theological Perspective," *Theology and Science*, 4.3: 309–20.

Grillmeier, A. 1996. *Christ in Christian Tradition*, trans. O.C. Dean. Louisville, KY: Westminster John Knox.

Grotius, Hugo. 1889 [1617]. *A Defence of the Catholic Faith concerning the Satisfaction of Christ against Faustus Socinus*, trans. F. H. Foster. Andover: Draper.

Gunton, Colin. 1988. *The Actuality of the Atonement: A Study of Metaphor, Rationality and the Christian Tradition*. Edinburgh: T&T Clark.

Guth, Alan H. 1997. *The Inflationary Universe: The Quest for a New Theory of Cosmic Origins*. Cambridge, MA: Perseus Books.

Habermas, Jürgen. 1987. *The Theory of Communicative Action*, vol. 2 *Lifeworld and System*, trans. Thomas McCarthy. Boston: Beacon Press.

Haight, Roger. 1999. *Jesus: The Symbol of God*. Maryknoll, NY: Orbis.

Hamerton-Kelly, Robert G. 1992. *Sacred Violence: Paul's Hermeneutic of the Cross*. Minneapolis: Fortress Press.

Hamerton-Kelly, Robert G. 1994. *The Gospel and the Sacred: Poetics of Violence in Mark*. Minneapolis: Fortress Press.

Haught, John F. 2000. *God After Darwin: A Theology of Evolution*. Boulder, CO: Westview.

Hawking, Stephen. 1988. *A Brief History of Time*. New York: Bantam.

Hefner, Phil. 1993. *The Human Factor: Evolution, Culture and Religion*. Minneapolis: Augsburg.

Heim, Mark. 2006. *Saved from Sacrifice: A Theology of the Cross*. Grand Rapids, MI: Eerdmans.

Heisenberg, Werner. 1971. *Physics and Beyond: Encounters and Conversations*, trans. A.J. Pomerans. New York: Harper.

Heyward, Carter. 1999. *Saving Jesus from Those Who are Right*. Minneapolis: Fortress Press.

Hick, John. 1977. *The Myth of God Incarnate*. Louisville, KY: Westminster John Knox.

Hill, Craig C. 2002. *In God's Time: The Bible and the Future*. Grand Rapids, MI: Eerdmans.

Hodge, Charles. 1981 [1872] *Systematic Theology*, 3 vols. Grand Rapids, MI: Eerdmans.

Hurtado, Larry W. 2003. *Lord Jesus Christ: Devotion to Jesus in Earliest Christianity*. Grand Rapids, MI: Eerdmans.

Huxley, Julian. 1942. *Evolution, the Modern Synthesis*. New York: Harper.

Inbody, Tyron L. 2002. *The Many Faces of Christology*. Nashville, TN: Abingdon.

Jammer, Max. 1993. *Concepts of Space: The History of Theories of Space in Physics*, 3rd enlarged edn. New York: Dover.

Jammer, Max. 1997. *Concepts of Mass in Classical and Modern Physics*. New York: Dover.

Jammer, Max. 1999 [1957]. *Concepts of Force: A Study in the Foundations of Dynamics*. Mineola, NY: Dover.

Jay, Nancy. 1994. *Throughout Your Generations Forever: Sacrifice, Religion, and Paternity*. Chicago: University of Chicago Press.

Jenson, Robert. 1969. *God after God: The God of the Past and the God of the Future, seen in the Work of Karl Barth*. Indianapolis: BobbsMerrill.

Jersak, Brad and Michael Hardin eds. 2007. *Stricken by God? Nonviolent Identification and the Victory of Christ*. Grand Rapids, MI: Eerdmans.

Juarrero, Alicia. 1999. *Dynamics In Action: Intentional Behavior as a Complex System*. Cambridge, MA: MIT Press.

Kähler, Martin. 1964 [1896]. *The So-Called Historical Jesus and the Historic Biblical Christ*, trans. and ed. Carl E. Braaten. Philadelphia: Fortress Press.

Kauffman, Stuart. 1995. *At Home in the Universe: The Search for the Laws of Self-Organization and Complexity*. Oxford: Oxford University Press.

Kauffman, Stuart. 2003. "The Emergence of Autonomous Agents." In Niels Gregersen, ed., *From Complexity to Life: On the Emergence of Life and Meaning*. Oxford: Oxford University Press, 47–71.

Kelly, J.N.D. 1978. *Early Christian Doctrines* San Francisco: Harper & Row.

König, Adrio. 1989. *The Eclipse of Christ in Eschatology*. Grand Rapids, MI: Eerdmans.

Korsmeyer, Jerry D. 1998. *Evolution & Eden: Balancing Original Sin and Contemporary Science*. New York: Paulist Press.

Küster, Volker. 2001. *The Many Faces of Jesus Christ*, trans. John Bowden. Maryknoll, NY: Orbis.

Kuhn, Thomas. 1996. *The Structure of Scientific Revolutions*. Chicago: University of Chicago Press.

Ladd, George Eldon. 2000 (1974). *The Presence of the Future*, revised edn. Grand Rapids, MI: Eerdmans.

Lakatos, Imre. 1980. *The Methodology of Scientific Research Programmes: Philosophical Papers*. Cambridge: Cambridge University Press.

Lambek, Michael, ed. 2002. *A Reader in the Anthropology of Religion*. Oxford: Blackwell.

Lang, U.M. 1998. "Anhypostatos-Enhypostatos: Church Fathers, Protestant Orthodoxy and Karl Barth," *Journal of Theological Studies*, NS 49.2: 630–57.

Levinas, Emmanuel. 2000. *Otherwise than Being: Or Beyond Essence*, trans. Alphonso Lingis. Pittsburg: Duquesne University Press.

Levi-Strauss, Claude. 1963. *Structural Anthropology*, trans. C. Jacobson and B.G. Schoepf. New York: Basic Books.

Lindberg, David C. and Ronald L. Numbers, eds. 1986. *God and Nature: Historical Essays on the Encounter between Christianity and Science.* Berkeley, CA: University of California Press.

Lovell, Terry. 2000. "Feminisms Transformed? Post-Structuralism and Postmodernism." In Bryan S. Turner, ed., *The Blackwell Companion to Social Theory,* 2nd edn. Oxford: Blackwell, 325–51.

Lüdemann, Gerd. 1998. *Virgin Birth?* Trans John Bowden. Harrisburg, PA: Trinity Press International.

Lyman, J. Rebecca. 1993. *Christology and Cosmology: Models of Divine Activity in Origen, Eusebius, and Athanasius.* Oxford: Clarendon Press.

MacIntyre, Alasdair. 1988. *Whose Justice? Which Rationality?* Notre Dame, IN: University of Notre Dame Press.

MacIntyre, Alasdair. 1999. *Dependent Rational Animals.* Chicago: Open Court.

McGrath, Alister. 2004. *Dawkin's God: Genes, Memes and the Meaning of Life.* Oxford: Blackwell.

McIntyre, John. 1992. *The Shape of Soteriology.* Edinburgh: T&T Clark.

McIntyre, John. 1998. *The Shape of Christology,* 2nd edn. Edinburgh: T&T Clark.

McKnight, Scot. 2007. *A Community Called Atonement.* Nashville, TN: Abingdon.

McMullin, Ernan. 1985. "Introduction: Evolution and Creation." In Ernan McMullin, ed., *Evolution and Creation.* Notre Dame, IN: University of Notre Dame Press, 1–56.

Milbank, John. 1990. *Theology and Social Theory.* Oxford: Basil Blackwell.

Milbank, John. 1997. *The Word Made Strange.* Oxford: Blackwell.

Milbank, John. 2003. *Being Reconciled: Ontology and Pardon.* London: Routledge.

Miller, Keith B., ed., 2003. *Perspectives on an Evolving Creation.* Grand Rapids, MI: Eerdmans.

Minns, Denis, O.P. 1998. "Traditional Doctrine and the Antique World-View: Two Case Studies, the Virgin Birth and Original Sin." In V. Pfitzner and Hilary Regan, eds., *The Task of Theology Today.* Grand Rapids, MI: Eerdmans, 139–62.

Mithen, Steven. 1996. *The Prehistory of the Mind: The Cognitive Origins of Art, Religion and Science.* London: Thames and Hudson.

Moltmann, Jürgen. 1985. *God in Creation,* trans. Margaret Kohl. San Francisco: Harper.

Moltmann, Jürgen. 1993. *The Way of Jesus Christ,* trans. Margaret Kohl. Minneapolis: Fortress Press.

Moltmann, Jürgen. 1996. *The Coming of God*, trans. Margaret Kohl. Minneapolis: Fortress Press.

Moltmann, Jürgen. 2003. *Science and Wisdom*, trans. Margaret Kohl. Minneapolis: Fortress Press.

Murphy, George L. 2003a. "Christology, Evolution and the Cross." In Keith B. Miller, ed., *Perspectives on an Evolving Creation*. Grand Rapids, MI: Eerdmans, 370–89.

Murphy George L. 2003b. *The Cosmos in Light of the Cross*. Harrisburg, PA: Trinity Press International.

Murphy, Nancey and George Ellis. 1996. *The Moral Nature of the Universe: Theology, Cosmology, and Ethics*. Minneapolis: Fortress Press.

Nellas, Panayiotis. 1997. *Deification in Christ*. Crestwood, NY: St Vladimir's Seminary Press.

Neville Robert C. 2001. *Symbols of Jesus: A Christology of Symbolic Engagement*. Cambridge: Cambridge University Press.

Niebuhr, H. Richard. 1951. *Christ and Culture*. New York: Harper & Row.

Nietzsche, Friedrich. 1989 [1887]. *The Genealogy of Morals*, trans W. Kaufmann. New York: Vintage.

O'Collins, Gerald. 1995. *Christology: A Biblical, Historical and Systematic Study of Jesus*. Oxford: Oxford University Press.

O'Donovan, Oliver. 1994. *Resurrection and Moral Order: An Outline for Evangelical Ethics*. Grand Rapids, MI: Eerdmans.

O'Donovan, Oliver and Joan Lockwood O'Donovan. 1999. *From Irenaeus to Grotius: A Sourcebook in Christian Political Thought*. Grand Rapids, MI: Eerdmans.

Padgett, Alan. 2003. *Science and the Study of God: A Mutuality Model for Theology and Science*. Grand Rapids, MI: Eerdmans.

Pannenberg, Wolfhart. 1969. *Theology and the Kingdom of God*. Philadelphia: Westminster Press.

Pannenberg, Wolfhart. 1993. *Toward a Theology of Nature*. Louisville: Westminster Press.

Pannenberg, Wolfhart. 1991–8. *Systematic Theology*, 3 vols. Grand Rapids, MI: Eerdmans.

Parsons, Talcott. 1968 [1937]. *Structure of Social Action*. New York: Free Press.

Peacocke, A.R. 1971. *Science and the Christian Experiment,* London: Oxford University Press.

Peacocke, A.R. 1979. *Creation and the World of Science* Oxford: Clarendon Press.

Peacocke, A.R. 1986. *God and the New Biology*, London: Dent.

Peacocke, A.R. 1993. *Theology for a Scientific Age: Being and Becoming – Natural, Divine, and Human*, expanded edn. Minneapolis: Fortress Press.

Peacocke, A.R.. 1996. "The Incarnation as the Informing Self-Expressive Word of God." In W. Mark Richardson and Wesley Wildman, eds., *Religion and Science: History, Method, Dialogue*. New York: Routledge, 321–39.

Peacocke, A.R. 1998. "Biological Evolution – a Positive Theological Appraisal." In Robert John Russell *et al.*, eds., *Evolutionary and Molecular Biology: Scientific Perspectives on Divine Action*. Berkeley, CA: Center for Theology and the Natural Sciences, 357–76.

Peacocke, A.R. 2001. "The Cost of New Life." In John Polkinghorne, ed., *The Work of Love: Creation as Kenosis* (Grand Rapids, MI: Eerdmans), 21–42.

Pelikan, Jaroslav. 1971. *The Emergence of the Catholic Tradition*. Chicago: University of Chicago Press.

Phan, Peter. 2003. *Christianity with an Asian Face: Asian American Theology in the Making*. Maryknoll, NY: Orbis.

Polanyi, Michael. 1962. *Personal Knowledge: Towards a Post-Critical Philosophy*. Chicago: University of Chicago Press.

Polkinghorne, John. 1994. *The Faith of a Physicist*. Princeton: Princeton University Press.

Polkinghorne, John. 1998. *Science & Theology: An Introduction*. Minneapolis: Fortress Press.

Polkinghorne, John. 2000. "Eschatology: Some Questions and Some Insights from Science." In John Polkinghorne and Michael Welker, eds., *The End of the Worlds and the Ends of God*. Harrisburg, PA: Trinity Press International, 29–41

Polkinghorne, John. 2002. *Quantum Theory: A Very Short Introduction*. Oxford: Oxford University Press.

Prigogine, Ilya and Isabella Stengers. 1984. *Order Out of Chaos*. New York: Bantam.

Rahner, Karl. 1966. "Christology within an Evolutionary View." In *Theological Investigations*. London: Darton, Longman and Todd, V, 157–92.

Rahner, Karl. 1978. *Foundations of Christian Faith*. New York: Crossroad.

Reichenbach, Hans. 1998 [1944]. *Philosophical Foundations of Quantum Mechanics*. Mineola, NY: Dover.

Reichenbach, Hans. 1958. *The Philosophy of Space and Time*. New York: Dover.

Repstad, Pål. 1996. "Between Idealism and Reductionism: Some Sociological Perspectives on Making Theology." In Pål Repstad, ed., *Religion and Modernity: Modes of Co-existence*. Oslo: Scandinavian University Press, 91–118.

Rescher, Nicholas. 1990. *A Useful Inheritance: Evolutionary Aspects of the Theory of Knowledge*. Savage, MD: Rowman and Littlefield.

Richardson, Mark W. *et al.*, eds. 2002. *Science and the Spiritual Quest: New Essays by Leading Scientists*. London: Routledge.

Robinson, John A.T. 1979. *Jesus and His Coming*. Philadelphia: Westminster Press.

Rue, Loyal. 2000. *Everybody's Story: Wising Up to the Epic of Evolution.* Albany: State University of New York Press.

Russell, R.J. 1988. "Contingency in Physics and Cosmology: A Critique of the Theology of Wolfhart Pannenberg," *Zygon* 23.1: 23–43.

Russell, R.J. 1994. "Cosmology from Alpha to Omega" *Zygon* 29.4: 557–77.

Russell, R.J. 1996. "T=0: Is it Theologically Significant?" In W. Mark Richardson and Wesley Wildman, eds., *Science and Religion: History, Method, Dialogue.* New York: Routledge, 201–24.

Russell, R.J. 1997a. "Cosmology and Eschatology: The Implications of Tipler's 'Omega-Point' Theory for Pannenberg's Theological Program." In C. Albright and J. Haugen, eds., *The End in the Beginning.* Chicago: Open Court, 195–316.

Russell, R.J. 1997b. "Does Creation have a Beginning?" *Dialog* 36.3: 180–9.

Russell, R.J. 1999. "Finite Creation without a Beginning: The Doctrine of Creation in Relation to Big Bang and Quantum Cosmologies." In Nancey C. Murphy *et al.*, eds., *Quantum Cosmology and the Laws of Nature: Perspectives on Divine Action*, 2nd edn. Berkeley, CA: Center for Theology and the Natural Sciences, 293–329.

Russell, R.J. 2000. "Time in Eternity: Special Relativity & Eschatology," *Dialog* 39.1: 46–55.

Russell, R.J. 2002a. "Bodily Resurrection, Eschatology, and Scientific Cosmology." In Ted Peters, R.J. Russell and M. Welker, eds., *Resurrection: Theological and Scientific Assessments.* Grand Rapids, MI: Eerdmans, 3–30.

Russell, R.J. 2002b. "Eschatology & Physical Cosmology: A Preliminary Reflection." In George Ellis, ed., *The Far-Future Universe: Eschatology from a Cosmic Perspective.* Philadelphia: Templeton Foundation Press, 266–315.

Russell, R.J. 2002c. "The Doctrine of Creation out of Nothing in Relation to Big Bang and Quantum Cosmologies." In *The Human Search for Truth: Philosophy, Science, Theology*, International Conference on Science and Faith. The Vatican, 23–25 May 2000. Philadelphia: Saint Joseph's University Press, 108–29.

Russell, R.J. 2003a. "Sin, Salvation, and Scientific Cosmology: Is Christian Eschatology Credible Today?" In Duncan Reid and Mark Worthing, eds., *Sin and Salvation.* Hindmarsh, Australia: ATF Press, 130–53.

Russell, R.J. 2003b. "Special Providence and Genetic Mutation: A New Defense of Theistic Evolution." In Keith B. Miller, ed., *Perspectives on an Evolving Creation*. Grand Rapids, MI: Eerdmans, 225–369.

Russell, R.J. 2005. "Natural Theodicy in an Evolutionary Context: The Need for an Eschatology of New Creation." In Bruce Barber and David Neville, eds., *Theodicy and Eschatology*. Hindmarsh, Australia: ATF Press, 121–52.

Russell, R.J. 2007 "Cosmology and Eschatology." In Jerry L. Walls, ed., *The Oxford Handbook of Eschatology*. Oxford: Oxford University Press, 563–80.

Schaff, Philip, ed. 1931. *The Creeds of Christendom: with a History and Critical Notes*, 6 vols. Vol II: The Greek and Latin Creeds with Translations. Grand Rapids, MI: Baker.

Schmiechen, Peter. 2005. *Saving Power: Theories of Atonement and the Forms of the Church*. Grand Rapids, MI: Eerdmans.

Schneewind, J.B. 1998. *The Invention of Autonomy: A History of Modern Moral Philosophy*. Cambridge: Cambridge University Press.

Schüssler Fiorenza, Elizabeth. 1995. *Miriam's Child, Sophia's Prophet*. New York: Continuum, 1995.

Schwarz, Hans. 1998. *Christology*. Grand Rapids, MI: Eerdmans.

Schwarz, Hans. 2000. *Eschatology*. Grand Rapids, MI: Eerdmans.

Segundo, Juan Luis, 1988. *An Evolutionary Approach to Jesus of Nazareth*. Maryknoll, NY: Orbis.

Shults, F. LeRon. 1996. "A Dubious Christological Formula: From Leontius of Byzantium to Karl Barth," *Theological Studies*, 57.3: 431–46.

Shults, F. LeRon. 1999. *The Postfoundationalist Task of Theology*. Grand Rapids, MI: Eerdmans.

Shults, F. LeRon. 2003. *Reforming Theological Anthropology: After the Philosophical Turn to Relationality*. Grand Rapids, MI: Eerdmans.

Shults, F. LeRon. 2005. *Reforming the Doctrine of God*. Grand Rapids, MI: Eerdmans.

Shults, F. LeRon, ed. 2006. *The Evolution of Rationality*. Grand Rapids, MI: Eerdmans, 2006.

Shults, F. LeRon. forthcoming. "The Philosophical Turn to Alterity." In F. LeRon Shults and B. Waters, eds., *Christology and Ethics*. Grand Rapids, MI: Eerdmans.

Shults, F. LeRon and Steven J. Sandage. 2003. *The Faces of Forgiveness: Searching for Wholeness and Salvation*. Grand Rapids, MI: Baker Academic.

Shults, F. LeRon and Steven J. Sandage. 2006. *Transforming Spirituality: Integrating Theology and Psychology*. Grand Rapids, MI: Baker Academic.

Smart, Barry. 2000. "Postmodern Social Theory." In Bryan S. Turner, ed., *The Blackwell Companion to Social Theory*, 2nd edn. Oxford: Blackwell, 447–80.

Sober, Elliot and David Sloan Wilson. 1999. *Unto Others: The Evolution and Psychology of Unselfish Behavior*. Boston, MA: Harvard University Press.

Sobrino, Jon. 1978. *Christology at the Crossroads*. Maryknoll, NY: Orbis.

Song, C.S. 1990. *Jesus, the Crucified People*. New York: Crossroad.

Stenmark, Mikael 2001. *Scientism: Science, Ethics and Religion*. Aldershot: Ashgate.

Stenmark, Mikael. 2004. *How to Relate Science and Religion*. Grand Rapids, MI: Eerdmans.

Stinton, Diane B. 2004. *Jesus of Africa: Voices of Contemporary African Christology*. Maryknoll, NY: Orbis.

Stone, Dianna L. and Eugene F. Stone-Romero. 2002. "The Religious Underpinnings of Social Justice Conceptions." In S.W. Gilliland *et al.*, eds., *Emerging Perspectives on Managing Organizational Justice*. Greenwich, CT: Information Age Publishing, 35–75.

Tanner, Kathryn. 1997. *Theories of Culture: A New Agenda for Theology*. Minneapolis: Fortress Press.

Teilhard de Chardin, Pierre. 1960. *The Divine Milieu*, trans. Bernard Wall. New York: Harper & Row.

Teilhard de Chardin, Pierre. 1964. *The Future of Man*, trans. Norman Denny. New York: Harper & Row.

Teilhard de Chardin, Pierre. 1968. *Science and Christ*, trans. René Hague. New York: Harper & Row.

Teilhard de Chardin, Pierre. 1970. *The Activation of Energy*, trans René Hague. New York: Harcourt Brace Jovanovich.

Teilhard de Chardin, Pierre. 1976. *The Phenomenon of Man*. New York: Harper & Row.

Terrell, JoAnne Marie. 1998. *Power in the Blood? The Cross in the African American Experience*. Maryknoll, NY: Orbis.

Theissen, Gerd. 1985. *Biblical Faith: An Evolutionary Approach*, trans. John Bowden. Philadelphia: Fortress Press.

Theissen, Gerd and Annette Merz. 1998. *The Historical Jesus: A Comprehensive Guide*, trans. John Bowden. Minneapolis: Fortress Press.

Tipler, Frank J. 1994. *The Physics of Immortality: Modern Cosmology, God and the Resurrection of the Dead*. New York: Anchor Books.

Torrance, T.F. 1969a. *Theological Science*. London: Oxford University Press.

Torrance, T.F. 1969b. *Space, Time and Incarnation*. London: Oxford University Press.

Torrance, T.F. 1976. *Space, Time and Resurrection.* Edinburgh: Handsel Press.

Torrance, T.F. ed. 1980a. *Belief in Science and in Christian Life.* Edinburgh: Handsel Press.

Torrance, T.F. 1980b. *Christian Theology and Scientific Culture.* Belfast: Christian Journals.

Torrance, T.F. 1981. *Divine and Contingent Order.* Oxford: Oxford University Press.

Torrance, T.F. 1984. *Transformation and Convergence in the Frame of Knowledge.* Grand Rapids, MI: Eerdmans.

Torrance, T.F. 1985. *Reality and Scientific Theology.* Edinburgh: Scottish Academic Press.

Torrance, T.F. 1989. *The Christian Frame of Mind: Reason, Order and Openness in Theology and Natural Science* Colorado Springs, CO: Helmers & Howard.

Trelstad, Marit, ed. 2006. *Cross Examinations: Readings on the Meaning of the Cross Today.* Minneapolis, MN: Augsburg.

van Huyssteen, J. Wentzel. 2006. *Alone in the World? Human Uniqueness in Science and Theology.* Grand Rapids, MI: Eerdmans.

Ward, Graham. 2005. *Cultural Transformation and Religious Practice.* Cambridge: Cambridge University Press.

Weaver, J. Denny. 2001. *The Nonviolent Atonement.* Grand Rapids, MI: Eerdmans.

Wessels, Cletus. 2003. *Jesus in the New Universe Story.* Maryknoll, NY: Orbis.

Wildiers, N. Max. 1982. *The Theologian and His Universe.* New York: Seabury Press.

Wildman, Wesley. *Fidelity with Plausibility: Modest Christologies in the Twentieth Century.* Albany: State University of New York Press, 1998.

Williams, Delores. *Sisters in the Wilderness: The Challenge of Womanist God-Talk.* Maryknoll, NY: Orbis, 1993.

Williams, Patricia. 2001. *Doing without Adam and Eve: Sociobiology and Original Sin.* Minneapolis: Augsburg.

Woodhead, Linda. 2006. "Apophatic Anthropology." In R. Kendall Soulen and Linda Woodhead, eds., *God and Human Dignity.* Grand Rapids, MI: Eerdmans, 233–46.

Worthing, Mark. 1996. *God, Creation and Contemporary Physics.* Minneapolis: Fortress Press.

Wright, N.T. 1992. *The New Testament and the People of God.* Minneapolis: Fortress Press.

Wright, N.T. 2003. *The Resurrection of the Son of God.* Minneapolis: Fortress Press.

Index